I0082913

THE QUANTUUM EFFECT

Saving our environment by changing the
measurement of economic performance

Raymond Samuels, ed.

Agora Books

Agora Books™
Ottawa, Canada

The Quantuum Effect: Saving our environment by changing the measurement of economic performance

© 2020, H. Raymond Samuels II

All Rights Reserved. No part of this book may be reproduced, stored in a retrieval system, or transmitted, in any form, or by any means, electronic, mechanical, photocopying, recording, or otherwise, without the expressed written consent of The Agora Cosmopolitan.

The views, opinions, and perceptions of the author and/or editor of the book herein expressed in this text are intended to support civil and creative joint academic and civic discussion.

Care has been taken to trace the ownership/source of any academic-reference material contained in the text. The publisher welcomes any information that will enable a rectification in subsequent edition(s), of any incorrect or omitted reference or credit.

Agora Books_{TM}
P.O. Box 24191
300 Eagleson Road
Kanata, Ontario K2M 2C3 CANADA

Agora Books is a self-publishing agency for authors that was launched by The Agora Cosmopolitan which is a registered not-for-profit corporation.

ISBN: 978-1-927538-50-0

Printed in Canada

Book cover art

General art work, by Raymond Samuels [Front cover];
Parliament Hill, Ottawa, Canada photo by Raymond Samuels [Back cover].

CONTENTS

ABSTRACT

❦

D O YOU SHARE a concern for an apparent on-going environmental destruction of the planet alongside talking among politicians that their course is the best way to nurture economic development and growth? Do you believe that the current responses of these politicians to protect our environment via various public policies which include "carbon taxes" are either woefully inadequate or misdirecting?

Do you also think that as human beings, we have no time to waste on correcting our course and yearn for an alternative approach that brings together our vital concern of safeguarding our environment that we ultimately rely on for our quality-of-survival with a desire for supporting the economic well-being of our dynamic modern societies? If you share an affinity toward such kind of queries, then this book was intended for your clearheaded reflection.

Environmental destruction has been conditioned by an economic discipline which teaches its students that after their graduation their role is to support a system which measures its own performance based on market-based criteria of viewing humans and the environment just as raw materials to be exploited. The growth viewed by the managers of the system is the result of the ability of its actors to exploit each other as well as the environment as raw materials towards achieving faster rates of exploitation that in the opinion of the gatekeepers of the system constitutes the "growth" that we are conditioned as societies to view as desirable.

Rather than putting an effort to deal with environmental destruction as a reaction to an economic system that is essentially dysfunctional to our quality of human survival which is associated to a flourishing environment, would it be more productive to deal with our conception of what economic progress is and how should we achieve it? That is what this book is all about – a rejuvenated conception of the economy which transforms the focus of our human species from a "market" prism centred on a dysfunctional context of exploitation to a holistic and heterodox conception of the economy which is associated to safeguarding the protection of our environment.

In fact, the framers of aggregate economic development policy have so far made themselves comfortable by looking primarily at changes at the aggregate levels of commerce. In the process, the prevailing economic aggregate development directorates now tend to lay emphasis on human economic agents as the pursuers of market-equivalent wealth rather than conscious, survival-centred entities who *also* participate in trade. Therefore, in the post-industrial society, the recognition of individuals, as entities who are using their resource and effort management to pursue quality-of-living targets, has been fundamentally overlooked.

In the Western societies, it has become a normal practice to regard aggregate resource management performance as a net financial yield from trade which is one of the components of GNP. How the program and policy initiatives of government have impacted the prevailing quality-of-life attainment has therefore been essentially made moot.

In contrast, the context of the "Quantum Effect" introduced in this book emphasises that the *consequences on people can be termed as the most important output of aggregate economic development initiatives.*

Mindful of the fact that **human development** is the ultimate target and the *conscious* human economic agents are using their effort and resource-manipulative activities to pursue it, the book also introduces the concept of Holistic Aggregate Economic Development Management. The concept emerges from the recognition that notwithstanding the historical oversight, the concept of "The New Economy", which is articulated via the initiatives of people rather than commercial profits from stocks of material resources, has existed since the initial commitment of human consciousness to "scarcity" management. Therefore, the presentation here elaborates the type of programming on which the societies need to focus if their intent is to bestow quality-of-living as a result of their economic development initiatives.

The Potential for an Emphasis on Human Development

by Horace Carby

Introduction

❧

I N HIS *Inquiry into the Theory and The Causes of the Wealth of Nations,* which he wrote in 1776, the classical economist Adam Smith laid emphasis on the productivity benefits that are forthcoming from the division of labour.

The modern industrial and post-industrial information-driven society pivots on the coordination that accompanies a high degree of division of labour. In the process of this technique, the convenience of money makes feasible innumerable private, formal and informal contracts that accompany trade and exchange.

Notably, the multitude of mixes of inter-personal, inter-regional, inter-societal and inter-temporal exchange contracts that accompany division of labour is also a part of the living that individuals experience. Therefore, mare market exchange contracts are involved in the economic management activities of the individuals.

Indeed, the consciousness which individuals have also mediates the selections of exchange choices, *into which* they respectively enter. Notwithstanding, market economists tend to emphasise the financial-equivalent attributes of the exchange choices, which form the trading activities that are revealed in a market.

Contrary to the commerce-centred focus of market economics, we are emphasising here that the mix of effort and resource commitment selections which individuals make is also substantively aimed at targets in living which they respectively have. Therefore, here it is being emphasised that the indicator of achievement is not necessarily represented by the forthcoming market-equivalent profits from trade.

Yet, it is recognised that the individuals pursue trade in order to acquire technical items which they will use in living as well as to earn net financial profit. It is also recognised that money has historically demonstrated its capacity to attract required items via trade. Essentially, the presence of money has enabled potential trading partners to stipulate the monetary quantities that they will accept in exchange for technical quantities of real goods and services that they contract to deliver (at bulk or at per unit financial-equivalent prices).

Money has come to act as the currency in which the exchange value of everyday (non-barter) transactions is expressed. Quotations for later settlements of current exchange transactions are usually also stated in money terms.

Money executes a pervasive role where people must trade in order to survive. Economists therefore impute that the presence of money enables technologically complex societies to emerge. These analysts also impute that the complex development that accompanies division of labour is forthcoming in concert with the activities of entrepreneurs, who are in quest of financial-equivalent profit.

Economic analysts also argue that the capability of money to function jointly as currency and as a store of value makes people enter into exchange in order *to hold on to* money. Indeed, the comprehensive role of privately negotiated money prices in "lubricating" trade acts as a system of coordination to the division of labour. As a result, societies (like the former Soviet Union) found it essentially impossible to execute a broad-based technically complex trading *environment* besides at the same time using a system of centralised bureaucratic pricing.

In economic development matters, the current overall tendency is to look upon persons as being (to a large extent) hunters of net financial gain. The result is that most technologically developed societies tend to compute the economic outcome from aggregate *resource* allocation in financial terms.

Notwithstanding that the focus of complex societies is on financial-equivalent results, here it is argued that economic **development** (as compared to economic growth) is indicated by the increases in the opportunity of the typical member of the society (at hand) in order to access preferred patterns of survival. We therefore argue that the achievement from development may be construed in terms of the extent to which the quality-of-living of the typical member of the society at hand has been enhanced.

We further argue that resulting development achievement must be determined from the *increases in the mix of critical services* which become accessible to human economic agents in the society at hand.

A quality-of-living focus on the achievements from aggregate economic development can be formulated. However, such a quality-of-living focus will require the aggregate economic development directorate to review how effectively prevailing trade that it facilitates is also associated with the production and the availability of outcomes on behalf of quality-of-life attainments. Yet, to date, the economists have concentrated on reporting on matters that they can associate with the prevailing financial-equivalent level of commerce.

Economists have adopted the route (of emphasising the relative size of aggregate market value) predominately by imputing a highly stilted analytical concept. The concept claims that an operating market leads to the presence of "equilibrium" prices. Their argument is that at the points of "equilibrium" prices for respective services (even if the points are fleeting), there is a "demonstrable" equivalence between the value in exchange, on the one hand, and market price (to the bulk of exchange participants), on the other hand.

This conceptual bulwark (of an imputed equivalence between exchange value and "equilibrium" price) is entrenched. As a result, the "high priests" of the economics profession used this declaration of the analytical substantiveness of the equilibrium price to denigrate the appropriateness of a real life presentation of economic reality that Staffan Linder had made.[1]

---

1. See, therefore the presentation in Staffan Linder, *The Harried Leisure Class*, (New York: Columbia University Press), 1969. Linder's eminently reasoned proposition was that high income earners tend to acquire high priced consumption goods, which they seek to "consume" in their leisure time. However, since time for leisure activities involved foregoing the earnings potential that could be secured during that time, these potential high income earners ended up with a feeling that they did not have enough time to pursue living as the enjoyment of their consumption goods. They therefore ended up with a feeling of being harried.

The response of the economics "high priests" was that Linder was essential-

Historically, economic analysts have also used this premise of the existence of equilibrium prices to persuade governmental policies regarding development (even though development is a condition of disequilibrium).

Specifically, these analysts have convinced governments that the market, in its normal functioning, will cause the delivery of adequate quantities of the (technical) real outputs which human economic agents seek. These economists have therefore convinced governments that government should pursue aggregate economic development.

Encouragement to market initiatives will cause sustained increases in the value of aggregate commerce. Under the influence of (capitalist) economists, governments have neglected to prioritise programmes that aim to enhance the experience of quality-of-life that will be forthcoming to the typical individual in the society.

In the process of emphasising that the competitive market mechanism is relatively superior for regulating the access that individuals have, economists have tended (for mainly political reasons) to make a number of glaring living-related oversights. These analysts have tended to overlook the lack of access to quality-of-living, which must be faced by persons who have limited cash to spend on their critical survival requirements.

These market economic analysts have also overlooked the accompanying context of existential "anomia" that people experience in the circumstances where development policy is oriented primarily at supporting aggregate market buoyancy (as shown by enhancement in 'GNP'/'GDP').

The condition of anomia exists where those persons who must sell the use of their skills in order to access the requirements for living find that the sale transaction is also accompanied by a dearth of participative meaningfulness in their daily sojourn. Anomia occurs because these individuals find that they fill the role of (and are regarded as) being primarily instruments/implements to profit generation as well as 'GNP'/'GDP' enhancement.

---

ly seeking to use arguments applicable to an "equilibrium" point transaction in order to make deductions about what they described as intra-equilibrium contexts. Therefore, they imputed Linder's implied criticism of the development guidance provided by economics reasoning should not be regarded as being valid.

In contrast, The New Economy, with a quality-of-living target, is one which seeks to minimise the generation, occurrence and incidence of anomia. Under its quality-of-life emphasis, *success in aggregate economic development programming will be revealed in the access of individuals to meaningful participation in how their environment evolves.*

However, so far, in Western societies, a *viable* lobby groupdoes not yet exist which *is not* a clone of the development management constituency that emphasises aggregate commercial attainment.

So far, institutions like the International Monetary Fund (IMF) do not include contribution to quality-of-life enhancement as a criterion for providing resources to economic development assistance. Rather, the facilitation which that organisation (and its sister institutions like the World Bank) offer is forthcoming to those societies which accept the imputation that 'GNP'/'GDP' enhancement is the target of aggregate economic development.

This type of (IMF and World Bank) prioritisation of development initiatives which are aimed at commercial sales in "the global market" has been a significant source of substantive cultural dysfunction and neo-colonial dominance. By virtue of their *calculated* oversight of the requirements for quality-of-life attainment, these instruments of (late twentieth and early twenty-first century) neo-colonialism have been quite content to facilitate or to perpetuate an indifference to the emergence of anomia in societies to which they provide "help".

Such institutional indifference to anomia has also allied itself with human capital contexts for executing aggregate economic development where the people who form the society are largely regarded as manipulatable and (if needs be) dispensable "tools/implements".[2]

---

2. Unfortunately, that has been the heritage which has evolved in association with the elaboration of the human capital context by Theodore Schultz and Gary Becker, (as principal proponents of a tradition that emerged out of the University of Chicago). Essentially, their formulation made the imputation that working people (as hunters of improved earning skills) represented human capital and were therefore essentially members of the capitalist class. That formulation provided an intellectual coup in the propaganda to the "Cold War". It essentially vitiated the arguments and the imputations of the

Raymond Samuels

When economic analysis accommodates these human "tools" as being primarily complements to profit generation, institutions like the IMF are content to focus primarily on financial balance sheet results. These Western dominated institutions of international financial "support" make themselves comfortable to overlook the reality of societies, as collectives of *persons*, that are in pursuit of *human development* targets.

This oversight of human development as the sought attainment allows these international institutions of financial "support" to facilitate the evolution of respective societies as clients to the multinational banking hegemony.

In contrast, toward the fruition of the *New Economy* (where the quality-of-living impacts of resource allocative programmes and policies are prioritised), the community and its economic development directorate must focus on people-centred survival achievements. An aggregate economic development directorate will need to focus on the mixes of human development features which its economic development programmes need to foster.

It happens, however, that an assessment of economic development programming initiatives in the light of their impacts on the survival of people can be made only after a society has also framed its critical people-centred achievement targets. When that framing of targets has been done, analysts will need to form indicators which will reveal how effectively prevailing aggregate economic development initiatives have enhanced the access of persons to the informed survival that makes their lives more tolerable. It means these analysts will need to develop an in-

---

Marxists and communists who were arguing class cleavages as a potential source of destruction of the capitalist society.

For a technical elaboration of the Human Capital regime, devoid of its highly political economic undertones, see T. W. Schultz, *Human Resources Policy Issues and Research Opportunities*, Gary Becker (ed.) Fiftieth Anniversary Colloquium VI, (New York: National Bureau of Economic Research), 1972. See, also, T. W. Schultz, "Human Capital", *American Economic Review*, Vol. 51, March 1961, pp. 1-17. In addition, See, Gary Becker, *Human Capital*, (New York: Columbia University Press for the National Bureau of Economic Research), 1964.

dicator which will reveal the extent to which individual empowerment is being facilitated.

One can talk with integrity that *"The New Economy"* is in place only when survival-centred empowerment is the principal outcome that is forthcoming from prevailing economic development programming.

The factory-centred economy developed out of the industrial revolution. However, in today's information-based economy, while persons are operating as employees, they are usually perceived as having merely the on-the-job rights of wage earners. They are therefore treated by employers as hired *implements*, yet persons at work are executing the operations of living. Furthermore, as members of their respective societies, they have accompanying existential rights.

However, market economic analysts have overlooked the need to accommodate resource allocative performance to incorporating the extent to which these existential targets in economic development that individuals have are being satisfied. They tend to rationalise that oversight by resorting to the evaluative assumption that the distributive effects on individuals which initiatives have are *statistically* "neutral".

In contrast, the context of a posited *New Economy* (with its focus on delivered quality-of-living) accommodates a performance evaluative context that pivots on an explicit distributive premise. This distributive premise makes the following stipulation: Effective development occurs in a society when *the representative* (responsible and Conscious) participating human economic agent finds (and accessible) the technical complements available to the informed survival which that agent seeks.

The quality-of-life context to *The New Economy* argues that *the evaluation of economic development performance must necessarily be based on the access of individuals to flows/mixes of critical technical complements on behalf of the informed survival which they seek.*

Under such circumstances, how stock markets have performed in terms of aggregate financial-equivalent value of commercial paper will be regarded as being not necessarily a primary indication of how effective aggregate economic development management has been.

However, the "scientific method" allows the analysts use analytical abstractions in order to formulate alternative perspectives on prevailing problems. Notwithstanding the potential that such scientific analysis has, the fact remains that the human economic agents (who operate in the pre-vailing economic development complex) are *owners* of their society. They may not be accommodated as merely (data) abstractions. Development outcomes will be impacting on their lives. Therefore, in the name of science, economic development analysts may not, with indifference, provide policy and programme recommendations which are based merely on the premise that the changes in net market results provide the appropriate objective indicator of the success of development.

In contrast, a posited *New Economy*, with its focus on quality-of-life and consciousness-centred human economic agents (as the operators), does not look upon individuals as being surrogate "machinery" that is being managed to complement market targets. In a posited *New Economy*, people who make up the society are not to be viewed as being essentially "bundles of skills" that may be hired, laid-off or discarded as expected market profits dictate.

Essentially, in an analytical context that is complementary to a posited *New Economy*, the persons who make up the society are not emphasised as serving (in their various capacities) the evolution of markets. Rather, these persons are emphasised as committing their resources and their skills to the pursuit of consciousness-directed survival-centred targets that they have in a political economy.

Regarding a *New Economy*, involved human economic agents are not appreciated as being indulgent and essentially hedonic pursuers of consumption "highs" that become satisfied when they buy and use items that get measured within a 'GNP'/'GDP' framework.

In contrast, individuals are recognised as forming an enlarged economic context in which the analytical context of the participation of individuals is placed in their overall strategies to execute the survival path (that is their lives), via their resource management initiatives.

Aggregate economic development directorates are therefore invited to develop and facilitate development strategies *that will stimulate deliveries of services* which are supportive of a high quality-of-living. However, to do so effectively, these directorates will need to *draw on a system of appraisal that ranks outcomes in the light of their consequences on people* rather than the changes in financial-equivalent results.

Yet, governments are likely to use such a ranking only under the prodding members of the particular society. These members of the society must be prepared to indicate that they *require* aggregate economic development programming in order to prioritise the survival targets to which members of the society are heirs.[3]

The following material will stress the management initiatives that governments will need to take towards the fruition of aggregate economic development results that have quality-of-life as their indicative outcomes. The material is mindful that although individuals are usually price takers for items that they acquire in trade, these individuals frequently make substitutes among products and services on the basis of the respective relative prices for those services and initiatives on behalf of their survival are correspondingly vital. More (short or long term) cash-equivalent outcomes are involved in the economic management operations to which individuals commit their resources and time.[4]

Additionally, it should be noted that the linkage of development to market disequilibria means that to justify economic performance via what financial computations show is tenuous. Indeed, where development is occurring, it cannot be argued (with integrity) that a one hundred dollar market expenditure on medical services (to treat any given sick child) is the economic equivalent of that same expenditure at any 'good' restaurant.

Towards an analytical focus which argues that impact on quality-of-survival is a prime indicator of economic development attainment, the first chapter of this book elaborates the required programme and policy issues. They also emphasise how oversight of targets in survival has also created the oversight of a quality-of-life focus to economic development.

---

3. Individuals who have been stimulated to make such a request to their governments are likely to be ones who recognise that the opportunity to pursue human development is the inheritance which they are seeking to sustain.

4. Individuals also place outputs in terms of their consistency with their survival targets. Accordingly, there is no imputation that as long as the expenditures are made under conditions of market competition, "a dollar yields a dollar of value wherever that dollar is spent".

Raymond Samuels

Subsequent chapters will incorporate some of the wider disciplinary thrusts (including constitutional features) that have also inhibited the evolution of a posited *New Economy* where attainments in quality-of-living are given primacy. These will then lead to the elaboration of the context of "Quantum Economics" and the first stage specification of relationships that must be approached when it is the tapestry of forthcoming human experience that will form the development indicator.

CHAPTER 1

The Economy, the Quality-of-Life Attainment

༄

THE NEW ECONOMY, where results are prioritised in terms of their impacts on people, requires that appraisals of aggregate economic development performance must also be so focused. Economic development analysts are required to recognise that individuals orient their resource management commitments at opportunities to secure the wherewithal on behalf of preferred *patterns of survival* at which they aim.

Analysts of aggregate economic development performance are required to appreciate that human economic agents are set out to manage their resources *and* time commitments. Furthermore, it must be recognised that in their effort management commitments, individuals seek to secure patterns of results which they associate with a high quality-of-living. Individuals also operate in the market with the intent to acquire the financial wherewithal to purchase services that they need. However, economic development analysts must also recognise individuals as entities who seek to acquire *mixes of services and opportunities* which they view as being complementary with their quality-of-living target.

Here, work and employment in which individuals engage themselves will be recognised as occupying a significant portion of the time-use commitments that human economic agents make as they go about their lives. These operations will be appreciated as comprising strategies in which individuals engage as they make the endeavours to secure *some of* the proximate technical components which they will use towards securing a high quality of living. Therefore, when quality-of-living is the development target, the appraisals of aggregate economic development must *also* clarify how supportive the prevailing administrative and the compensation underpinnings to work have been.

Here, private individuals are recognised as measuring the results from their effort-commitment activities in living-centred terms. It is argued that when analysts measure aggregate economic development performance, they must be mindful to incorporate the extent to which the living-centred targets at which human economic agents aim have also been serviced.

In particular, economic development analysts are required to be mindful that although development is executed with the assistance of markets, measurements of economic performance may not overlook the *living*-centred attainment focus on resource management outcomes which human economic agents have.

As a result, *measurements of aggregate economic development performance must be required to appraise the extent to which the typical individual in the society has access to a survival path that exhibits high quality time-use opportunities.*

A society that seeks to execute the union of market activity and the delivery of services which enable individuals to access the requirements to high quality of time-use opportunities will need to adjust the programme context of its economic development. It will need to accommodate a context of Holistic Aggregate Economic Development assessment because that context promotes economic development programming which emphasises the human development targets that individuals have for themselves *and for their heirs.* Essentially, Holistic Aggregate Economic Development management is particularly mindful that the respective human economic agents who make up the society *need to be able to exercise informed management of the time-use* which manifests/houses their survival.[5]

Under Holistic Aggregate Economic Development management, decisions are informed and are guided by the relative impact of (potential)

---

5. For an elaboration of such a context, see, Horace Carby-Samuels, *Work, the Economy, and Human Development*, (Ottawa, Canada, The Agora Publishing Consortium) forthcoming, 2002, (ISBN 09681906-1-8).

programme initiatives on the quality-of-living of the typical member of the society. The framework looks upon the commercial relationships such as employment and sales, which arise in an environment as being among the instruments which are brought into play in the delivery of many sought services. At the same time, the Holistic focus is also mindful that in any particular society what individuals achieve depends on the information that is available the ability of individuals to handle that information and how power is structured and managed in the prevailing society.

Economic Development framework looks upon the items in trade as being technical outcomes that arise in response to prevailing resource allocative tolerances and information flows in the particular society. As a result, forthcoming outcomes are placed in a social context. For example, the Holistic Economic Development context is reconciled to the principle that an agrarian based society, which is managed under the principles of religious fundamentalism, will portray corresponding trade relationships. Therefore, it is inappropriate to expect that such a society will develop and manifest a brisk trade in personal computers. However, to accommodate the variety of societies that do exist, the Holistic emphasis is on attributive technical features, the mixes and the flows of attainments that individuals secure from their time-utilisation commitments and opportunities.

Consistent with its emphasis on a social context to resource allocation and management, the Holistic Aggregate Economic Development approach views the market economy as arising from a socio-political pact on behalf of *an emphasis* on financial-equivalent outcomes to resource allocation. In fact, the market economic emphasis seeks to preserve dominance by financial interests rather than to preserve representative democracy. Accordingly, Holistic Aggregate Economic Development does not promote the inter-personal structural features which accompany reliance on purely financial-equivalent weighing of outcomes.

The aegis of the market economy operates via a rule system wherein it is the success of individuals in transforming the components of reality into financial-equivalent property that regulates their access to the wherewithal for survival and other levers of power. In contrast to the market economic society, which accommodates human economic agents largely as merchandisers of their time (and other designated property), the Holistic Aggregate Economic Development emphasises individuals as managing their time in order to bring quality to how they live.

The market economy does not prioritise satisfying the needs of people. It is a society where prevailing resources become available to deliver the complements to the material survival of individuals *only* if a desired profit rate can be associated with the particular delivery. To that end, in the market economy, an active system of trading in resources and outputs toward generating financial profit operates in concert with a system of financial payments and settlements. This payments system and an accompanying system of market-determined pricing smooth out the inconvenience which would arise in trading via barter. However, in the process of providing the convenience in the settlements of accounts, the financial intermediation system legitimates for itself claims on *a share* in the net revenues that accompany the creating and the trading of property.

The convenience of this financial arrangements network that facilitates payments settlements with regard to features *that are defined as property* breeds a covert coalition between the politically and the commercially dominant operators in the society. This coalition operates on behalf of financial-equivalent accumulation. Accordingly, notwithstanding popular statements which *profess* that constitutional democracy is the operating norm, in the capitalist society, government as the institutionalised political arm of that coalition operates as the "orchestral conductor" on behalf of results that the commercial arm desires.

The market economy assigns government the responsibility for promoting/cultivating conditions which are consistent with "relative stability" to the changes in the perceived value of the property which the coalition has legitimated. Accordingly, in the name of preserving "peace, order and good government", formal and informal programmes of "education" are covertly used to foster among the population acquiescence to features that are consistent with a commercial thrust to living. In contrast, there is no corresponding coalition which requires governments to emphasise the delivery of the quality-of-life features out of which access to human development will emerge.

Accordingly, where Holistic Aggregate Economic Development programming is *absent*, development programming, which is touted as "education", "security" and "justice" initiatives, is unlikely to be more than tactics on behalf of stable and secure commercial growth. Under these circumstances, the accompanying development programmes are usually marshalled *to reinforce the SOCIETAL ACCEPTANCE OF PROFIT-DICTATED RESOURCE ALLOCATION*along with promoting acceptance of the coalition(s) such as the World Trade Organisation (WTO) which focuses on the profit which markets spawn.

In such circumstances, the prevailing political and economic management coalitions aim to *stymie discussions* which promote the premise that government also has people-centred economic development responsibilities. Holistic Aggregate Economic Development management emphasises that these responsibilities of government are beyond the legitimating of private (tradable) property as well as structural support to the likely forthcoming generation of market profit. However, currently, in Western societies, the "education" and communications system neglects to stimulate awareness that *government has responsibilities with regards to the quality-of-living targets that individuals have.* Therefore, *government needs to ensure that its tolerance of commerce is not at the expense of those quality-of-living targets.*

The prevailing market-centred "education" and communications system(s) have as a target more than distracting people regarding the responsibilities of governments. These "education", communications and skills delivery systems are also used to generate specific types of "people production" results. For example, these programs tend to concentrate on packaging besides emphasising in subtle ways the imputation that the overriding economic development role of government is to protect and defend the rights of wealth holders and private ownership of property.

This system of education and socialization is also set out to *lead citizens* and support the proposition that governments should allow all items which have identifiable and controllable boundaries (with the exception of the person of the citizen) to be treated as market-alienated property. As a result, in Western economies, the idea of "a common property resource" of the prevailing society is substantively becoming viewed as being almost an anachronism.

Meanwhile, the high degree of division of labour which has accompanied the technological evolution of Western societies requires a system of formal and informal education that is tailored to the delivery of the required technical skills. Currently, the training and skills development system appears to have also been assigned the implicit mandate to communicate and reinforce at least two commerce-centred development-related messages.

The first of these assigned (and to be delivered) messages is that facilitating the private ownership of (profit yielding) property is one of the principal reasons for having government. The next message, which is the (commerce-centred education) system, "assigned" to communicate is that the skills of individuals are being effectively used when the commitment contributes to changes in the aggregate level of commerce (and thus to measured GNP).

With this policy context in mind, the prevailing curricula of respective skills development programmes are not oriented at complementing Holistic Aggregate Economic Development. Significantly, if prevailing curricula had integrity in matters which are related to human consciousness, they would be designed to either reinforce or be supportive of the recognition that technically empowered survival-centred citizens are the substantive output and target of a knowledge-delivery industry.

In contrast to the overlooked Holistic focus, in Western market-centred societies, *information transference* is given relevance primarily in terms of *how* extensively the activities of individuals who have been exposed to the information will lead to GNP enhancement. The result is that in these market-centred societies, individuals are essentially socialised to hold the view that "if no money can be made" from acquiring the piece of information, the material is not worthy of being given much due attention.

However, human development is one of the principal outcomes which will arise where education programming is designed to communicate information that will complement the technical as well as the time-use management empowerment of individuals. Therefore, *human development will be forthcoming where accessible prevailing outputs of goods and services enable individuals to secure time-use opportunities out of which a high quality-of-living will arise.*

Conscious human economic agents are rational and survival-centred entities. They respectively have their survival-centred attainment targets and they make private estimates about how much their quality-of-living will be furthered by the outcomes of respective prospective initiatives. However, it must first be resolved that what exactly are these targets/ achievements that the prevailing resource and effort management commitments need to satisfy. It is only after such designation that statistical measurements of development performance that aim to facilitate the effectiveness of individuals in achieving the quality-of-living targets that they have can be made.

Correspondingly, the success of development programming in fostering the quality-of living of members of the society can be measured only after the society at hand indicates the levels and mixes of critical services that it will use its programming to become available to its typical members.

For example, post-apartheid South Africa (1987-98) stated that its aim was to shift to a people-centred appraisal of prevailing economic development results. To that end, the African National Congress (ANC) had previously formulated a Reconstruction and Development Program (RDP). The ANC had indicated that *empowerment* of the total citizenry would be the target of the economic development programming of the post-apartheid government.

Evidently, the ANC did not want an environment where the economic importance of the persons that it represents is viewed as being equivalent to the extent of the market contribution of the individual in respective functional roles which these persons executed in the generation of GNP. Arguably, the RDP document *as initially formulated* by the African National Congress aimed to achieve a domain where human development, rather than "wage slavery", would emerge.

Yet, to achieve the contemplated human development outcomes, the government of the New South Africa would need to indicate target empowerment achievements against which its development programming should be judged. The government would also need to ensure that members of the population are exposed to formal and informal education/ communications initiatives which will cultivate the skills, with which quality-of-life attainment will be serviced.

Additionally the programmes of the post-apartheid South Africa government would also need to emphasise and make clear that *development rewards will be forthcoming only to individuals who exercise responsible participation in effort commitment and resource management.* A mass of citizenry which is awaiting a generous bestowal of transfer payments (government hand-outs) is not a structural base from which development as empowerment will emerge.

It happens, however, that the typical Western-trained economist is in service to market mobilization (and to subsequent commercial attainments). These analysts do not focus on how effectively such commerce is complementing quality-of-life attainment. Furthermore, although quality-of-life attainment is a private experience, the contributory features become accessible to the typical individual as direct outcomes from the priorities at which prevailing aggregate economic development management initiatives are aimed. However, unfortunately, the prevailing economic development literature offers the governments of countries such as the New South Africa little guidance to policy and programming that may draw towards prioritising the features out of which the empowerment at which it aims will emerge.

High quality-of-life attainment levels are forthcoming to individuals when they have access to *mixes of outputs and opportunities* which will facilitate or support the survival targets to which their consciousness leads them. Therefore, as the author has elaborated elsewhere, analysts will need to identify these targets and the technical complements with which the targets may be best serviced.

However, one starts with the premise that individuals (as conscious entities) seek to structure a preferred time-path to their survival. Therefore, their quality-of-living is revealed in their prevailing time-use patterns. The forthcoming patterns will need to show the opportunity and ability of individuals to participate in controlling the respective forces which impact their lives. Accordingly, in any reference period, the quality-of-life pointers will be revealed in the *changes* in the access of respective individuals *to critical mixes* of attainments.

Performance inquiries about quality-of-life attainment are therefore essentially about whether prevailing aggregate economic development programming is *fostering* the access of individuals to the critical complements to survival as time-use patterns that they seek. As a result, the analyst can talk about forthcoming improvements in quality-of-living only after first clarifying what are the attainment targets that form the quality-of-life pointers at which a prevailing aggregate economic development domain aims.

Holistic Aggregate Economic Development management seeks to take initiatives to mitigate or remove access bottlenecks to the critical mixes of services that frame the survival targets of consciousness-centred human economic agents. However, access changes will be forthcoming under a variety of circumstances.

For example, there are mixes of services (such as roads and public health) that become available from investment that facilitates effective use of common property resources of a society. Other services such as the availability of meat and potatoes will be forthcoming from investment that complements private market exchanges. There are also some sought technical services such as consumer protection in the market that will arise only if the government decides to execute oversight rules. For example, government may decide to orient the administrative support that it provides largely to those trade and exchange operations that service the survival priorities of citizens.

When performance is gauged by how much aggregate financial-equivalent wealth has been generated, the *details* of the mixes of available services do not form a point of focus because under those circumstances, when it is financial-equivalent price that weighs the economic importance of the exchanges that are conducted, items are usually considered important because they are associated with aggregate commerce. In contrast, when a government seeks to foster quality-of-life attainment, it will need to guide its investment by a paradigm that correspondingly emphasises survival-centred consequences on people.

In these circumstances, governments must be prepared to recognise that towards executing their human development objectives, human economic agents have historically been economizers on how they commit their time. It is particularly on how effectively individuals are able to execute that (time) budgeting commitment which government will need to facilitate. Government will therefore need to require development data to reveal how extensively the complements to the time-use patterns (out of which human development will arise) will become available to the typical member of the society.

Yet, the technical variety of items which individuals require and the substitution possibilities that arise among them make trade a vital instrument in service to the delivery of not a few of the technical complements to quality-of-living. It is also the fact that individuals secure a high quality-of-living by budgeting the allocation of their time. There are therefore in operation living-centred time-prices as well as financial-equivalent market prices. As a result, Quantum Economics emerges in recognition of the living (as duration) and consciousness-enhancement as its infinite horizon which intersects the trading decisions which individuals make as they go about their lives. As a result, the context of the New Economy which is envisaged here imputes that economic development initiatives which aim to enhance the net market value of trade do not represent the superior development management technique on which a society must concentrate.

———•———

The Background to Date

To date, in Western society, the norm is to measure in financial terms exchanges of the effective involved technical quantities. The result is that Western society socialises individuals to gauge, in terms of capitalised (net accruing) market-equivalent value, the bulk of the interactions which form their lives. Individuals in Western societies are socialised to weigh their current or their planned selections among resource management (and even their personal interaction) options in terms of the expected financial results.

In Western societies, particularly in the North American versions, individuals have been largely socialised to judge in expected commercial terms the success of their prevailing path in living. Remarkably, individuals who have been so socialised *also* tend to weigh their selections among inter-personal encounters in terms of the potential, direct or indirect, net private financial-equivalent gain, which the potential encounter promises.

Notwithstanding the underlying socialization which is being promoted across the globe via international agreements and "conferences" on behalf of "trade globalisation", humans also recognise their mortality. Therefore, as conscious entities, human (economic agents) also want to use their resource and time commitments to secure attainments which give expression to (or which are centred to) *what* being alive means to them.

Humans make time and effort management commitments in the light of the background which is provided by their consciousness and their sense of being. Therefore, in the economizing that they do, the human economic agents as private, survival-centred entities also tend to weight their expected success at achieving the living-centred targets that they have.

The traditional market economic approach deals with the market efficiency of committed financial equivalent resources/funds. The traditional market economic focus does not have a measurement basis for addressing queries about how effectively the survival targets of the involved consciousness-centred individuals in the environment at hand are being serviced.

Essentially, the effectiveness of service to targets in survival is indicated by the extent to which the available mix of opportunities of individuals to commit their time (on and off the job) meets the quality indicators in the survival at which they aim. Development performance will therefore be revealed by examining the patterns of the technical mixes of services and time-use opportunities that become available to the typical individual in the society at hand.

To appraise performance, analysts must therefore verify the extent to which the prevailing patterns of access to the technical complements of living in the society at hand enable the *typical* individual to satisfy the respective survival-centred time-use goals in living which that individual has. For example, the individual must have access to mixes of goods and services which minister to the critical needs that he/she must satisfy to survive as a biological and conscious entity; the requisites for basic human needs such as food, clothing, shelter and a sense of security. However, evaluative/computational problems are presented by features such as the technical variety to the components that comprise of the mixes of critical services, the differences in the technical complexity of the component items as well as their non-standardisation and the practice of measuring the diverse mix (and their supportive resource complement) in market value terms.

Economic performance as delivered quality-of-life attainment in the environment at hand must also reveal the extent to which *respective* human economic agents have rights to manage how and where their time and efforts are committed. A New Economy which has a quality-of-life delivery as its attainment indicator may therefore not treat as being subsidiary the availability of these management rights.

Market value computations of delivered outputs do not directly address either the presence of time-use management rights or the composition of the mixes of services that become available. Rather, the market price of respective services is largely a "ballot" on matters regarding the financial-equivalent value of the PROPERTY that is associated with the items. The associated price quotations indicate how much money value (as "liquid" property) individuals are being asked to be willing to surrender in exchange in order to secure the *ownership* rights to the less financially liquid piece of property.

Essentially, market economists argue that it is the expectation of at least equivalent value in exchange or the expectation of profit that is behind the transactions which markets reveal. Accordingly, the imputation is that when a society treats the complements to survival as being marketable property, the extent to which they will become available in needed quantities will depend upon how profitable their delivery will be as items of trade because normally the possibility of profit from product delivery via sales on the market acts as a context for steering the outputs to which resources will be committed. However, normally there are private as well as social costs to all production arrangements and a New Economy, which has a quality-of-living focus, is sensitive to how these costs are being distributed.

Not surprisingly, what becomes profitable to private producers of outputs is also linked to the tolerances that the society decides to exercise about how the associated social costs will be borne. For example, entrepreneurs can make a profit if the society does not make them liable for discomfitures such as environmental destruction or pollution that their selection of production techniques causes.

The system of governance in The New Economy also needs to be mindful that geographic space and the non-renewable natural endowment to which the society as a whole has been treated comprises of a significant portion of its societal assets. Furthermore, how the society decides to handle these assets is a significant feature in its economic development strategies. For example, Western governments give to entrepreneurs rights to buy and sell as private property respective partitions of the geographic endowment, even though that endowment belongs to the society as a whole.

Within the operating markets, the principle of "buyer beware" holds. However, via the court system, which the society institutes, the prevailing government operates as an implicit eventual guarantor of trade contracts. The result is that respective individuals expect implicit performance guarantees from items which they acquire in any trade contract that government will empower the adjudicative offices of the courts in order to require the buyer to also honour. The overriding result is that essentially government effectively underwrites the integrity of the trading environment. It does so by providing a legitimated currency as well as a credible set of adjudicative mechanisms (courts, and a system of weights and measures) for *unquestionable* settlements of contract disputes regarding delivery or payments.

Unless participants have confidence in *how* these facilitative mechanisms (which the society under-writes via its government) are functioning, there is unlikely to be any widespread, sustained and effective trade in that environment. However, there are potential negative spin-off outcomes which frequently accompany operations of private production for sales. Therefore, an administrative regime which seeks to use trade and exchange as a vehicle in quality-of-life delivery must also make decisions about the extent to which it *will cause* the remainder of the society to absorb these spin-off environmental and other costs to production for trade. For example, a high quality-of-living will not be forthcoming in trade environments where governments allow the proliferation of consumer fraud of the sort that Warren Magnuson and Jean Carper (1968) presented. There is also a plethora of additional environmental costs, which are addressed later in this book, on which an aggregate economic development directorate must focus if complementing the access of individuals to quality-of-life attainment is its target.

The responsibility that government exercises in providing currency and the courts system, as a support to prevailing trade, makes government a silent partner to ALL trade and exchange in the market. Therefore, when political economic "conservatives" argue that they support getting government out of prevailing economic operations, they betray a deplorable level of unawareness about the administrative pillars on which private exchange contract evolves. Furthermore, inferences about performance that are drawn from what changes in the financial value of trade show are valid *only* in the presence of a system of governance that polices the monetary supply and the presence of conditions of market competition.

Analysts who recognise quality-of life as the target of individuals and at the same time recognise that access to time-use management opportunities is the principal aggregate economic development performance indicator will also need to emphasise the facilitative role which governments must play in order to achieve quality-of-life results. For example, empowerment as an attribute of quality-of-life will be feasible only if individuals have access to critical information. Only then can they approach making the efficient technical substitutions which will enable them to overcome their limited access to purchasing power (money), time and other resources.

Government initiatives TO LIMIT the incidence of institutional barriers that will cause restriction of the capability of individuals to access and process information are a particularly powerful empowerment-oriented economic developmental tool. Therefore, when governments condone the formation and the operation of monopolies (and cross media ownerships) in the press and public information media, they are evidently *not* committed to facilitating the access of individuals to quality-of-living.

In the post-World War II era (1947), Karl Polanyi (1968) had used his essay the "Obsolete Market Mentality", which was later republished in other material, to elaborate the myopia of using primarily a market focus to appreciate occurrences and results in the environment of development. Furthermore, even though the production, delivery and acquisition of information usually have a cost, the feature does not justify the evaluation of economic performance primarily on market value terms.

Historically, the outcomes which individuals have sought from their time and resource allocation include more assured access to the means of their subsistence, (food, clothing, shelter), security of person, good health and information about their world and how it works. The New Economy, which recognises conscious, mortal human beings as the operators who have quality-of-living as their substantive target, emphasises the market as *the service sector*. The market is not emphasised (as capitalist economics does) as the dictating effort and resource management context into which individuals must fit and by which the management priorities of governments must be guided.

It is the civilisation (as indicated in quality-of-life attainment) and not the sales value of collections of tradable trinkets which is the aggregate output of the time and the resource management operations of human economic agents. Therefore, if analysts are to deal with that reality, the presentation of the philosopher Michael Polanyi (1966) regarding how humans recognise and cope with information is germane.

Essentially, Michael Polanyi clarified the information absorption background regarding how understanding operates.

In matters regarding economic development, the logic to the Michael Polanyi presentation points to the feature that *it is consciousness-centred human economic agents who are recognising resources and are also executing and managing combinations of them*. His presentation regarding how individuals focus makes it easy to appreciate the circumstance that it is a sought survival with preferred attributes that is the target at which human economic agents respectively aim their time and resource commitments.

In the light of that Michael Polanyi pointer regarding how individuals operate, policy makers in The New Economy are called on to be mindful of the attributes of the quality-of-life targets at which individuals aim. They are then called upon to formulate policy in recognition that success of their decisions will be indicated by the level of quality-of-living attainment that becomes available. These policy framers are therefore required to look at forthcoming results in the light of the appreciation that human economic agents execute scarcity management towards achieving the targets in *human development* that they respectively have. The aggregate economic development management directorate will therefore need to look at the access of individuals to technical complements which will foster consumption attainments of the sort that is associated with survival and consciousness enhancement.

The New Economy therefore requires that observed activities in wealth management must be appreciated as being technical strategic operations on which *socialised* human economic agents draw to *leverage* the achievement of their targets in human development.

As a philosopher, Hans Jonas (1969) pointed out that a provision for heirs represents one of the substantive commitments on behalf of human development which mediates the choices of resource commitments that human economic agents select.[6]

This appreciation that human development is the target emerges from the recognition that conscious human economic agents (on having rejected suicide) seek the capability and the opportunities to better *execute how they live*. Over the process of human evolution, efforts to secure living of a higher quality comprise of the time-use commitments of conscious human economic agents. Notably, the time-use achievements against which the forthcoming quality-of-survival of individuals must be measured also include the access that they have to participate in opportunities for leisure, celebrations and rest and recreation.

Individuals judge the quality of the survival which they have attained by ranking alternative levels of access that they secure to mixes of critical features. These critical features include:

(a) Mixes of the components which they need for material survival (subsistence)
(b) Empowerment to manage their (survival) time in preferred ways
(c) Environments/eco-systems that are not destroyed in the process of market exploitation.

6. See, therefore, Hans Jonas, "Economic Knowledge and the Critique of Goals", in *Economic Means and Social Ends*, Robert Heilbroner (ed.) (Englewood Cliffs, New Jersey: Prentice-Hall Inc.) 1969, pp. 67-87.

Purchase of technical components in the market is one route through which individuals acquire many of the complements to their sought attainments. However, where human development is the economic development target, the emphasis on prevailing development programmes must be on *the opportunity* of the typical individual in the society to secure *mixes* of critical services that they need (on behalf of their quality-of-survival).

Therefore, even though markets exist for products as well as skills, the net commercial equivalent value of outputs may not be used as the indicator of development vitality.

The time that individuals spend in working is also a part of their time that is spent in living. As a result, individuals also appraise the returns to their time and resource commitment efforts in living-related terms. These terms are not fully captured by what prevailing opportunities to purchase show.

When individuals offer their time-housed efforts in employment, the involved human economic agents set out to judiciously combine their time with other resources that they do not currently control. Via those employment-linked time-use combinations, individuals aim to acquire financial capability. In addition, they aim to contribute to outcomes which will complement and give enhanced content to the path of survival at which they aim (as conscious entities). As a result, The New Economy that operates under Holistic Aggregate Economic Development management recognises development outcomes as being indicated by how much enhancement has occurred in the access of individuals to mixes of critical complements to their survival. Furthermore, one of those survival attainments will be indicated by the opportunities for informed management of how their lives evolve that individuals secure.

The required information about the access of the typical individual in the society to critical technical services that are associated with quality-of-life attainment is not yet being systematically collected. In addition, the management of the typical market economic society is not concerned with (and therefore neglects to appraise) the extent to which prevailing trade also complements the survival needs of the typical member of the society.

In contrast, The New Economy that has quality of life as its attainment focus assigns government the aggregate economic management responsibility in respect of the environment in which survival occurs. Government will need to monitor the extent to which that environment is being compromised and it must also monitor access of the typical individual to mixes of critical services on which their quality of survival depends.

Government is then required to take policy programming and management steps to ensure that the market practices which it legitimates are also consistent with the access of individuals to flows of services which they need to secure a high quality-of-living.

Notwithstanding the convenience of money in trade-related matters, governments need not allow the profit dictates of the providers of footloose, internationally mobile property-equivalent value (that resides in money), to orient their selections of development initiatives. Instead, the strategy of Holistic Aggregate Economic Development requires governments to take initiatives to improve access of individuals to the background facts that they need to make informed trades. Government is also required to facilitate the access of individuals to the flows of mixes of critical services which make a high quality-of-survival.

Information which elaborates how extensively and rapidly the aggregate market value of wealth is increasing will not communicate about whether there has been improvements in the access of individuals to mixes of critical services (out of which the high quality-of-living arises).

———•———

Delivery Issues

Where services become available under the auspices of the market, it is expectation of profit from the items that are offered for sale which will dictate the mixes of products and services that become available. Correspondingly, in the market dominated economic development contexts, it is the expected profitability of sold outputs that will influence the mixes of resources in addition to the technology which will be attracted for use in the delivery of respective outputs.

Yet, mixes of services which become available in trade and the governments are prepared to cause to become available don't just happen. What any level of output delivery flow happens to be is also under the influence of institutional tolerances. Some of these institutional tolerances have traditionally operated as government-provided subsidies such as administrative features (for example zoning regulations) regarding how resources in a particular area may be used and stipulations regarding how the spin-off costs from prevailing techniques of production will be borne. Issues such as tolerable environmental impacts, the on-the-job rights of individuals and licensing regulations (that may also be quality-of-life oriented) are other administrative relationships to which forthcoming production flows in development initiatives may be required to conform.

An example of an implicitly existent government stipulated prohibition is the circumstance that persons are not allowed to accept current financial payments from potential employers on the promise that their children will be later available to work for that employer. Another example of government impact is that, narcotics and other hard drugs are not usually regarded as items which are included in the everyday trade that government legitimates.

One more example of government impact on profit expectations arises out of government regulations which require firms to build paid vacation time into the work year income of employees. Comparably, when firms are not required to bear the costs of environmental and other spill-over damages which their operations generate, governments are then essentially providing these firms implicit subsidies.

Most outputs which are forthcoming through trade are usually also accompanied by the usage of space and other common property resources of the society. However, historically, via their selections of emphases among investments in common property resources (such as communications and roads, security and health and safety), governments have also leveraged the mix and the spatial source of forthcoming trade outcomes.

In addition, governments have also used initiatives such as zoning and health and safety regulations to place caveats on how designated respective parts of the geographic space of the society are utilised in production.

In the performance evaluation matrix that may be applied to development outcomes, there are two streams. One performance stream arises as the prevailing market exchange opportunities (for the planning period at hand). The appraisal concern is the effectiveness with which offerings in the market assist or enable individuals to make efficient commitments of their time.

The other performance stream is the consistency with which the prevailing administrative initiatives within which the prevailing aggregate economic development directorate operates complement the access of individuals to their quality-of-living targets. [7]

Human development is a perpetuity at which conscious individuals respectively aim and the aggregate economic development management directorate is charged with the responsibility to monitor and execute the preservation of an environment that nurtures the access of individuals to the attendant evolutionary opportunities.

When individuals use the flexibility of money to make substitutes among the technical items that are offered in trade, these substitution operations do not signal that these individuals have subordinated wealth targets for the quality-of living ones that they have. Indeed, as economists fully recognise, the private price at which individuals are prepared to make certain purchases or make a particular sale is an idiosyncratic fact in their respective lives and is not necessarily the "market" price. When it is the fostering of sought living-centred impacts at which prevailing time and resource management aims, the presence of free and competitive markets (so called "equilibrium prices" for resources and popularly

---

7. The operation of this latter performance stream is emphasised in the later chapters of this book, whereas statistical computational matters in respect of the first performance stream are elaborated in detail elsewhere. See, therefore, *Work, The Economy and Human Development*; Ottawa, Canada, Agora Publishing Consortium, ISBN 0-9681906-2-6, (Forthcoming, 2003).

traded outputs) does not provide either a necessary or a sufficient guide to program decisions.[8]

For example, feature outputs such as food, clothing, shelter and access to justice and participation in how their environment evolves comprise of services which individuals typically seek. Acquisition in the market has been one of the ways through which individuals have accessed these outputs. Yet, requiring human economic agents to pay prices that purchasers of resources require to make their output profitable does not exhaust the techniques through which the required flows of critical outputs may be caused to become available.

Indeed, as far back as the post-World War II period (1947), Karl Polanyi (1968) had pointed out that the universalization of an "Obsolete Market Mentality" has had dysfunctional effects on our society. However, the ever increasing complexity of division of labour together with the institutionalisation of access rights via earnings has also required individuals to cope with the principle of survival via their capability to offer market value in monetary terms.

The result is that within the premise that an expectation of market-equivalent gain is behind the exchanges that individuals make, Gary Becker (1975) elaborated a performance appraisal context which viewed the human living space (that is their time-use commitments) as being all about trade and markets. The Becker focus complements the imputation that the responsibility of the aggregate economic development directorate is to facilitate stable markets which will deliver the saleable merchandise that individuals (in the normal and customary process of living) will seek to acquire.

In contrast, in The New Economy that has quality-of-life enhancement as its target requires achievements to be indicated by the access of individ-

---

8. An emphasis on quality-of-life as an outcome may not be overlooked by using the assumption that where market prices prevail, distributive effects may be treated as being neutral. The one hundred dollars that a drug dealer spends on flamboyant consumption does not provide an equivalent development yield with the identical amount that is spent on subsistence for children in an orphanage. As a result, the development directorate needs to concern itself about the impacts of its investment on the delivery of *the living-centred priorities* with which the society (as a civilization) seeks to characterise itself.

uals to critical complements to the time-utilization targets that they have as they pursue their survival. Therefore, economists may not (as Simon Kuznets (1963) pointed out) substitute statements that address matters regarding how a logically defined trade-centred whole has been affected and thereby overlook a focus on how results affect the people in a society.[9]

So far, governments have tended to *not* communicate about how their stewardship has contributed to the quality-of-living of the typical member of the society. Oversight of that delivery impact is largely due to the collusions (between the government, the commercial sector and economic spokes-persons) on behalf of generating financial flows which the politicians and dominant groups in commerce want to see accelerated. Accordingly, the principal development "advice" which Western economists (as a part of that collusive context) give to the governments in developing economies is that steps should be taken to ensure that market competition prevails.

Governments are also advised to concentrate on investment initiatives which lead the members of the society (whom the government is supposed to represent) to become better "tools" and "earning instruments" in prevailing commerce. The advice of the economic spokes-persons is that the participating members of the polity (of the typical economic society) must be trained to become better human capital (essentially purchasable tools) in the competitive market for skills and outputs.[10]

---

9. See, therefore, Simon Kuznets, (1963) "Parts and Wholes in Economics" in *Parts and Wholes*, Daniel Learner (ed.), (New York: The Free Press of Glencoe). Essentially, there, Kuznets pointed to the interesting conundrums that can emerge in economics as a discipline.

   In the name of science, the discipline can structure, for analytical purposes, *defined* wholes. Thereby, the discipline can conveniently remove itself from the need/responsibility to deal with the *functioning* wholes that create the access dysfunctions (such as those in subsistence, health care and control over their lives) with which people are called upon to live.

10. This current human capital nexus emanated around the University of Chicago in concert with the separate and also the collaborative works of Theodore Schultz, Gary Becker, (1972) and others. In contrast, there is the human capital context which Fritz Machlup was developing and he was unable to finish and publish prior to his death. Machlup had his human

Essentially, the economic literature presents manpower training and corresponding strategies of creating earning-skills called "human capital formation" as the "yellow brick road" to the attainment of development. The governments of countries with low aggregate market activity are therefore also advised to take the necessary steps to structure their financial institutions so as to ensure that their currency is internationally convertible (so as to smooth the evolution of "globalisation" of trade).

Outputs tend to become available through the manipulation of renewable as well as non-renewable resources as individuals seek to access their preferred survival path development as enhanced quality-of-life attainment may need to draw on some components that become accessible only via prevailing market operations. However, in the living that they do, individuals are in search of the most effective technique for securing the enhanced consciousness at which they aim.

Living as an economising operation comprises (survival-centred) of time-use management operations where individuals seek to manoeuvre towards goals in survival that they have (as conscious entities).

In the process, they secure living of a preferred quality by acquiring enhanced technical capability to control, access and accommodate the features that impact the survival path which they seek.

Individuals acquire money for its convenience and they then spend it in patterns which can enable them to acquire resources (inclusive of outcomes from research capability) on behalf of their survival-centred targets. The aggregate market value from prevailing trade does not tell whether the typical individual in the society at hand is securing the opportunities and capabilities in order to secure preferred patterns of survival. Therefore, on order to communicate about quality-of-life attainment of such human economic agents, measurements of economic performance must tell the success which they respectively had in securing

---

capital focus on the technical, managerial and environmental structuring capabilities which generate an evolutionary path for conscious effort managers. He especially regarded these effort managers as respective societally-vital decision-making units. His focus was on the structured resource management whole and how knowledge mediates the effectiveness of the consciousness-driven evolutionary initiatives on which individuals decide to concentrate.

the critical technical components of the informed and enhanced survival at which they aim.

Accordingly, The New Economy (that has quality-of-life attainment as its focus) emphasises economic management success as being indicated by the access of individuals to flows of technical services that complement their survival-centred time-commitment opportunities/patterns. The achievement of individuals will also become manifest as their enhanced capability to forge informed trade-offs in pursuit of sought subsistence as well as on behalf of control over how their environment evolves.

In the market-managed economy, rich people can buy more "influence" as well as larger and more varied quantities and mixes of subsistence goods and services. However, where quality-of-living is the target, the development techniques in a constitutional democracy will need to aim at delivering time-use management empowerment to the typical citizen. Therefore, the investment and the other economic management initiatives of the government must aim at delivering enhanced understanding that can be converted into enhanced resource, time and effort management skills. As a result, unlike what the prevailing "human capital" approach emphasises, government investment initiatives that are directed at impacting on people need not be aimed principally at enhancing their earning skills.[11]

A viable currency is an indispensable component in any society that produces or uses a variety of outputs. Accessible information is the other component which must be in place in order to facilitate exchange among products that are not technically standardised. Indeed, it can be argued that the presence of markets demonstrates two principal features. One is the willingness of individuals to exchange real goods for currency and the other is the adaptability in face of variety to which human consciousness leads. However, in the light of the market oversights (including stipulations of environment usage tolerances which government must execute), it is the patterns of critical services which become available from those

---

11. A context for appraising the effectiveness of government investment as indicated by prevailing output deliveries which retains analytical roots in Marshallian economics has been elaborated by Horace Carby-Samuels. See therefore, *Work, The Economy, and Human Development*, (Ottawa, Canada, Agora Publishing Consortium; forthcoming, 2003); ISBN 0-9681906-1-8.

markets that will demonstrate prevailing aggregate economic development performance.

Individuals face the need to execute the critical trade-offs on behalf of a high quality-of-survival. Therefore, a development directorate has particular tasks if it aims to cause its operations to be complementary to the survival needs which individuals have. The directorate will need to discourage or remove barriers which systematically seek to inhibit the access of individuals to the information (that they will need to make the living-centred trade-offs to which they are committed).

It is the pattern of the mixes of critical services among which individuals are able to choose that will reveal the time-use opportunities which are open to them. It is also from informed exchanges that a high quality-of-living will be forthcoming. Therefore, an aggregate economic development directorate will need to:

(a) Verify the extent to which its prevailing administrative support to trade complements the access of individuals to critical technical mixes of services on behalf of their quality-of-living.
(b) Discourage blockages to the flow of information which individuals will need to make their survival-oriented trade-offs effective and efficient.

---·•·---

The Way Forward

In proceeding forward, an aggregate economic development directorate needs to recognise that it faces two sets of relationships which it needs to coordinate. It must facilitate deliveries in respect of critical services that individuals need in order to access opportunities for quality-of-life attainment. However, as a part of its responsibilities to facilitate the delivery of mixes of these critical services on behalf of a high quality-of-survival, an aggregate economic development directorate also has responsibilities to police and facilitate the type of environmental preservation that a high quality of survival requires.

Tradable outputs (in varying degrees) are forthcoming from inputs that are common property items as well as from others that are own-able renewable resources. Therefore, in matters regarding the access of individuals to critical survival-oriented services, a development directorate must execute a balancing act. The items that become available through trade are largely ones where producers are able to "attract" and use available resources to create them and then sell them at a profit. The resources on which these sellers draw to deliver those outputs include those which they own; those which become accessible via fee-for-service from the use of common property resources as well as government initiated institutional support (inclusive of a court system, subsidies, "zoning" regulations, tariffs and international trade treaties). There is also the behind the scenes "bully pulpit" of its military capability that government uses as "influence" on behalf of its favourite clientele groups in the economy.

The (direct and indirect) costs which are associated with attracting these sources of inputs into production decisions are likely to influence the price at which respective sought outputs (inclusive of those on behalf of a high quality of living) will be made available.

At the same time, there is also competition among possible outputs for access to available resources. Therefore, when an aggregate economic development directorate identifies the critical delivery mixes which it will seek to facilitate, there are accompanying issues regarding the resource access to which it will commit itself in the light of potential variations in the technology of production. However, there is a variety of techniques through which governments may influence forthcoming output availability or influence how it plans to include in forthcoming output impact on the environment.

These impact techniques that governments have on forthcoming patterns of output start from how government uses its legislative power to execute its function as custodian of the common property resources of the society. Another impact technique on forthcoming patterns of deliveries operates via the power of government to structure and levy direct and indirect taxes (including tariffs) and to offer subsidies. However, when a government decides to measure performance via the access of individuals to critical services, it will need a correspondingly focused quality-of-life-oriented measurement system to guide its attempt to remedy shortfalls efficiently.

At the same time, when a government decides that the indicator of performance will be the levels of availabilities and access to critical services, it will also have decided to not necessarily leave the vagaries of the "free" market to resolve questions regarding "Who gets what" and "How much". Such a development directorate will therefore need to collect data which reveal where and how extensively shortfalls in access to critical (targeted) services are present. Implicitly, the directorate will be guided by statements and stipulations (listings) of the identity and the levels of the critical services for which the availability shortfalls will be computed.

Information about development performance as it affects private individuals must therefore show:

(a) The levels of access that the typical member of the society has to these critical technical services
(b) The extent of progress that has been made towards the removal of bottlenecks to the production and the delivery of those services
(c) The extent to which the time-use opportunities that are available to individuals complements their access to the quality-of-survival targets at which they respectively aim.

However, in order to fully support the attainment of a high quality-of-living, government will also need to discharge its policing and protection responsibilities in respect of the environment. Therefore, government will also need to assure itself that there are available scientific data on which it needs to draw (in order to monitor the extent of departures from attainment targets and preferred environmental states which are consistent with a high quality-of-living).

CHAPTER 2

CITIZENS WITH CIVIL RIGHTS OR
HUMAN CAPITAL?

⌒⌒⌒

C ITIZENS ARE THE BASIC components of prevailing polities. The term citizen is essentially linked to ideas about people (in groups). The term is also linked to considerations about the constitutionally articulated and entrenched rights that the member individuals of the polity have. In contrast, the economy comprises of or is represented by, institutionally integrated collections of prevailing sets of trade and exchange arrangements that arise in association with negotiated prices.

An economy, therefore, emerges in concert with a number of trading-centred institutional provisions. Typically, the institutional underpinnings to the economy tend to end up operating as an extra-constitutional governance system that operates via alliances between prevailing governments and groups that have secured access to and ownership rights over financial equivalent wealth.

The result is that what ends up being tolerated in trade-related matters usually ends up being at the convenience of and also being on behalf of the interests of these extra-constitutional management institutions. Implicitly and explicitly, the government-stipulated tolerances usually dictate what items will be handled as property. Furthermore, the rules under which the complements to survival will be distributed among members of a polity comprise of an integral part of the government legitimated functioning economy.

Starkly put, the concept of an economy is normally applied to an environment where on the basis of their information and their accessible resources, individuals create outputs and then execute voluntary trade and exchange operations at the negotiated prices. It should also be noted that substantively, these negotiated prices signal the agreed upon compensation at which re-arranging of the ownership of the traded property is being made.

In the quality-of-life-oriented New Economy, markets and negotiated prices also exist. However, the economic development focus is not on the market value of the associated trade. Rather, the economic management emphasis will be on evolving strategies that will promote the use of the available resource base of the society towards the delivery of the critical technical complements to survival. In the context of the New Economy, the aim of economic performance appraisal is to determine the extent to which usage of the prevailing resource base has enabled responsible participating members of the society to access critical quantities of these survival complements.

Therefore, outcomes of the prevailing resource base will not be weighed primarily in market value terms. As a result, even though private individuals will be making purchases and sales in the market, the effectiveness of aggregate output will not necessarily be measured by the net value of prevailing commerce.

Human economic agents will be recognised as entities who seek the capability and the understanding to use their time and resource commitments to cause forthcoming outcomes in their lives in order to have the configuration that they associate with an enhanced quality-of-living. They are appreciated as seeking to use their time and resource commitments to generate and secure mixes of outcomes which promise to give them a preferred linkage to how their environment evolves.

The New Economy, with its focus on quality-of-life attainment, recognises that the target of individuals is the configuration of events which populate their lives. Therefore, performance appraisal looks at the outcomes of resource and effort management operations as portraying flows of time-use operations and opportunities. Furthermore, it is the flow of time-use commitment operations/opportunities that substantively manifest the economy at hand. That is why economic development performance must be appreciated as being indicated by the availability of the critical services that enable individuals to secure the time-use opportunities at which they aim.

What must be appraised, therefore, is the consistency of the manifest access data with the time-use opportunities that human economic agents (over their evolution) have associated with the achievement of a high quality-of-living.

As they participate in prevailing production and trade, respective human economic agents operate in a number of roles such as producers, consumers, merchandisers, brokers, financiers, providers of labour skills, entrepreneurs and functionaries for government. The features that condition the operating roles which individuals respectively execute are:

(a) The pervasiveness of the production efficiencies that arise via the practice of division of labour
(b) The variety of the conclusions which individuals tend to form about the potential trading opportunities that are likely to become accessible to them
(c) The windows on understanding which their socialisation has led them to hold.

The pervasiveness of division of labour ensures that individuals must jointly focus significantly on financial compensation which they secure as well as the expected prices which sellers will ask for critical services which they will need on behalf of their survival. Therefore, in a technologically complex society, individuals recognise that financial manipulation is required of them. The result is that capitalist governments use the premise that forthcoming net realised increase in financial-equivalent value portrays the "prosperity" to which the development policies of the government have contributed.

This capitalist emphasis on development as a process of fostering (financial-equivalent) "prosperity" operates as a mantra. That focus legitimates and reinforces the market/commercial weight to what entails economic achievement. The result is that quality-of-survival as forthcoming time-use opportunities is ignored and overlooked.

When the focus is on financial "prosperity", governments tend to construe towards achieving the ensuing commercially measured development. The business and financial managers in the corporate culture, which delivers the bulk of the items which are bought and sold, comprise of the pivotal technical instrumentality whose requirements must be serviced.

However, quality-of-life as the achievement joins together the idea of a citizen and the idea of an economy. Therefore, development achievement in quality-of-life terms also becomes a conjoint context. It requires that although the indicator of performance may talk about trading results, it must also express the enhancement in the access to survival wherewithal which the typical consciousness-directed citizen is securing.

The prevailing commercial robustness of an economy is pertinent only if the prevailing data that are associated to that robustness also show the access of the typical citizen to mixes of services which will enhance that citizen's quality-of-life attainment. It will not be sufficient to draw on data that reveal relative changes in the Consumer Price Index (CPI). Rather, if quality-of-life attainment is to be the indication of performance, the data that portray the (aggregate or the pattern of) results from resource allocation and management must also tell about outcomes which portray the pattern of time-use access that the typical individual in the society secures.

Economic performance reports, which overlook how the time-use targets of conscious individuals have been served, are appropriate only if it is also deemed that the principal (and overwhelming) responsibility of policy framers is primarily to provide support for profit-oriented trade.

The New Economy (that is focused on quality-of-life attainment) operates on the economic development premise that under the mediation of their consciousness, human economic agents seek to use their time and resource commitments to give content and quality to their survival. In the prevailing environment in which the development is occurring, the economic activities of these agents extend beyond their respective market-centred capacities such as hired providers of effort (labour), purchasers of the commodities that are offered for sale (customers) and entrepreneurs and their surrogates (who provide and co-ordinate the investment and the marketing that delivers profitable sales). Yet, the political economic background of the market economic focus uses prevailing programmes of formal and informal education to perpetuate the understanding that persons are linked to the economy, largely via these foregoing functional market operative roles.

It is true that in the market managed society, individuals typically see the complements of their environment as carrying associated money prices. It also happens that in the accompanying environment, informal education leads human economic agents to understand that in order to gain access to their survival wherewithal, they must seek to acquire money in requisite quantities.

Consequent to the socialisation, individuals are led to formulate estimates of the quantity of money that they will need in order to access legitimately their requirements to survive.

Yet, if those who are so socialised are sufficiently alert, they soon recognise that the bulk of the information and communication which is flowing around them is also largely designed to seduce them out of whatever funds that they have succeeded in acquiring. As a result, persons in the prevailing market economic socialisation soon come to recognise that they become respectively valued to the extent that they can operate as sources of money or instruments (human capital), which others may use in their own pursuit of money.

However, in support of the critical living-centred permanencies at which persons respectively aim and within the stipulations of their political economic environment, human economic agents also set out to use the convenience of money to secure mixes of outputs that they seek. Essentially, their aim is to try and secure mixes of availabilities (goods and opportunities) which will deliver/support the time-use patterns at which they aim.

Therefore, mindful of the fact that time-use patterns comprise of the target, The New Economy appraises development attainment via the resulting changes in access of the typical member of the particular society to critical time-use opportunities which such an individual (as a consciousness-guided entity) seeks to achieve. Outcome data from aggregate resource allocated management are therefore required to reveal how much enhancement has occurred in the opportunity and the capabilities of such individuals to achieve/secure preferred patterns of time-use.

In the quality-of-life oriented New Economy, time on the job and time that is spent in living are not treated as either separate or separable domains. Therefore, the extent of the rights and the opportunities of employees to participate in the management of the time which they respectively spend on-the-job is one of the indicative political economic development outputs.

Individuals seek to achieve subsequent preferred time-use opportunities by currently directing their efforts to acquiring critical mixes of technical services, which will enable them to attain their living-centred permanencies. In the process, they measure costs of pursuing alternative survival paths via financial value that they must surrender or forego. They also measure costs via what they see as the potential impact on their self-evolution which their selection will have.

It follows, therefore, that education programming must facilitate the capabilities of individuals to execute the financial as well as the survival-centred costing, on which they respectively draw. Only by being exposed to education, which enables them to be discriminating appraisers of their reality, individuals (as managers of their lives) can deal cost effectively with construing their survival.

Education programming must accommodate that dual (financial and living-centred) focus to costing that human economic agents do is necessary, because conscious resource-manipulating humans are not "blank slates" on which packaged information (that is favourable to market-oriented development management) is to be imprinted. Like birds that have evolved, having a programmed ability to build nests (of the sort that is characteristic to respective species), over the eons of their evolution in communities, humans have also evolved consciousness. This consciousness exists as a survival-centred synergy that individuals forge. Furthermore, the extent of it is forthcoming from the information that reality reveals (sometimes under prodding) about the parts of its components that are accessible to manipulation.

With survival, displayed as experience on a time path, consciousness (as a feature) reveals itself in the mixes of effort and resource management initiatives that individuals are able to take, so as to remove/lessen uncertainty from how the passage of time impacts them.

Consciousness and its economic linkage to how time is managed operates on the creation, selection and usage of technology. As soon as humans began to recognize that there are alternative techniques to securing any particular outcome, they began to select the strategy which gives them the more efficient use of their time.

Traditional societies also follow rhythms of time-use efficiency in the technical strategies which they use. In his writings, the classical economist David Ricardo (1817), (1911) had also argued that it was the efforts of human economic agents to enhance the net output from the allocation of their available time and efforts which provided their impetus to make trades.

The Ricardian emphasis on individuals, as pursuing enhanced effectiveness to their time-use, is unlike the emphasis of the early economists on the mercantilist tradition (who emphasized those who make trades as pursuing enhanced financial-equivalent capability). The Ricardian emphasis is also unlike the emphasis of today's neo-mercantilist market proponents. They focus on trade as being *primarily* linked to net profit opportunities. They emphasize trade as a technique which individuals mobilize towards securing from market operations, net "monetary" gains and financial-equivalent profits. As a result, these neo-mercantilist analysts of today overlook the outcome from trade that arises as time-use enhancement which is complementary to heightened quality of survival. In contrast, The New Economy emphasizes attained quality-of-living. Therefore, it requires that the trade which a government supports must explicitly complement the delivered time-use opportunities out of which quality-of-living will be forthcoming.

The role of money, in "lubricating" the co-ordination of owned resources with hired ones and providing compensation for use of accessible common property resources that are drawn into the delivery of traded outputs, is recognized. However, in order to recognize that money plays a role does not impute that if economic development is to be successful, matters must be everywhere consistent with financial prioritization. Therefore, the quality-of-life-oriented New Economy makes no stipulation that an aggregate economic development directorate must allow the results from the monetization of exchange to guide the ranking that it applies to alternative collections of resource allocative outcomes.

Here, an economic development directorate is therefore NOT encouraged to use education programmes to socialize individuals to link their success in living with their capability to "chase money" (or to secure market equivalent gain).

In the society at hand, the synergy that is consciousness-evolution flows from opportunities which individuals have in order to understand their environment besides managing their survival, so as to secure a preferred experience in living. Quality-of-life-oriented development emerges out of the availability of the mixes of services which will facilitate the opportunities of individuals to execute informed survival. Therefore, for any reference period, The New Economy emphasizes that an economic development directorate will foster the micro economic survival successes at which individuals aim by fostering enhancement in their access to *mixes* of these critical services that will enable them to pursue the consciousness-enhancement synergy.

Measurements can be formulated to guide the living centred efficiency with which the society is pursuing the achievement targets for respective critical services. However, the aggregate economic development directorate also has responsibilities for the protection of the environment out of which these respective services will be forthcoming. Therefore, appraisals of the success of the directorate in fostering product flows at the micro level may not be formed with indifference to relative success of that directorate at environmental protection.

Also, in order to assure that the required mixes of critical quality-of-life oriented micro outputs will be forthcoming, the society will need to have in place structural provisions which will assure that the resources that are necessary for the delivery of those flows of critical services will become available. It follows, therefore, that if quality-of-life is to be the outcome, individuals must have the rights, opportunities and capabilities to direct their choices of how and where their time and resources will be allocated. Accordingly, the society can have a viable commitment to individual freedom only in the presence of policy targets that monitor the technical achievement flows from the prevailing resource base. Therefore, the society must make programme and policy commitments on matters regarding what features will be treated as own-able property.

In an environment with a high degree of division of labour, there are structural as well as institutional matters that end up significantly determining the prevailing earnings of individuals in respective skills groups. Monetization, in association with division of labour, offers individuals flexibilities in the trading which they use to access mixes of services which they require. However, at the same time, a society needs to take steps to ameliorate or have removed prevailing structural barriers that are likely to prevent individuals from securing affordable access to services on which their quality-of-life attainment depends.

Laying emphasis on the need for a societal emphasis on discouraging the formation of barriers to preferred patterns of time-use management that individuals face does not contradict Milton Friedman's permanent income hypothesis. He argued that over their lifetime, individuals (as earners and managers of their financial income) choose to operate either as net borrowers or net savers of that financial income.[12] Rather, the argument here is that notwithstanding what individuals do with their earnings (pursuant to their quality-of-living targets), they are also budgeting the allocation of the time for living which they have/anticipate. Therefore, a development directorate is required to be mindful of how its programme and policy initiatives complement that living-centred time and resource budgeting operation by individuals.

The development managers of the New Economy (which has a quality-of-life focus) will need to recognize that human economic agents seek to make their time-use commitments and exercises on self-validation and consciousness reinforcement. Such an analytical focus on human development as being the target of consciousness-directed individuals is con-

---

12. For more details on the idea of the permanent income to date, see Milton Friedman, *A Theory of the Consumption Function*, (Princeton: Princeton University Press) 1957. There, he characterised human economic agents as having market income profiles that are divided into two parts; one part permanent, and the other part transitory. Consistent with that financial focus, he argued that in their approach to financial resources, respective human economic agents behave as either net borrowers or net savers (The behavioural decision was supposed to depend on whether, as per their expectations, individuals viewed the "transitory component" of their prevailing income/earnings as being either negative or positive).

trary to traditional market centred emphasis on human economic agents as primarily pursuing financial-equivalent efficiency targets. Rather, the human development focus recognizes human economic agents as seeking efficiency in their time-use commitments. Therefore, it emphasizes individuals as seeking to enter into those time-use operations which will validate and reinforce their prior conclusion/expectation that their decision to remain alive would be accompanied by opportunities for enhanced meaningful participation.

Towards achieving that survival target with the support of their micro economic management operations, human economic agents tend to treat their time as a "currency" that they must also budget. However, that "currency" is neither storable in the conventional sense nor it is physically transferable (like money) to others. Yet, under the understanding/agreement that a present commitment will be later reciprocated, the time of individuals can also be voluntarily committed to currently executing outputs on behalf of others. At the same time, individuals measure the quantity (to them) of their time "currency" in duration. They also measure returns to its "expenditure"/commitment as the (expected) relative levels of informed discretionary participation and control over their environment which the usage or the time commitment allows/yields.

Recall that the mere passage of time is also the space in which human economic agents execute living as survival-centred mixes of effort and resource management operations. As a result, in budgeting their time as a "currency", persons set out to vary systematically the duration that they commit among various types of operations.

Notably, what constitutes saving or borrowing of the time "currency" is different in substance from the context which Friedman presented in his *Theory of the Consumption Function* (where individuals are budgeting financial earnings). Additionally, the capabilities which individuals bring to their time-use management decisions are also subject to variation (among individuals). As a result, in the early portion of their lives, individuals set out to enhance parts of that capability by committing time to acquiring skills which they can apply in later years to securing greater control over the flow of outcomes which their environment will deliver to their time-housed efforts.

It follows, therefore, that a society which seeks to foster development can use the technique of providing time and resource support to skills training which enables individuals to acquire and enhance capabilities which they can subsequently commit to production.

When individuals make decisions regarding where they will commit their time and their resources, targets in living as well as targets in the form of financial expectations operate as the guidance mechanism which they use. Indeed, currently, the Republic of Cuba is an example of a society which is seeking to cope with how these conjoint (time-use and financial) efficiency contexts which individuals use can operate as structural guidance features in its economic development planning. The Cuban economic development directorate has committed itself to creating a skills base (on behalf of facilitating access of individuals to the complements of survival). However, the economic development directorate of that society appears to have not accommodated itself to accepting the linkage which exists between the quality-of-living of individuals and their rights to decide where their personal savings and time are committed.

Indeed, Cuba's desire to not re-experience the neo-colonial features which accompanied off-shore ownership and management of its resources influences its current approach to its development policy. However, the New Economy, with its quality-of-life-oriented focus on human time-use management, provides a context with the use of which Cuban society can become the vanguard to the fostering of human development in the twenty first century.

————◆————

The Cuban Context to the Human Development Issue

In matters regarding the evolution of human development, the Cuban environment presents a particularly unique context. The revolution of the mid nineteen fifties (which framed Cuba's prevailing political economy) had been substantively led by (what may be described as) a group of dedicated constructive patriots. Their aim was liberation of the Cuban society from a then prevailing neo-colonial regime, where the quality-of-living of the typical Cuban was not a development priority. However, the international political economic realities of the Cold War at that time led the revolutionary patriots to proclaim subsequently that Cuba would operate as a Marxist-Leninist socialist state.

Initially, there was an underlying quality-of-life focus to this Cuban revolution. Therefore, the Cuba environment of 2002 contains a significant portion of the fundamentals on which The New Economy of the twenty first century (with its emphasis on human development) can evolve. Yet, to reach that twenty first century type of evolution, an interplay of local and off-shore demographic and other currents which Cuba faces will be pivotal.

On the one hand, there is the population which remained in Cuba to benefit from the health care, advanced education and local input into governance that formed the quality-of-living emphases of the new Revolution. On the other hand, there is the other demographic group which is comprised of expatriate Cubans and their descendants (hoping to return), but who now reside in the United States. This latter group subscribes to the profit and the environmental manipulative priorities and emphases of market capitalism.

In the absence of external military and political interference, a significant potential exists in Cuba for a synergy on behalf of The New Economy. This outcome will emerge from the ensuing interplay between the currently off-shore Cubans (who subscribe to the emphasis on empowerment via wealth possession) and the resident Cubans (who learnt from the revolution, a community-centred focus that carries with it distributive entitlements).

However, as a monetized society, Cuba also operates via the principles of division of labour. Therefore, currently, the domestic as well as international trading (out of which enhanced time-use effectiveness can arise) is being sought via financial as well as international barter arrangements.[13]

On having removed land from being treated as *alienatable* property, the government of Cuba decided to link land-use to the access that can be secured (by the typical Cuban citizen) to critical development complements.

Continuance of that common property focus on land is likely to be the flash point in future developments as the off-shore Cuban community (with the likely support of the U. S. government) seeks to re-establish pre-revolutionary patterns of private ownership and management of Cuba's non-renewable resources.

Yet, Western societies do have "zoning" regulations which put conditions on the use to which specified critical resources (in specified regions) may be put. Therefore, pursuant to its commitment to quality-of-life delivery, the government of Cuba is not necessarily ill advised to make its entire country a critical region for "zoning" purposes.

However, towards the delivery of The New Economy of the twenty first century and to take advantage of the benefits of monetization (among other things), the government of the Republic of Cuba will need to develop a separate ownership focus for renewable as compared to non-renewable resources.

When individuals have ownership rights to property in which they may invest, innovations are usually forthcoming. To complement quality-of-life enhancement, the government of post-Revolutionary Cuba has the option to create or foster circumstances in which such innovations may be attracted. Therefore, the forthcoming government will need to also accommodate its development programming to rights of ownership by private individuals. Specifically, it will need to distinguish significantly between the ownership regulations which it will apply to renewable as compared to non-renewable resources.

---

13. That latter tactic was possible, because the government of post-revolutionary Cuba had defined land and geographic space as a common property resource. It therefore decided to exchange its output of sugar for bundles of manufactured goods.

In particular, the forthcoming government of Cuba will need to agree to private ownership of renewable resources that have been created from private investment of savings and effort (Investment that has been created by the use of funds from international sources is a separate matter that must be tackled within regulations governing the banking system).

Allowing private ownership of the renewable resources that have been forthcoming from savings and investment does not prevent the government from removing the non-renewable resources from becoming private property merely through simple purchase of these resources from the open market.

On designating the components of endowment as common property resources, the Post-Revolutionary Government of Cuba can make access to their use conditional on how extensively or how effectively the proposed usage contributes to delivering outputs that are supportive of quality-of-life enhancement of the typical Cuban.

On the basis of the experience of its people, prior to the Revolution, the Government of Cuba is appropriately cautious about any "investment" venture, which would appear as a surrender of parts of the society to off-shore dictates and management. However, if, constitutionally, land and geographic space in Cuba are defined as a national resource whose parts can only be conditionally leased, the patriotic governments would be able to ensure that the pre-revolution circumstances of neo-colonial dominance do not re-occur.

If the Cuban Revolution is able to operate as a jumping-off position to the execution of aggregate economic development management that has a focus on human development, Cuba's twenty first century heritage needs not to be re-colonization.

The government of Cuba faces the management challenge to find the combinations of taxes and subsidies that will (in the prevailing societal milieu) stimulate the evolution of trade which complements quality-of-life enhancement.

Flows of critical services as well as the access of individuals to survival which affords them opportunities for knowledge-guided creativity are parts of development as quality-of-life attainment. Development of that sort requires that individuals must also be empowered to participate in the management of the flow of events which impact their existence.

Therefore, if the government of Revolutionary Cuba is to cause human development to accompany its evolution into the twenty first century, some re-focus of its guidance framework will be necessary. Programming to enhance quality-of-life, as an experience of individuals, is not readily reconcilable to a Marxist-communist guidance on how economic development programming must be structured.

————•————

The Education Vehicle

In respective collectives/societies, education functions as the lubricant to the understanding that individuals develop about how the world and its parts work. Education also functions as the cement to allegiance within a society as members interact during the process of creating paths of survival at which they respectively aim. As a result, historically, the holders of power in respective societies have recognized the manipulative capacity that their control over public education provides. Accordingly, these power groups tend to use education programming to encourage understanding and attitudes, which will complement reinforce both the allegiance that the power group seeks to foster as well as the outcomes which it targets.

Education programmes are therefore usually aimed at forming, in those who have been exposed to associated respective packages, particular types of allegiance; appreciation, capabilities and patterns of responses.

Notably, the monetization of societies tends to operate as an instrument of informal education. Monetization tends to condition individuals to become aware of the productivity of division of labour. As a result, monetization of human interactions in traditional societies tends to lead individuals quickly to begin to focus and plan, on the basis of expected financial returns, their resource and effort commitments.

The convenience of monetization tends to lead individuals to focus on the financial value with which items that can be traded may be associated. In such an environment of informal education, operators/trainees as well as the managers of formal education programmes tend to end up making themselves comfortable with education which has been packaged to operate as manpower development in support of the environment of trade.

Educational programming, as manpower development, exposes individuals to a highly restricted partial understanding of the environment. In such programmes, trainees are typically indoctrinated into as much information as will make them better operating instruments (hired or self-directed) towards making more profitable the "machinery" out of which enhanced commercially profitable output is forthcoming.

Historically, division of labour has also been linked to technological discoveries. It is a matter of record that in the face of opportunities to trade, entrepreneurs have tended to weave into commercial opportunities and the discoveries about manipulative possibilities that the environment offers.

These technological evolutions that individuals have evolved have usually been forthcoming from opportunities for enhanced understanding (and insight) to which they have respectively been exposed. Historically, education programmes have the opportunity to communicate such enhanced understanding to a larger audience. The result is that the forthcoming results of education programmes extend beyond impacts on commerce.

Understanding has the capability to reinforce or modify the competence of individuals to execute the time-use opportunities, out of which human development is forthcoming. However, understanding, as an outcome, is significantly a personal attainment of members of the society. Typically, the power elites of the society want an education package which reinforces and complements its military and commercial targets. Therefore, the packaging of education to create and facilitate the type of understanding, out of which human development is forthcoming, is not currently being emphasized in prevailing economic development programming.

Paulo Freire, for example, elaborated the background. He argued that the circumstances which typically operate in developing societies are usually of the sort where one finds that education programming is used to create covert relative dominance. He pointed out that in colonial and neo-colonial societies the prevailing educational programming typically socializes already disenfranchised persons to interpret their environment contrary to their own best interests.[14]

In contrast, an educational system, which seeks to service the evolution of the New Economy (where enhancement of quality-of-life and associated human development is the target) has two joint tasks that it must execute. Prevailing education programmes are required to foster technical capabilities, which will assist individuals to operate as efficient manpower. In addition, prevailing education programming is also required to cultivate and foster in all exposed individuals their capability to handle information. Thus, execute the living-centred allocation of their time that they seek.

The late Fritz Machlup may be credited with evolving the most perceptually comprehensive context to approaching the linkages that cause education to yield economic development with a quality-of-living ambiance.[15] His untimely death prevented his eventual communication of the empirical and intellectual evolution on which he had embarked.

In parallel with the Machlup focus, this writer informs the citizens that the education support from government must foster the manpower capabilities as well as enhanced understanding. Only with the support that dual programme targets, it is likely that the time-use permanencies out of which a high quality-of-living arises will be forthcoming.

---

14. See, therefore Paulo Freire, *Pedagogy of the Oppressed*, Myra Bergman Ramos (tr.), (New York: The Seabury Press), 1970.

15. See, therefore, Fritz Machlup, *The Production and Distribution of Knowledge in the United States*, (Princeton: Princeton University Press), 1962; where he emphasized a close human capital context to the role of education. However, in his next book, *Knowledge, Its Creation, Distribution and Economic Significance*, Vol. I, (Princeton: Princeton University Press) 1980; Machlup broadened beyond manpower development, toward the function of the citizen participant, the economic function of knowledge. That is why his untimely death and the presentation of his last manuscript, *The Economics of Information and Human Capital*, T. W. Schultz (ed.), (Princeton, Princeton University Press) 1984, via the insights of T. W. Schultz, was so unfortunate.

On account of Machlup's untimely death and a subsequent editing of the manuscript by T. W. Schultz, a clear-cut emphasis on that dual focus was not forthcoming from Machlup's last book. In fact, it can be emphatically argued that in the editing, Schultz had allowed *his own* emphases (with that of Gary Becker) on "human Capital" to guide his interpretation of the income permanencies in Machlup's focus. Accordingly, Schultz also interpreted Machlup's arguments regarding how individuals used information, from within the earnings-potential focus, rather than from a living-centred time-use one.[16]

Schools and schooling (primary, secondary, post-secondary and post graduate) comprise of the formal delivery parts to the cultivation of understanding via education. Informal education arises within skills 7development and training programmes; within on-the-job training and from newspapers, magazines, books, radio, television and the cinema. Additionally, individuals also receive a significant quantity of their "education" via their informal fraternal associations.

The context of The New Economy requires formal education in order to service the *capability* of individuals to recognize and manipulate the critical complements with which their sought quality-of-survival may be sustained. Human development, as the targeted achievement of individuals (that education programming is supposed to serve), is accompanied by the opportunities of affected human economic agents to secure the permanencies in survival to which they aspire. Achievement of such permanencies will be forthcoming, only when individuals acquire the capability to comprehend, rationally organize and technically manipulate their environment.

The New Economy requires education and skills development programmes to facilitate the delivery of those capability attributes. It also

---

16. However, Schultz was very much aware that Machlup was saying something with a wider context. For example, on reading the drafts of number of papers which the writer had prepared prior to Machlup's death and on account of the similarity that he saw between Machlup's emphasis and that of the writer, Schultz had strongly suggested to the writer that he should familiarise himself with Machlup's writings in the human capital area. He had also wanted the publisher to show the writer the "galley" copies of Malchup's book prior to the final printing. However, that did not occur.

requires education programmes to recognize and present respective outputs from resource and time commitments, as technical complements, which individuals create and use on behalf of securing their living-centred permanencies.

The emphasis on the need to focus on the technical composition of outputs contrasts with the emphasis of the market economic socialization, which conditions people to look upon outputs as largely financial-equivalent wealth objects. Additionally, although The New Economy recognizes the importance of division of labour and the potential for market competition among skills, its substantive emphasis is on humans as budgeters of their time. In the process, it recognizes individuals as committing their efforts towards achieving sought permanencies to their survival.[17] The quality-of-life oriented *New Economy* does not allow the convenience of money and expected financial returns from time-use to confuse issues regarding forthcoming quality-of-living outcomes. Therefore, The New Economy prioritises education programming which encourages and *empowers* individuals to take steps to operate as managers of their lives.

In any economy, *the policy decision regarding HOW access to resources is legitimated and sustained* is an ideologically dictated one. Programme formation in The New Economy is not constrained by the ideological dictate to the effect that access to the technical complements to living must be rationed by (or must pivot on) access to money. Therefore, the accompanying educational programming in this development context does not impute that individuals must be socialized (educated) into perceiving that "making money" is the principal rational survival task/tactic to which they must commit their skills.

However, prevailing education programmes must be appraised for their consistency with delivering capable manpower and must also be appraised for their effectiveness in enabling individuals to understand and impact in preferred ways on their environment.

By virtue of their stake in the delivery of many common property outputs (such as public health), governments have a stake in the delivery

---

17. Indeed, in the process of formulating the human capital context, which Gary Becker elaborated, Theodore Schultz had emphasized human economic agents as being seekers after "*sources* of Permanent income streams".

of not a few technical attainments that will provide the quality-of-living that human economic agents seek. In addition, government stipulations regarding how many services (such as justice) will be accessed also form another example of a significant responsibility that a government must execute in facilitating the access of individuals to the complements of quality-of-life attainment.[18]

It happens, however, that until the education system primes the citizenry to appreciate (as an indication of prevailing economic development performance) the access of individuals to flows of critical technical services (on behalf of a high quality-of-living), an aggregate economic development directorate is unlikely to focus on such attainments. In addition, when the prevailing education programming *socializes individuals to ignore government's inattention* to issues regarding the *access* of individuals to a high quality-of-life, the effect is to impute that quality-of-life attainment is *exclusively* a personal responsibility.

It is the combined pattern of time-use (on and off the job) which accompanies the employment and other time and resource commitments of individuals that will indicate quality-of-life attainment. As a result, the context of The New Economy stipulates that skills development and training programmes may not prepare trainees, as if when individuals become hired labour, they surrender management rights to how their time is used.

The structure and the curricula of prevailing education and skills development programmes must service enhancement of the capability of trainees to participate in the informed management of the forces, which impact their lives (on and off the job).

It will not be sufficient for these training programmes to prepare trainees to view their on-the-job role as showing up on time, executing assigned tasks and in the process performing the necessary job-centred communications.

---

18. For example, in some countries (such as Canada), government operates a legal system which stipulates that persons experiencing injustice can secure legal representation only by first meeting the financial retainer that private lawyers call for. Thereby, the government ensures that only the financially powerful and the financially well connected will be able to challenge how prevailing entrenched power operates.

Instead, individuals in education, training and skills development programmes must be accommodated as seeking to earn and to be also creative in the execution of the time-usage which is their lives. Therefore, the trainees must be recognized as having *rights* and desires to use the application of their time and their skills to cause the prevailing environment to yield preferred mixes of flows of outcomes.

In the light of that recognition (of the role of training and skills development programmes), The New Economy emphasizes that as conscious entities, working people seek to have on-the-job rights in respect of how their time is committed.

The quality-of-life centred New Economy is therefore *viewed as dysfunctional*, educational programmes which accommodate trainees as if they are being conditioned to operate primarily as hired *implements* and market functionaries (I.e., prevailing programmes may not prepare trainees to operate, primarily in respective roles as "hired stiffs" or as astute "bottom-line"-oriented managers).

Holistic Aggregate Economic Development

The New Economy that emphasizes quality-of-living as an outcome will emerge only from a context of Holistic Aggregate Economic Development programming. Although prevailing outputs arise in a highly refined system of division of labour, the prevailing prices at which items are sold need not be the "competitive" market ones that economists idealize. Rather, Holistic Economics economic development programming recognizes that costs as well as selling prices can be deliberately impacted by institutional interventions (such as various types of taxes, government regulations which aim to protect the rights of individuals as well as the environment). Accordingly, Holistic Aggregate Economic

Raymond Samuels

Development management does not argue that economic development out of which quality-of-life attainment is forthcoming emerges under an economic regime on behalf of private gain that is guided by an Adam Smith type of "invisible hand". Instead, it explicitly recognizes that for quality-of-life enhancement to emerge as the outcome, the "visible hand" of a government must monitor and act to impact the prevailing rates of access of the typical individual to critical survival-centred services. The Holistic Aggregate Economic Development framework then argues that towards remedying access disparities, government must execute administrative initiatives regarding skills development and how the non-renewable resources and the common property resources of the society are marshalled.

The governments that have decided to promote the ideology of the market-managed economy typically use formal and informal education to condition the expectations of citizens about the responsibilities of government in their access to survival. In particular, individuals are conditioned to accept the principle that their rights of access to the resources and the outputs in the society depend on the discretionary control which their private efforts allow them to secure over the market value of property and currency. However, as Hirshman and Rothschild (1973) pointed out, to be without substantive financial income is not necessarily to be without substantive economic power.[19]

These authors argued the political economic proposition that groups of individuals who are without wealth also have the potential to make themselves important via their capacity to generate substantive negative wealth impacts. Therefore, the imputation is that even after building more jails (to dissuade the economically disenfranchised from generating prohibitive negative aggregate costs), a market-centred aggregate economic management directorate will still need to give due accommodation to distributive outcomes.

In recognition of the need for such accommodation to distributive results, Holistic Aggregate Economic Development Management starts

---

19. Hirshman, Albert O. and Michael Rothschild (1973) "The Changing Tolerance for Inequality in Development", *Quarterly Journal of Economics*, Vol. LXXXVII, pp. 544-566.

with a built-in political-economic distributive focus. It argues that human economic agents (as consciousness-centred entities) commit themselves to time-use operations which they want to operate as venues of respective mutual impacts between themselves and their society.

The supportive premise to that argument is that these agents have rights (as well as responsibilities and privileges) to manage their time-use commitments. The Holistic Aggregate Economic Development context obligates programmes of education, training and skills development to also cultivate in trainees the capabilities which enable persons at work to be joint participants in the management of their work environment. The Holistic Aggregate Economic Development management context recognizes that at the base of the resource management, the commitments of individuals are expectations of financial profit *as well as* expectations of achieving more effective control over the configuration of their survival. It also recognizes that towards using their time and resource commitments to achieve the permanencies in survival at which they respectively aim, individuals seek to acquire enhanced understanding as well as the enhanced capability to purchase supportive services that are offered for sale in the market. That is why The New Economy also invites educational programmes to recognize and communicate the truth that the trade and exchange operations of individuals have always been intermediary procedures in the fruition of the targets in human development which these individuals have.[20]

---

20. A metaphor reflecting the presence of market operations as an intermediary procedure in the delivery of human development is found in human biological evolution. There is a stage in the living that individuals do, where they are respectively robust specimens, with the attributes of mutual physical sexual attraction on which the material survival of the human species depends. It may be argued that the market operations, in which delivered outputs emerge, are, to human development, what sexual activity and energy is, to the synergy of consciousness evolution. In the same way, the *raison d'être* to living (as an exercise in consciousness) is not only to execute and preserve the reproductive imperative; the achievement that human economic agents seek from resource management, is not primarily demonstrated by what the level of market activity indicates.

Against that background, Holistic Aggregate Economic Development management challenges the aggregate economic development directorate to facilitate the availability of critical services as well as the enhanced understanding that conscious human economic agents seek.

The directorate must therefore foster a production and marketing environment which attracts entrepreneurs to reconcile, with their pursuit of profit, the delivery of outputs which individuals require on behalf of their quality-of-survival.

Attainment from Holistic Aggregate Economic Development will be portrayed by the reduction (or the removal) of shortfalls in the access of individuals to minimum targeted availability levels for respective critical services.

When a society sets such attainment targets, it will become necessary to have "zoning" regulations in order to assure resource access. The expected profitability of the sales from discretionary outputs in the open market will not be the principal method for leveraging how resources (that could contribute to remedying production shortfalls in access) will become available. However, performance appraisal which is based on the access of individuals to minimum critical services, on behalf of their quality-of-life attainment, can be executed only after the society is prepared to make statements about what the critical availability targets are.

The result is that the aggregate economic management directorate will also need to state what are the shortfalls in availability of critical services which it will refuse to tolerate.

When economic development success is judged on the basis of the relative access of individuals to critical technical services, market data are regarded as being contributory to, rather than as being definitive of performance. The effectiveness of educational programming is executed in fostering the search of individuals for enhanced understanding. That, in turn, will be portrayed by the extensiveness of the commitments of human economic agents to pursue innovation. Therefore, the educational system may not operate as if its mandate is to deliver "human capital" and pliant "consumers" of services that are being marketed by corporations on behalf of their own profit targets.

Consistent with Western social philosophy, Holistic Aggregate Economic Development management imputes that individuals are entitled to have access to information of the sort which allows them to make informed decisions about how to live and how to manage their lives. Therefore, the Holistic context stipulates that the skills delivery system must deliver graduates the capability to execute informed control over the evolution of their own lives.

It was a system of education which was largely in service to the foregoing principle in Western social philosophy which delivered the "flower power" generation that came of age in the 1960s. In contrast, during the 1990s, fearful of the "liberation" to which that type of education had led, the corporations have joined the political economic elite to dictate a different educational emphasis. In this latter period, the management elite is requiring that prevailing education programmes must concentrate on the delivery of employable labour-power that the "market" needs.[21]

Encouraging students to express their capability for independent thinking is the key to promoting the evolution of consciousness as an "output". Therefore, towards such an evolution, Holistic Aggregate Economic Development Management emphasizes as its output what happens to people (rather than to commerce). As a result, the Holistic system stipulates that an educational system must be committed to produce graduates who will be prepared to understand, tolerate, respect and explore the variety and the complexity that is reality.

In Holistic Aggregate Economic Development Management, the prime economic function of education is not necessarily to cause individuals to operate with or in lieu of machines. In the Holistic Aggregate Economic Management focus, the responsibility of educational programming to deliver empowered citizens is not being set aside. Therefore, the emphasis is not on training people for jobs. As a result, unlike the current Western economic management focus, the Holistic Aggregate Economic Development context does not substantively describe the execution of education programming as a process of "human capital formation".

---

21. As a result, one now finds on university campuses blocks of buildings, classrooms or auditoriums that are explicitly under the sponsorship and "educational" programme support of large private commercial "donor" corporations.

When the educational industry neglects to communicate about the historical commitment of conscious human economic agents to human development, it feeds the myopia which results in an emphasis on aggregate commerce. In these circumstances, the education industry becomes primarily "tooled" to prepare people in earning skills.

The result of such type of educational concentration is the creation of societies prevailing inter-personal relationships are largely instrumental and utilitarian. In these circumstances, growth in commerce will be facilitated. Unfortunately, on socializing individuals to infer and also to complement the *instrumentalization* of their human interaction, the education system also complements a social environment where legitimated predation is treated as a societal norm.

People who have been so socialized (into construing an instrumental context to human interaction) end up either using-up each other or in executing operations where they apply various strategies with the aim to manoeuvre each other out of held assets.

A society neglects to foster Holistic Aggregate Economic Development when the prevailing educational industry neglects to encourages students to question. One can therefore ask whether students are currently being rewarded for demonstrating creative thinking.

The apparent prevailing educational norm is that students are rewarded for memorizing and reproducing (like automatons) the "information" and "messages" that the authority figures (as teachers and professors) have communicated and legitimated.

When preparing people to fit into prevailing commerce is the target, the typical classroom is not likely to communicate to students a sense of wonder about reality. Rather, what emerge are classrooms that communicate process, boredom and ennui. Those tactics accompany a socialization in which education is cleverly packaged to reinforce in trainees a commerce-centred message. The communicated message is that responsible citizenship requires them to make themselves effective parts of the "market" by making themselves more financially prosperous (either as compensation-extracting "tools" or ingenious seducers and exploiters of "resources" and of each other).

In this background of using the schools to cultivate complements to commerce, school boards, in recognition of the political role that they play (as dispensers of tax revenue at the primary and secondary level), have bought into the perspective that construes education as human capital formation. Accordingly, as the thrust for "a more business-like view on education" has gained currency, these school boards have been quite willing to shepherd the process in which the primary and secondary schools operate as "manpower-development kindergartens".

School board trustees are politically alert individuals. They recognize that currently individuals with interests in how the schools have serviced the needs of commercial business will gain access to as well as rewards from a viable political constituency. As a result, in a society where the political economic directorate has so far not been prepared to articulate its human development goals, it is also unlikely that one would also find school board trustees with commitments to fostering such goals.

The prevailing school boards in societies with no stated or no implicit commitment toward human development are therefore unlikely to call for curricula that will develop in graduates the skills which they will require in order to exercise informed control over the evolution of their own lives.

Where delivering graduates who have the required skills to process information discriminatingly is not a priority in the prevailing schooling system, the teachers in the various classrooms in the society are not likely to be operating as mentors. Instead, they will operate as "authority figures" who prepare students to fit into a world of commerce-centred work. The aim of prevailing teachers will be to produce graduates who at work will be willing to execute unquestioningly the *instructions* that a corresponding authority figure (the boss) has given them.

Not surprisingly, it appears that the formal education industry even up to the university level is currently being "tooled" (and reinforced via commercially dedicated/sponsored halls and classrooms on campuses) to supervise the moulding of graduates who will function as paid automatons and paid "slaves".

A "mass society" (that has been organized around the principles of division of labour and profit-centred selections of resource allocative commitments) is approached by fostering a quiescent, undiscriminating and manipulable populace. Surprise!!! An individual who is prepared to fit comfortably into that type of societal environment is what our educational system is now turning out.

The result is that in the North American educational milieu, the likelihood of having graduates with the questioning, quarrelsome rebelliousness of the 1960s, has been effectively suppressed by the powers Notably, in Canada, as an authority-centred and neo-colonial domain, the roots of a '60s type of rebelliousness had not been deep anyway. Therefore, in Canada, the use of formal and informal educational programmes to suppress and eradicate any wholesale desire by members of the society to query authority was not difficult on this side of the international border.

———•———

Programme Reconciliations

When a society decides to make the focus of its economic development programming the access of individuals to the complements of human development, it still has to execute critical monetary policy. For example, such a society still has the responsibility to *police* and *preserve* the conditions that contribute to the integrity of the currency. However, aggregate economic development directorates (governments) also have political constituencies which they will seek to service in order to remain in power. Accordingly, governments seek tax revenues as resources with which they will be able to promote projects and thereby give their critical constituents access opportunities on behalf of their private earning and other financial accumulation targets.

By facilitating the presence of a robust commercial sector, governments are also able to secure a less cluttered access to tax revenues. Therefore, when economists use market value terms to compute the state of a prevailing economic union, the analytical focus also complements the tax-base reference which governments desire.

Correspondingly, when economists neglect to compute performance from prevailing programme initiatives, as the quality-of-life attainment that is forthcoming to the typical member of the society, governments also find that type of lack of analytical emphasis on their performance to be very convenient.

So far, there is no active political constituency which monitors the performance of government development policy in terms of how the quality-of-life access of the typical citizen has been enhanced. Furthermore, a government will also neglect to monitor the access of citizens to flows of critical survival complements if it does not accept that its responsibility is to facilitate the access of individuals to the complements of quality-of-living. Therefore, the governments of prevailing market economies are unlikely to regard prevailing levels of homelessness, hunger and insufficiency in access to health care as indications of their development failures. Instead, the buoyancy of profits from speculation in commercial paper that is traded on the prevailing stock market is utilized by Western governments as being a surrogate "index" of the appropriateness of prevailing aggregate economic development paths (as viewed by "investors").

Yet, while operating as facilitators of development, governments also have responsibilities for the stewardship of the common property resources of the society. These common property resources include the geographic space (land) which the society claims, its roads and harbours, the electronic communications spectrum; an environment that must be preserved for posterity, non-degraded, non-polluted and free of garbage and a system of adjudication, where justice is not essentially a purchased commodity.

Indeed, how a government construes and discharges its management responsibilities in respect of common property resources essentially communicates to individuals whether service to their quality-of-living is also a government target.

Normally, after observing the prevailing environment of aggregate output delivery, individuals tend to develop anticipations of outcomes that are likely to be forthcoming to them (consequent to prevailing institutional as well as pricing arrangements).

It happens also that in respective societies, members of respective groups of individuals also tend to construe that prevailing ethnic and cultural allegiance carries with it access entitlements. Therefore, when respective members who benefit from the prevailing allegiances begin to construe that the patterns of access, which they expect, will not be forthcoming, their tendency is to look for sources outside of the allegiance group which they can blame for the shortfall.

The context of The New Economy argues that the economic manipulative role of government (and its linkage to political allegiances) places entitlement issues at the base of how individuals appraise prevailing economic development results.

The feature which demonstrates performance will therefore be the extent of relative availabilities as compared to entitlements which individuals construe or that have been formulated. As a result, Holistic Aggregate Economic Development charges the aggregate economic development directorate with focusing on quality-of-life entitlements. The directorate is required to identify and facilitate a mix of critical product flows and access entitlements that are consistent with its prevailing culturally centred targets in quality-of-life attainment.

Ideally, what these target levels are, will be forthcoming from conventions that have been adapted out of prevailing citizenship. Furthermore, assigning governments the duty to focus on how such availabilities are being serviced is a management obligation which is no less appropriate than the oversight responsibilities that the market economic context has assigned to government. The government is expected to discharge the development responsibility to facilitate and otherwise service a competitive market environment which complements the pursuit of market profit by entrepreneurs.

The commercial operations of conscious human economic agents may be regarded as enabling transactions on behalf of securing the resources with which they plan to execute their survival (as respectively preferred paths in being).

Appraisers of aggregate economic development performance are therefore invited to link the prevailing commercial panorama with the extent of the opportunities that individuals have to service their targets in human development.

Aggregate economic development analysts are therefore invited to focus on the prevailing access of the typical citizen to the complements of survival at which they aim. These analysts must then measure how effectively the flows of critical consumption and activity opportunities complement the attainment of human development in the prevailing environment.

CHAPTER 3

LIVING AND ECONOMISING AS TIME-USE MANAGEMENT

∽☙∾

To conscious human economic agents, living is not merely a series of operations, with which they aim to maximise their opportunities for self-indulgence. To them, the achievement from resource management is not indicated by the market value of the self-indulgence possibilities which individuals (or collectives of them) have corralled.

Instead, Holistic Aggregate Economic Development Management regards the outcomes from resource management as being pursued complements to the living which individuals do. Furthermore, the context emphasises that notwithstanding the presence of operations in the market, selections of time-use allocation represent the substantive economising operation at hand, into which individuals enter. The Holistic focus also emphasises that securing the complements to a high quality-of-survival is the economic management target. Therefore, over any period of time, the achievement from the management of prevailing resources and available time is not revealed merely in terms of what prevailing market value data show.

So far, in Western economic society, the living that human economic agents pursue is essentially appreciated as a biological operation which portrays an *organic* fruition. In Western society, the manifest operations as living, which individuals execute via their resource and time-use management, are not linked to economic management operations. Rather, any concept of living that Western market economics has construes the organic operation that living is a feature that is occurring within respective socio-cultural contexts. Here, individuals are seen as organising their operations around the achievement of "role" and "status" attributes.

This emphasis on living, fundamentally as an organic operation that is accompanied by cell division and the behaviours that are associated with the respective species, does not emphasise the effort-management operation. As a result, this focus socio-intellectually dissembles, manipulates and beclouds. It is necessary to recognise that the political economic management outcomes *are* the substantive access opportunities which individuals secure. It is therefore the mix of forthcoming access that must be used to judge outcomes in living. However, the beclouding of the issue regarding access via a focus on living as an organic operation makes it convenient for economic discourse to neglect to look on how effectively prevailing production and exchange operations have impacted the quality-of-living of members of the society.

When the living-centred effectiveness of resource allocation contributions is neglected, the net profitability of market operations is allowed to form the indicator of resource management achievement.

Mindful that such oversights can occur, The New Economy recognises that consciousness is at the base of the systematic resource manipulation into which human economic agents enter and it motivates them to seek to enhance the quality of their forthcoming survival. The New Economy is also mindful that the typical individual has historically sought to execute time and resource management selections on the basis of his/her judgements about how consistent the selection will be, with securing access to the features of quality-of-survival at which he/she aims.

Performance appraisal in The New Economy inquiries about how supportive of such survival requirements which individuals have are the prevailing strategies of aggregate economic development.

Therefore, the focus necessitates measurements of performance to communicate the extent to which the data show the presence of the critical mixes of structures and the outcomes out of which a high quality-of-living becomes accessible to individuals.

Quality of survival is shown by patterns of results that accompany the usage of time by individuals. However, analysts, such as Gary Becker, in the "Theory of Allocation of Time", have emphasised human time-usage as contributing to commerce-equivalent adjusted GNP. He posited that places such as the households of private individuals represent (market equivalent) production centres.

Becker did *not* accommodate private households as places where individuals co-ordinate the management of their survival. Accordingly, he argued that aggregate economic performance would be better revealed if surrogate market prices could be found to weight and include in output the quantities of (market equivalent) outputs that are produced in households.

Other analysts have, on the other hand, focused on including in output the negative spin-off results from market operations that arise as outputs such as pollution and environmental degradation. They necessitate that these generated results should be correspondingly price-weighted. They argued that price-weighted inclusion of such results (even if negative) in a substantive (objective) indicator of outcomes would provide a more appropriate statement of what has been delivered.

Even though the prevailing features that lead to a high quality of life have objective components, the conclusions which individuals draw about the quality of their living are private. Therefore, one cannot find market prices with which one may state the objective exchange value of the forthcoming achievements which individuals secure. As a result, the selection of the development policy that is centred on quality-of-life attainment cannot be guided by a balancing exercise where the net financial "harm" which outcomes can cause to "losers" is compared with the net financial rewards that beneficiaries of the initiative may receive. Therefore, development programming may not start out by relying on the (market-centred) assumption that neutral distributive effects will accompany programme and policy initiatives.

Living, as a consciousness-directed collection of resource and time-use management operations, by individuals where they aim to secure mixes of opportunities/experience that are consistent with a structural ideal imputes the pursuit of self-interest. However, what individuals construe as being in their self-interest is significantly based on the understanding that they have about how their material environment functions.

The New Economy emphasizes individuals as integrating into their consciousness the understanding that they deduce and then applying the deduced inferences towards furthering the evolution of a survival path which they respectively seek. In the process, The New Economy underscores sustenance and technical discovery as being among the principal vectors on the path of human development to which individuals are committed.

The framers of development programming are therefore invited to recognise that when conscious human economic agents make selections among resource commitment operations, their targets are self-discovery, self-affirmation and self-sustenance.

These achievements aimed at a high quality-of-living will emerge only in an environment where members of the polity have access to informed time-use opportunities. In order to generate such results, aggregate economic development programming must facilitate the capability and opportunity of individuals to access and decipher information about how their environment functions.

Living occurs over succeeding short-run periods of time. Duration is a critical feature of survival. Via their quality-of-living commitment, individuals bring a long-term (durational) reference context to their effort management choices. As a result, The New Economy emphasizes human economic agents as seeking to have an environment which allows them to access flows of preferred items and opportunities which will complement their survival.

Under these circumstances, development performance will be revealed in the changes in the access of individuals to critical survival-centred attributes/features of a high quality-of-living. Development data must therefore show how much access to discretionary time-use opportunities and mixes of critical survival-supportive technical outputs is available to the typical individuals in the society. The data should also show the extent to which prevailing natural environment and eco-system remain non-threatened and in the process complements that access.

Although informed individuals are willing to make technical substitutions among available services, they also have preferred patterns of time-use that they want to secure.

However, typically, Western society construes human economic agents as seeking out financial earnings as their "passport' (so to speak) to acquiring the technical complements to "living" that they need. The closest, which that Western society has come to acknowledging the mixes of available services must be framed into an indicator of performance, is the formation of the Consumer Price Index (CPI) that it computes. That index is arrived at by first forming a collection (market basket) of representative services whose availabilities are deemed to be vital.

Currently, inferences regarding "development" performance are frequently drawn depending on the extent to which average earnings are changing at higher or lower rates than the quantity of money which is required to purchase the "market basket" in the CPI.

The focus which the society puts on the CPI fits into its imputation that socialising individuals to chase money and manage the quantity that they have secured is the way to pursue quality-of-life attainment. Yet, the principle of stipulating a "market basket" of critical commodities also approaches the recognition that mixes of technical attainments of services are imperative.

Therefore, when the society decides to overlook the access of individuals to actual mixes of critical services, economists haul out the CPI as the primary reference about how markets and the accompanying changes in prices have been affecting how individuals live.

Yet, notwithstanding the convenience of money, development attainment is not about the level of commerce in necessities, toys and consumption "trinkets" that has occurred. Rather, development attainment is about the access of individuals to time-use opportunities which will enable them to reinforce and enhance their self-value, thereby confirming the appropriateness of their decision to remain alive.

Governments will need to focus on the mixes of initiatives they will need to take to complement the relative access of individuals to the wherewithal that delivers a high quality of time-use. It follows, therefore, that a government which has set *no* targets in access to technical services indicates that *it*, on its part, has no commitment to fostering high quality time-use opportunities in the society.

Mixes of critical services which will complement quality-of-life attainment are associated with time-use opportunities. As a result, governments have the opportunity to measure performance via indexing the distribution of shortfalls in access to these critical services that the typical citizen faces.[22]

———•———

The Time-use Focus to Date

In the current information-driven post-industrial society, it is largely overlooked that individuals seek to use their selections of resource and time commitments in order to execute and enhance their self-fulfillment besides giving dimension to their survival. However, division of labour also requires persons to fit their choice of effort commitments into acquiring the financial wherewithal with which they will purchase the complements of their survival.

Usually, capitalist trading arrangements accommodate all and sundry efforts and outputs for which there are buyers and sellers. Whether the prevailing trade arrangements complement the access of individuals to time and effort allocated choices that foster living as self-expression has so far been overlooked. Instead, Western society ends up viewing the economising operations of persons as mixes of strategies where they are set out to acquire or manage *money*.

Economic development directorates which recognise that the market merely functions as an instrument will want to know how effectively the prevailing operations complement the quality-of-living targets that individuals have.

---

22. One approach set will be further elaborated here later within the context of Quantum Economics. The other is elaborated in Horace Carby-Samuels, *Work, the Economy, and Human Development*, (Ottawa, Canada, The Agora Publishing Consortium); Forthcoming, winter, 2003, ISBN 0-9681906-1-8.

However, it must first be recognised that living is revealed in the selections of time-use operations into which human economic agents enter. Appraisers of attainment must also recognise that the consciousness of individuals leads them to seek to execute/secure respective technical features with which they plan to support their survival.

The technical composition of the components which manifest choices in time-use and the mixes of sought outcomes will differ for different periods and also among different individuals. However, the data that are associated with these choices will have identifiable attributes out of which associated quality-of-life impact may be deduced.

Historically, economists have usually computed outcomes as the market value of flows of trade-linked data with which collectives of individuals are associated over elapsed periods of time. Additionally, that duration is usually measured as man-hours, man-days, man-weeks or man-years. These analysts have also regarded the resources which entrepreneurs provide as having been committed for periods of elapsed *economic time.*

One such elapse, for example, is the production time i.e. the duration between the start-up of production co-ordination and the subsequent event where the generated output is sold to the customer. In that genre of economic time, one frequently used computation is the aggregate commercial value of marketed output and the changes in the aggregate market value of inventory in a production year. As a result, the Gross National Product (GNP) for the society in a production year becomes a significant indicator of aggregate economic performance.

Over the period of evolution of economics as an analytical discipline, analysts have used selected time horizons to communicate about the levels of exchanges that have occurred in the supportive features that have contributed to the measured outcomes. For example, the classical economists had pointed out that money, as capital investment or loans, is committed for time periods.

The classical economists had also argued, for example, that when money is committed as loans, interest charges represented a payment *obligation* which borrowers incurred for having use of the money over the elapsed time between the offering of the loan and its subsequent repayment. In *their* view, it was the borrower, rather than the lender, who had used the loaned funds over the time period that the loan was outstanding.

However, Irving Fisher (1930), (1961) *emphasised time as a space, over which human economic agents executed business development opportunities.* He argued that over the time when the loan is outstanding, lenders (as entrepreneurs) needed to protect the wealth power of their committed funds. However, Fisher did not give recognition to the feature that in any time space, human economic agents are normally operating as managers of their resources and their lives (as a time-space).

Fisher was emphasising the economic operation which comprises of the business of money management towards delivering rates of command over market-measured wealth. However, there is a second and no less important economic management operation which individuals are normally at the same time conducting. The other (largely overlooked) economic management operation by human economic agents comprises of the business of living.

As was emphasised above, living as an economic activity comprises of mixes of operations that function as survival-oriented choices which individuals make among opportunities for effort and time commitment. Results are indicated by the success of persons at using available information and resources to give sought direction and content to their survival.

The initiatives which individuals will take in the business of living will depend upon what the context of their understanding of the available technology enables them to recognise and the type of future which they desire. In contrast, Irving Fisher's concentration on how time was involved was on establishing the logic to the right of entrepreneurs to use interest payments to preserve or protect the wealth power of their currency in face of the variety in earning potential that business operations offered.

Fisher's focus construed economic activity as being largely aimed at the business of *earning*. He pointed out that technical developments in association with new capital investments are likely to cause falls in the productivity of old capital investments to emerge over time. His essential proposition was that over the time period of the loan, the interest became a form of "insurance" in order to "index" the wealth power of the cash which the lender had advanced. Fisher's argument was, therefore, in the support of the right of lenders to use interest payments to protect over time the "wealth power" of their loaned funds.[23]

The borrowing and the lending of funds comprise of legitimate business operations. However, when the delivered quality-of-living is seen as the indicator of development performance, the commercial activity that accompanies financial investment does not clearly declare the level of performance in respect of quality-of-life attainment.

The data that point to the buoyancy of commerce may not stand alone. Rather, in the society at hand, the relevance of that data must be weighted in terms of how the business of living has been facilitated.

The forthcoming aggregate market data must complement the access of individuals to time-use options which make a high quality-of-living. In particular, the data must reveal the opportunities of persons to access the technical complements that are critical to the survival of individuals in the time period at hand. Accordingly, the collected data must show the extent to which prevailing public policy enables the typical working person to achieve targets in survival and to at the same time manage the commitment and usage of his/her time.

The tolerances which industrial relations legislation legitimates form one of the principal vehicles for co-ordinating the business of living with the cash economy. That legislation must protect the investment of entrepreneurs from irresponsible action by hired labour. However, it must at the same time also complement the rights of working people to participate in the management of how their time on-the-job is committed.

The presence of such enabling work-rules regarding how individuals use their time on the job is not sufficient. In the context of economic development, it is the structure and distribution of the opportunities which individuals have to use their total time that is the defining feature to quality-of-living. That is why, on behalf of the time-use opportunities of individuals, a government which is committed to facilitating human development must foster features additional to industrial relations.

Specifically, to facilitate the time-use opportunities out of which quality-of-living will arise, the government must also be prepared to proceed

---

23. See, therefore, Irving Fisher, *The Theory of Interest* (New York: Augustus M Kelley) 1930, and 1961.

on the principle that not everything in the society at hand has an effectively attached "For Sale" sign.

Targets in human development are not likely to be served when the access of respective individuals to justice as an output is regulated by how much that individual can pay. Space is a component in most technical production. Although the use of elevation as in sky scrapers in the real estate industry enables expansion of the functional usage of the limited geographic space at hand, prevailing space is a *non*-renewable resource. Geographic space as in territory is therefore a rationed component.

How such available non-renewable resources are used represents a critical feature that will impact on the mixes of technical outputs that become available.

Even in the face of technical innovation that extends the effectiveness of the usage of prevailing resources, current usages will ration the availability of non-renewable resources for producing other outputs. Furthermore, when the performance target is quality-of-life as access opportunities on behalf of human development and is not necessarily net financial returns, resource rationing arrangements will have to be adjusted.

When quality-of-life is the target, a number of propositions must be challenged. Among those is the capitalist one that the mere payment of an asking price in the market gives entrepreneurs essentially unalloyed rights to decide how the services of the land and other *non*-renewable resources in an environment may be used.

As far back as the near post World War II era, Karl Polanyi had argued that an "Obsolete Market Mentality" has limited our ability to understand economising that human economic agents do in their societies.[24] Therefore, in the spirit of that background, it must be appreciated that although operations which are aimed at the business of earning may be ranked with the use of money prices as the weights, there are also operations regarding the business of living that may not be so ranked. These

---

24. See, therefore, Karl Polanyi; "Our Obsolete Market Mentality", in *Primitive, Archaic, And Modern Economies: Essays of Karl Polanyi*, George Dalton (ed.), (Boston, Mass.: Beacon Press), 1968, pp. 59-77.

other operations are aimed at targets that persons have. There, achievement uses a different ranking context.

In a society where the creating and the using of new technology is the norm, human economic agents may not be relegated into being accompanying service-providing robots and automatons. Furthermore, the development operations in which conscious human economic agents engage themselves are mediated by both the targets in earning and the targets in being that they have. As a result, it is inappropriate for the framers of aggregate economic development to plan as if human economic agents like corporations are primarily marketing the allocation of their effort and time towards cash-flow targets.

Instead, development planners need to recognise that typically based on their understanding, human economic agents commit their resources and efforts towards crafting the pattern of survival as time-use that they desire.

The framers of aggregate economic development programmes are therefore required to foster conditions which complement the technical capabilities to facilitate a high quality to their survival that responsible individuals seek. As a result, for any time period, the performance data must point to where resource and information bottlenecks are preventing members of the populace from crafting the associated informed resource and time-use management opportunities that they seek.

It will not be sufficient for these development performance reports to tell of how extensively investment policy has executed manpower development programming that meets the market demand of employers for skills.

In The New Economy that is aimed at a high quality of survival over any time period, servicing the availability of a manpower pool on behalf of "wage slavery" and commercial "prosperity" is not the principal economic development obligation of responsible governments.

———•———

Raymond Samuels

Living and Economising

Under the influence of their consciousness, human economic agents commit their resources and time towards securing mixes of outcomes which will assist them to reach the quality-of-life targets to which they aspire. From the outcomes with which their resource and time commitments are associated, human economic agents respectively seek to deduce confirmation that their decision to remain alive was meaningful and worthwhile.

The New Economy sets out to promote the blending of the business of living with the business of commerce. At the same time, it recognises that although division of labour marks improvements in the economic effectiveness of time usage, there are also survival targets at the base of the economic management initiatives into which human economic agents enter.

Towards the blending of the business of living and the business of commerce so as to foster quality-of-life attainment, The New Economy construes as an activity context the resource and time-use management into which individuals enter. As a result, living in economic terms can be recognised as patterns of opportunities and access. Therefore, in the context of economic development, living becomes patterns of survival.

Living as an economic activity is an output which is manifested in the *managed* allocation of resources and time in which individuals engage themselves towards securing preferred technical patterns in the time-consumption that forms survival.

Therefore, for human economic agents, living was not merely a biological event that one observes. Furthermore, although it is an output, it has a particularly unique resume. The delivery of living of a high quality does not happen to be one of those outputs which, because of its attractiveness as a profit centre, are dispensed on the market. As a result, The New Economy comprises of a promoting agency on behalf of generating a high quality-of-living. It mandates the aggregate economic development directorate to stipulate an underlying rule system to trade such that associated operations are also consistent with performance that is measured via quality-of-life enhancement.

Conclusions about how quality-of-living has been serviced by prevailing trade will emerge from what the data show about how much access individuals have secured to the permanencies in survival that they seek.

The imputation that there are underlying permanencies to the attainment targets at which human economic agents aim their effort commitments is not new to the economics literature. However, when it is recognised that economic management targets comprise of the business of earning as well as the business of living, further elucidation of the targeted permanencies background becomes necessary.

Consider, for example, that in introducing the context of human capital, Schultz (1964) started out by modifying the financial emphasis to Milton Friedman's "Permanent Income Hypothesis". However, the Schultz modification of that hypothesis emphasised human economic agents as being seekers of "sources of permanent income streams". Furthermore, in that formulation, Schultz had also blended the economic activities of individuals in business of earning with their efforts in respect of the business of *living*.[25] Notably, unlike our emphasis here, at that time Schultz did not explicitly consider the quality of the natural environment as one of the "sources of permanent income streams".

Living occurs on and off the job. It should be noted, therefore, that although the providers of skills are pursuing earnings which they will then allocate among available services, they are also at the same time going about the business of living.

How much quality-of-living these human economic agents achieve will not necessarily be indicated by the size of the market basket to which their acquired earnings give them access. Rather, that achievement will be indicated by the mixes of critical services that have become available to them and by their access to informed time-use management opportunities. Thereby, they will be enabled to achieve the survival at which they aim.

---

25. See, therefore, T. W. Schultz, *Transforming Traditional Agriculture*; (New Haven, Yale University Press), (1964). See, especially Chapter 5, pp.71 – 82.

A Holistic approach to aggregate economic management is an administrative context. The approach is set out to pursue development policies and programmes that blend targets which individuals have in the *business of living* with their opportunities to earn.

As a result, the Holistic approach requires economic development analysis to discover and point out administrative and investment initiatives that will relieve or mitigate bottlenecks to informed survival that individuals face.

These analysts will also need to point out the extent to which the common property resources of the society are being efficiently used to service the survival targets of the typical individual in the society.

Holistic Aggregate Economic Development programming recognises that although individuals are pursuing the business of living, their opportunities to obtain survival wherewithal also depend on their opportunities to earn. Where division of labour is the norm, to a large extent, it is the initiatives of entrepreneurs to secure profit that tends to generate these opportunities of individuals to earn. However, Holistic Aggregate Economic Development argues that although individuals may not be high income earners, they still have rights to time-use opportunities which are consistent with a high quality-of-living.

It is a vulgar civilization which operates on the principle that only earners of high money income have rights to a high quality-of-living. Accordingly, where individuals can gain access to the critical means of their survival only if they function as hired disposable labour that seekers after-market profit require, a type of "wage slavery" is the tolerated societal norm.[26]

Holistic Aggregate Economic Development Management grows out of a context where respective societies are prepared to ask themselves, *"How will the emphases of their prevailing economic development programming facilitate the rights to survival that their participating members have?"*

---

26. Historically, Western colonialism advanced itself by taking over the administrative systems of traditional economies and thence forcing the indigenous peoples into various strategies of wage slavery. That experience is also likely to arise where conditions such as racism are used to ration the access of targeted groups to capital markets and managerial positions in corporate organisations.

However, some economists have raised issues regarding a guaranteed financial income in the typical market economy. The Holistic context to economic development places its focus on the availability of critical services. It invites the society to stipulate what are the availability minima in respect of critical services which it will use programme initiatives to facilitate or guarantee.

It is true that so far, in the market managed economy, control over money and other property has functioned as the doorway through which individuals gain access to the complements of their survival. However, the Holistic context to aggregate economic development challenges the society to indicate whether "wage slavery" is the access norm with which it is comfortable.

At the same time, if access in accordance with wage earnings is not the condition of existence in the society, governments will need to decide what management initiatives they will respectively take to complement the availability of critical services to the typical individual in the society.

Ever since the days of Adam Smith, market economists have argued that individuals are in a better position than government to make exchange decisions on behalf of their own self-interest. Accordingly, Western economists have historically argued that governments should not interfere in the establishment of the prices at which goods and services get traded.

Yet, in addition to levying various types of taxes on trade and outputs, some countries have frequently initiated programmes to subsidise the access of citizens to quantities of critically sought consumption/survival services. Housing, health care, food, fuel, security, transportation, education, access to justice and environmental non-pollution are some of the outputs where availability levels have frequently been forthcoming due to government programming initiatives.

Holistic Aggregate Economic Development recognises that the providers of labour effort have a right to expect financial compensation that is linked to the market productivity of the effort which they provided. However, the context also focuses on how individuals share total output. It recognises that individuals also contribute to total output directly via the skills that they provide and indirectly via their association with the power relationships to which they give allegiance. Recall therefore that historically the political power alliances which individuals make in a society have been typically aimed at accessing or preserving shares in aggregate output.

There is the additional distributive consideration that the increases in aggregate output which forms economic development arise in concert with conditions of market *dis*equilibria. As a result, it is inappropriate for economists to use arguments that hold for conditions of equilibrium where output is stable to prescribe or stipulate how output must be shared where development is occurring.

Accordingly, currently one sees the circumstances where the governor of the United States Federal Reserve Bank is imputing that things are normal and are as they should be when corporate profits are rising, while the earnings of labour remain stable. The Governor of the Federal Reserve System then imputes, as inflationary, statistical indications which show that the providers of effort are seeking to share the extra-equilibrium profits from business.

Holistic Aggregate Economic Development recognises that economic development can be linked to management initiatives which entrepreneurs undertake with property over which they have control. However, it also recognises that ownership as rights to manage and convey property is a feature that is ascribed and supported by the governance at hand. In addition, money has become supreme property by virtue of its acceptability in exchange together with its associated flexibility of conveyance. Furthermore, when the currency becomes primarily fiduciary, its designation and quantity are also government regulated.

The trade that circumscribes economic reality emerges within the background of government participation/protection of property designation and its conditions of conveyance. The Holistic Aggregate economic Development context makes no imputation that distribution should be outside of the concern of government. Therefore, it also makes no imputation that only high income earners deserve the access to a high quality-of-life.

Additionally, the Holistic Aggregate Economic Management context does not make the imputation that highest quality-of-living will be forthcoming in a society only if all of the scarce resources and the sought outputs inclusive of environmental non-pollution are treated as conveyable property. The context does not impute that in order to have equitable and efficient economic allocation, all outputs and property must respectively have a "for sale" sign placed on them. Instead, the Holistic context is based on the proposition that governments have an economic development obligation to take initiatives that complement the access of individuals to critical mixes of outputs on behalf of a high quality-of-survival.

Where division of labour is the effort allocated norm, a stable environment of money prices for skills and respective property holdings arises out of the smooth predictable functioning of prevailing exchange alliances. In those circumstances, groups that have been allowed to control the flow of the information on which individuals make exchange decisions are able to influence favourably the quantity of money property which will be forthcoming to themselves and their allies.

For example, in the prevailing market economic civilization and circumstances involving a "legitimated employment contract", the contributor of the money part to the exchange transaction is typically vested with management authority in the project at hand. The society vests the provider of the money with the right to stipulate at the workplace the choices of production techniques and the choice of output targets. Yet, when a society decides to make quality-of-living the attainment target, it also has responsibilities to protect the typical individual against the evolution of "wage slavery". In particular, the society needs to take explicit steps to ensure that the assigned rights that financial entrepreneurs have to manage invested financial capital are not used by them as leverage which enables them to contractually compromise the living-centred rights of hired labour.

To avoid the likelihood of such inappropriate compromises, Holistic Aggregate Economic Development management calls for industrial relations regulations and legislation which accommodate the providers of effort as partners with the providers of capital in output delivery.

The recognition that it is a partnership that exists views the attempts of individuals to acquire technical skills partly on behalf of their strategies to earn and partly directed at their attempts to impact how their environment evolves. Accordingly, the government of a society has the responsibility to put in place industrial relations programmes that are extensions of empowerment-oriented training and skills development programming.

Curricula, libraries and capable faculty that do not regard trainees as manpower which they are preparing for employment in the market will be the technical instruments to the delivery of Holistic Aggregate Economic Development. It follows, therefore, that except in those limited circumstances where military security is involved, citizens should be assured the rights of unimpeded access to information that has been generated with the use of public resources.

Where such conditions of access to information are in place and where individuals have participatory rights in how their work environment functions, wage earners can better place themselves in time-commitment operations which they associate with meaningful survival.

When the classical economist Alfred Marshall (1890) formed the term "real income", he imputed that individuals prior to deciding whether to shift to alternative offered employment reflected on the type of survival with which they wanted to associate with their time-usage.[27] Furthermore, when labour unions require "work rules" and "working conditions" of given sorts to be written into the employment contract, they too are aiming at the living that occurs on-the-job.

It follows, therefore, that governments communicate an important implied indifference to quality-of-living when they put in place industrial relations legislation which allows corporations to accommodate wage earners primarily as "paid stiffs" rather than as "partners in the production operation". The message is that these governments have neither the real income nor the quality-of-living of their citizens as development targets.[28]

---

27. See, therefore, Alfred Marshall, *Principles of Economics*, Eighth Edition, (London: MacMillan), 1890, 1964.

28. Capital can always be discarded when it becomes obsolescent or becomes worn.out. Therefore, when the economic view of governments is that the human providers of skills and technical capacity comprise "human capital", that focus becomes a convenient stratagem which these governments can use to overlook the right of the providers of effort to have a meaningful participatory work environment.

Normally, individuals bring to their economic development participation the variety in their capabilities, personal histories and stocks of accessible discretionary resources. As a result, there is a variety to the attainment mixes which respective persons will seek out in the market. Therefore, the details of the mixes of services which individuals will respectively want to bring to their technology of living will differ. Yet, when an aggregate economic development directorate decides to make the quality-of-life attainment of its typical citizen its target, it must make decisions about what are the *mixes* of critical deliveries which it will foster.

It is true that the tendency of human economic agents to make technical substitutions among scarce services suggests that the services need not be made available in fixed proportions to each other. However, the willingness of individuals to make technical substitutions does not justify an oversight of delivered technical quantities in favour of an emphasis on the market exchange values of delivered/available technical services.

The New Economy recognises that typically towards executing their financial survival, corporations make management and resource allocated decisions which they expect to enhance their profits. However, at the same time, the context of the New Economy appreciates individuals as pursuing action opportunities. It recognises that these action opportunities are comprised of technical time and resource trade-offs. The individuals expect to secure the enhanced sustenance and enhanced understanding which they associate with a heightened quality-of-living.

Earnings attainment may also accrue from some of the time-use commitments which are included in those technical trade-offs that individuals make among alternative action opportunities. However, the aggregate economic development directorate needs to appreciate that although net financial-equivalent earnings are the indicator of successful corporate performance, the outcome does not provide a measurement of the survival attainment from human time-use commitment.

———•———

Raymond Samuels

Working and Living; Some Additional Issues

On recognising that living as an economic operation is manifested by the selections of time-use commitments into which individuals enter, it becomes evident that working and living do not comprise of separate spheres of human endeavour. As a result, notwithstanding common parlance in an economic development context, work and employment are not interchangeable.

Employment is normally associated with implicit or explicit wage (compensation) contracts for services rendered, whereas one only needs to think of what housewives do to see that work does not need to involve any such formal or informal compensation arrangement.

The economics literature has also usually stated that work and leisure form the functional alternative activity sets into which human economic agents normally commit their time. The imputation in that economics literature is that to individual human economic agents in operational terms, these two action paths are supposed to exhaust the time that individuals have available for effort commitment. However, when human economic agents are appreciated as committing *their understanding and resources* to arrive at targets in *survival*, the complexity of their objective must be appreciated. Therefore, it is inappropriate to see work and leisure as operations which exhaust the manifested action paths.

The time and the resources which individuals commit for enhancing, clarifying or reinforcing their understanding of how their environment is operating is a serious investment activity. Such survival oriented operations neither belong to work-time nor to the time which individuals commit to leisure. Furthermore, a commitment to life-long learning makes individuals and those in search for a high quality-of-life aware. Their search for understanding is not limited to the time that they spend in formal research and formal schooling.

Holistic Aggregate Economic Management recognises that the business of living and the business of earning are substantively joint understanding-guided activities. As a result, it appreciates that towards making their survival more meaningful, individuals typically co-ordinate their effort commitments among selections of information-yielding technical operations. However, in that co-ordination out of which they expect to secure enhanced meaningfulness, individuals also seek to determine the extent of the presence of enhanced opportunities to secure the complements of their subsistence.

In the light of that recognition, the Holistic focus on aggregate economic development rejects the imputation that the time which individuals spend in work and the enjoyment of leisure jointly exhausts the time-allocated economic activity patterns in which they are occupied.

Quality-of-living and the meaningful survival emerge in concert. Respective aggregate economic development directorates are therefore required to make their selections among programme and policy initiatives on the basis of forthcoming expected impact that the selection will make on the opportunities of individuals for meaningful survival.[29] Prevailing education programming and the industrial relations legislation will be also required to operate in service of enabling individuals to secure enhanced meaningfulness in their time-use commitments.

The legislation and regulations out of which the industrial relations and education programming of post-World War II West Germany had evolved were in service to such an implicit (human development oriented) reference context. The framers of the constitution and administrative structures of West Germany had accommodated the providers of labour-effort as valid and valuable participants in the economic development process. The "legislated" economic development arrangement had been framed as a strategy which was calculated to move that country from its Nazi past. Therefore, the industrial relations context of West Germany essentially accommodated working people as investors of their living-centred time. Accordingly, in West Germany, the industrial relations regulations had stipulated worker/employee representation on the decision-making boards of all respective industrial corporations.

---

29. The evaluation of aggregate economic development performance within that context is presented in Horace Carby-Samuels, *Work, the Economy, and Human Development*, Ottawa, Canada, (Agora Publishing Consortium), Winter 2003, ISBN 0-9681906-1-8.

In a more informal organisational context, largely to capture the productivity and profit benefits that accompany lower industrial unrest, Japanese corporations developed the "quality circles" context, wherein towards encouraging greater apparent participation in authority at the work site, assignments on the job are managed within the "quality circle" which the particular work group comprised.

The North American economic development milieu presents a time-use management context which contrasts with that which had been developed for West Germany. In North America, the rate of profit that accrues to corporations after they make their wage payments is construed as the principal indicator of economic performance.

In contrast to the milieu which had been framed for West Germany, the dominant North American Labour relations scene regards the providers of financial capital (entrepreneurs, bond holders and the banks) as the essential investors. The providers of effort and of skills are not accommodated as quality-of-life-centred economic investors of a portion of their living time. Instead, in North America, when all of the public relations statements and the propaganda about the superiority of the American style market economy is stripped away, the providers of human effort as hired labour are largely accommodated as no more than "Working Stiffs" that must be provided wages.

The officials of the typical North American labour union essentially handle their membership as a "commodity" that is being peddled by these union officials, who function as "hired advocates" for their particular "commodity"/"affinity" group. As a result, in North America, the norm is that officials of labour unions see their task as to earn their own pay by "negotiating" "shop floor" pay and work conditions *on* behalf of the providers of effort.

Under the political economic doctrine of the "globalisation" of markets, the view of the labour as an "instrument" and as a provider of effort commitment that is treated as a purchasable commodity is executed via colonial and neo-colonial techniques on the domain of "third world" countries. When such attitude transferences (regarding labour providers as hired implements) are made, economists overlook the impact on bargaining power of the effort providers who of course have uneven access to information and who typically are under the control of politicians that have usually been "bought out".

Such an oversight of the targets of working people as citizens parallels the neglect of economists to recognise that individuals have meaningfulness in living as an effort management target. These economists, instead, argue the alleged superiority of economic management via the "free market". As a result, they overlook how "wage slavery" is used as an instrument in the globalisation of markets at which their propaganda support aims. The extent of the contribution of exploitive wage payments practices to the forthcoming high profits that fuel the stock market prices of multinational corporations is accommodated by economists as merely good business.

Only a societal commitment to fostering development as meaningful time-use commitment by informed human economic agents will lead to the evolution of the quality-of-life-oriented New Economy.

Towards a Critique and Renaissance of Economics

by H. Raymond Samuels II

Introduction

❧

THIS SECTION has been developed to support a broad based critical appreciation of "contemporary economics". It has also been developed to hopefully illuminate critical areas of economics which have been omitted from the societal application of the discipline. In addition, this section presents 'quantum economics' towards the disciplinary renaissance of 'economics'.

Economics has evolved from an intellectual context that is concerned with 'the management of scare resources'. This section's introductory chapter, *The Individual, Work and Economic Society*, further illuminates critical socio-intellectual foundations of a posited rejuvenated New Economy. The next chapter, *'What is Capitalism?'* presents general intellectual parameters of a political economic ideological ascendancy. It elaborates how "contemporary economics" has evolved from a mixture of certain apparent identifiable "world views", assumptions and ensuing computational systems. These systems associated with *'traditional economics'* that forms the basis of modern capitalism include an 'implied Social Darwinism', 'Commercial Utilitarianism', "Free Market" 'economic colonialism', 'Human Capital', the linked corollary of 'limited government', 'Corporatization' and "Capitalistocracy" towards an induced state of "institutionalised fascism". What is the elaborated context of these pivotal subcomponent areas of the current capitalist economic paradigm?

Social Darwinism refers to a reactionary socio-biological and economic philosophy that views society within the premise that accepts the "survival of the fittest". *'Commercial Utilitarianism'* accommodates the contemporary economic approach to market 'resource utilisation'. *'Human*

Capital' refers to the implicit existential domination of individuals in general by "contemporary economics", and specifically by 'market-based economics'. As induced by so-called 'Globalisation', the work-related activities of human beings in the form of 'labour' with civil rights are transformed into a political economic role of 'chattel'.

Human Capital was a theoretical approach to economics that was developed by University of Chicago's internationally renowned and prestigious School of Economics in the early 1960's. The concept has been successfully proselytised into the axiomatic intellectual paradigm of the so-called '*New Economy*'. In the overall milieu of 'economic colonialism' into which the concept has been fitted, money has implicitly become a valued economic feature in itself and the role that it plays is stressed in the attributed righteousness of the "*free market*" in capitalism.

This section will explore the extent to which 'contemporary economics' has emerged to essentially legitimate the process of 'colonisation' and foster a modernised '*economic colonialism*'. For example, is the so-called corporate-led "free market" interested to expand markets as exemplified by 'globalisation' about assisting "expanding prosperity" and democracy or is it about entrenching a form of *neo-colonialism* that has been built into the intellectual framework of modern capitalism?

To what extent has an ensuing form of *fascism* been institutionalised into the norms of a political economic milieu that has become divested to a private enterprise culture that is dominated by Trans National Corporations? The chapter on *International Fascism* explores the forces of "economic globalisation" that is based on the market-based economics paradigm. "Economic Globalisation" is supporting an apparent dysfunctional ascending globalised neo-fascist political economic system. This developmental milieu of "economic globalisation" undermines the very democratisation that the champions of "economic globalisation" purport to support. With this in mind, is the so-called '*New Economy*' really new, or is the so-called '*New Economy*' the pseudonym for what is really the unleashing of the imperial and predatory forces of the '*Old Economy*' against the world? *What is the apparent role of "limited government" that is prescribed by the Apostles and disciples of capitalism towards how a capitalistic society should operate?*

The chapter on *"Capitalistocracy"* and related 'globalisation' presents some publicised examples of the perniciousness that is associated with 'globalisation' and some identified and apparent pivotal intellectual sub-components of "contemporary free-market economics".

The section also provides a corresponding intellectual basis for an alternative approach to economics. This alternative approach is inspired by quantum science and enlightened or holistic approaches to economics that have so far been displaced by the University of Chicago School's successful proselytising of a 'positive economics' that has also been synonymous to "contemporary economics". Critically omitted areas of a perhaps more enlightened approach to economics could pivot on an alternative application that relies on a "science of living" rather than the current relative preoccupation with a 'science of money'.

Identifiable components towards the renaissance of economics on which this section focuses include community as an alternative to the current *'modus operandi'* of 'economic globalisation', 'Quantum Economics' and 'Quality of Living'. Indeed, 'positive economics' as championed by Milton Friedman from the Chicago School via his book entitled *Essays in Positive Economics* (1953, 1962) together with Friedman's somewhat more polemical and also ideological presentation, *Capitalism and Freedom* (1962), have become the entire basis for the evolution of post-World War II American economics. The result has been a 'globalised' postCold War era which has been driven by the corporate priorities of 'market capitalism'.

In the popular constitutional context that is associated with civil rights, the substantive relationship between capitalism and freedom and equality is antagonistic. Freedom via a posited axiomatic human developmental context of "cosmopolitan constitutionalism" is concerned with an ethical system of governance that rests upon tenets of supporting and protecting civil rights and equality as the basis of the pursuit of freedom by individuals in a pluralistic society associated with the 'ecology of survival'. In contrast, "freedom" in capitalism as the pseudonym of the "free market" is preoccupied with the furtherance of the pursuit of predatory commercial interests largely revolving around firms within a "market" as an environment of commercial entities with purchasing power. *'Quantum economics'* is a rejuvenated quality of survival context of economic development in contradistinction to the apparent apocalyptic development context of market-based economics.

'Modern capitalism' that relies on applied "positive economics" supports the premise that the economy, notwithstanding the role of government concerning monetary policy, is a "self-regulating" context. Protagonists of the 'positive economics' paradigm refer to what Adam Smith in the well-known book entitled *Wealth of Nations* (1776) referred to as the 'invisible hand' as the basis of their approach to the 'management of scarce resources'. According to that premise, "unnecessary intrusion" by government into the self-regulating functioning of the economy can only serve to distort its attributed distributive optimisation via trade, specialisation and liquidity.

The empirical approach that the application of "positive economics" relies upon emphasises the rational choices of consumers and households. The approach also draws attention to the accompanying initiatives by government to facilitate the flow of these aggregate relationships as well as to facilitate the orderly patterns of market-negotiated prices. The critical apparent deficiency with 'market economics'-driven globalisation is its parochial constriction of *contemporary economics* into being an instrument of commercial interests, *where human beings are valued only up to the extent to which these entities, as 'capital', have money or 'purchasing power' and receive earnings form servicing these commercial interests via work and employment.*

In market-oriented 'capitalistocratic'-driven 'globalisation', 'wage slavery' is the outcome when persons become 'human capital' that is servicing the 'commercial society' via the institution of work.

'Capitalistocratic'-driven globalisation substantively denies the delivery of 'quality-of-life' as the critical focus of economic development. In doing so, the 'capitalistocratic'-driven globalisation subverts existential meaningfulness in conditions of work. Therefore, in this genre, the very nature of work as being alternatively oriented at 'quality-of-living' in a rejuvenated economic system is being subverted. With this in mind, the last chapter of this book is so-to-speak a 'Retrospective'.

CHAPTER 4

The Individual, Work and Economic Society

⚜

T HE TECHNOLOGICALLY developed societies of the industrialised West have become a role model for "less developed" societies. The societies of the industrialised West have evolved vibrant democracies of varying sophistications. Indeed, diverse individuals in these societies often take for granted so-to-speak their evolved political civil rights in comparison to many other societies. Sweden, Denmark, Switzerland and Canada are at the forefront of these "political democracies". However, the developed nature of Western industrialised societies in the 'political realm' has by and large not been as reflected in the 'economic realm'.

"Economic globalisation" has hastened a type of "democratic credibility gap" between the stated official political and the effective economic 'modus operandi' of these societies. In other words, the Western industrialised societies that have 'developed' politically could be viewed to be operating comparatively 'underdeveloped' in the economic realm. The simultaneous operation of a relatively high level of sophisticated political development and reactionary economic development is an apparent paradox within western industrialised societies. Notwithstanding this, discourse has continued to focus on the presented desirability of these so-called "developing" societies striving to achieve the "development" standards of the "advanced" West.

The reference to countries as being "developed" as compared to "developing" implicitly relies on a premise of what constitutes "progress".

Accordingly, the democracies of the industrialised West as recognised "developed" societies are represented as having achieved a more desirable progress as compared to "developing societies". However, it can be legitimately argued that many societies throughout history with perhaps less extensively articulated political constitutional systems have been more 'progressive' and sophisticated in the "economic realm". This representation is with particular reference to the "management of scare resource" that is axiomatic to economics.

Societies which have been referred by somewhat perhaps "Eurocentric" scholars as "traditional" have frequently been based on an economic developmental paradigm of ecologically-sensitised sustainability. These societies have included the aboriginal civilizations in Canada, the U.S., some Kingdoms in Africa and diverse civilizations before European economic colonial interpenetration. "Traditional" societies operate on a great amount of accumulated wisdom for the organisation of "economic society" that West has substantively ignored. This type of oversight has been done to the apparent peril of fostering prospective economic sustainability in the West. The adoption of 'the market' model as the basis of achieving a "developed" economy has evolved upon a context which has ignored the vital quality of survival considerations that have formed the critical basis of many sophisticated 'pre-European colonial' civilizations.

The author of this section of this book posits that the evolution of a society with a politically sophisticated constitutional system which also has a correspondent economically sophisticated milieu of human development would more credibly support claims of being a "developed" society. Such a posited context of human development would be linked with quality of survival considerations in relationship to a rejuvenated context of 'modernisation'. There is an apparent paradox between a desired 'democracy' in Western societal "political" articulation and a simultaneous non-democratic functioning "economic" realm in the industrialised West. Indeed, having not acknowledged the presence of this apparent paradox, the West therefore does not provide an unqualified basis for developmental emulation.

————•————

The Individual and Work

Many employed individuals in so-called "developed" societies spend a considerable portion of the day at their workplace and work linked operations. Usually, these workplaces are located in various office buildings, shopping malls or other locations away from the residences of these individuals. Commuting to and from work is also a required part of the time-budgeting for work. Work has functioned in the predominately urbanised socio-economic milieu of societies in the geo-political West as providing critically needed 'earnings' needed to support subsistence requirements. Work in the West, indeed, has been institutionally developed in response to the 'demands' of a market economic framework. Within this societal context, leisure and other important areas of human living are subordinated to the time-budgeting of an institution of work that has been shaped in the image of the market economy.

The typical individual needs about an average of eight hours of sleep in order to work without requiring too much coffee. It might take that employed individual about an hour is prepared to go to work and one more hour to commute to work. In American cities, many persons live far out in the suburbs to get away from what in their view constitutes areas of inner city poverty and crime. Frequently, these 'suburbanites' may require two hours just getting to work in the morning. The typical employed individual in Canada and the U.S. formally commits to eight hours of work as "wage earners". By the time, these "wage earners" have hopefully been able to leave work by 4:00 PM or 5:00 PM and get back home – notwithstanding persons who are on shift work or variable working hours – they would have committed to a work-related time-budgeting of nineteen to twenty-one hours of a twenty-hour day. That estimate includes work-related sleep time budgeting and specific scheduling accommodation in the evening of eight hours plus work preparation and commuting time and eight hours in the workplace itself.

Indeed, by the time these "wage earners" get back to their residence, they have just enough time to have dinner, watch TV for an hour and do some household maintenance or go to a concert or movie theatre for two hours and then prepare for the next workday. This preparation may include recriminating about the induced job-related stresses of that day and contemplating the job-related assignments of the next day.

Work as an institution of "wage earning" is institutionally concerned with the salaries that a management apparatus chooses to pay to the employed individuals for skills, services and production rendered. Individuals who secure employment opportunities in association with work as an institution of the marketplace are viewed as freely choosing between various firms, offering various salaries that encompass monetary and other "fringe benefits". The market paradigm affirms that management has a right to manage and employed individuals who are "so privileged to be hired" shall respond to the direction of management notwithstanding nominal labour law standards and *collective bargaining* considerations.

However, work can be viewed within a broadened context. This broadened context is associated with the process of living within the context of the time which individuals allocate to their quality of survival. This broadened context is also correspondingly associated with the relationship between the experience of work by conscious individuals and the operation of a political economy of a so-called "developed" society.

The experience of work as a prominent part of the living of employed individuals has frequently become a milieu of anomia. Labour unions, management, academics and other researches and government institutions have documented high turnover, labour grievances and illness as being among other indications of anomia in the modern workplace. When the employed individual gets to work, he or she is frequently confronted by hostile supervisors who often make unreasonable demands in some way because of pressures from their own supervisors, antagonistic fellow employees and poor air quality among other horrendous environmental conditions. The operation of the market capitalism-based economy divests work from an integral part of 'living' into work as being in an economic milieu of commerce.

Indeed, "developed" societies have readily accepted the exercise of rights in a political context. However, the vital economic consideration of work as an expression of living has not been regarded in the contemporary market-operation context of work. Work as an expression of living has been denied a needed correspondent entrenched rights framework. In other words, the individual in association with the institution of work has not been provided a correspondent "economic system" of rights that can critically complement and serve to reinforce the affirmation of political rights. The persistent apparent discontinuity between political rights and comparatively "underdeveloped" economic rights manifests a "credibility gap". The apparent "credibility gap" is between a represented vital political context in the West that has attracted many immigrants and a markedly contrasting 'market'-induced anomia. An affirmed economics rights framework concerning 'work' in a posited rejuvenated New Economy would be mandated to complement 'work' as an expression of living associated with human development.

The anomia associated to the institution of work includes workplaces and limited alternative opportunities where individuals may perceive that they are ill-treated by management. Work in the West is often accompanied by a feeling of marginalisation by the individual in the 'modus operandi' of the business organisation. This feeling of marginalisation includes substantive exclusion from meaningful decision-making process in association with general representations of managerially perpetrated ill-treatment. The experience of anomia by employed individuals also includes correspondent callously maintained poor working conditions overall. In addition, anomia is experienced by individuals in relationship to 'work' where wages are perceived to have been kept systemically low in a manner that institutionalises poverty and "areas of despair" in effected constituencies and the entire societies. These "areas of despair" form socio-economic milieus of hopelessness. Extreme examples of these areas of despair are homelessness in urban areas and huge shantytowns totally deprived of clean drinking water and sanitation infrastructure on the outskirts of urban areas like those found in Brazil and South Africa. These areas of despair have become institutionalised in America's inner city via 'ghettos' with sub-standard high-density housing and horrendous living conditions that are sometimes juxtapose relatively 'affluent' areas. These "areas of despair" are also in rural areas like growing areas of Africa, where famine is the result from so-economic disenfranchisement of farmers' lands by transnational enterprises.

These areas of despair in general are frequently characterised by deprivation from access to healthcare resulting in rampant diseases, hunger, chronic drug abuse and ensuing crime. These areas of despair within the milieu of Western Industrialized societies are particularly prevalent in the United States, with its comparatively orthodox market economic developmental framework. However, as other societies are encouraged to embrace "economic globalisation", these areas of despair are becoming more common internationally. This has occurred as the ability of governments to serve quality of life. The attainment of its citizens has been undermined by the repressive doctrine of "economic globalisation".

Within the framework of market doctrine related to "economic globalisation", the individual has been deprived of an "economic citizenship" that pivots on the institution of work. In the process, the meaningfulness of the "political citizenship" of the individual has been subverted, eroded and undermined. While modern economic society recognises the previously outlined "management rights" towards "market efficiency", individuals have been treated as merely "the masses" that provide a labour pool of capital and purchasing power for offered goods and services that are created by the efficient "management of capital". Such treatment denies the notion of an "economic society" which embraces an "economic citizenship" of conscious individuals who are associated with an environment that is supportive to human development.

The institution of work in a market-based economic society has become relegated to a wage-earning context, in which the individuals essentially sell a predominant part of their time-budgeting associated with living to the alienated market-related demands of management. Thus, a predominant part of the survival strategies of market-based society requires the necessity to take employment as an operation of wage earning. This wage-earning emphasis often detracts from the desire of individuals to pursue their self-actualised targets in human development as conscious individuals. The growth of the union movement has been a popular response by individuals in the workforce to the need to ameliorate conditions in the workplace including improved wages. In union-management relations, the efforts of union to countervail the efforts of management to depress wages have been viewed by the economic directorate to be a source of "market inefficiency", in the pursuit of maximised profit by management on behalf of shareholders. Notwithstanding this, corporations particularly in the United States have rolled back many historical gains of the union movement with the support of "capitalistocratic" government. This has been done, in part, by corporate pressures on government to make it more difficult to organise unions. This has also been done by undermining the legal support associated with the bargaining power of organised unions. This has also been done by allowing management in certain jurisdictions to intimidate employed individuals to de-certify existing collective bargaining units.

While the union movement has made a tremendous contribution to ameliorating the conditions of 'wage slavery' associated with the institution of work, it has had much less success in alleviating the ideological persistence of a quasi-"master" and "indentured servant" relationship that is the prevailing organisational dynamic of workplaces in the West. This dynamic is central to a work culture of 'wage slavery' in market-based economics. Indeed, wage slavery has a socio-economic dynamic that extends beyond the workplace into the individual's relationship to a political economy.

Indeed, one approach to dealing with such an apparent "master" and "indentured servant" relationship in the workplace might be to quit such a workplace and find and alternative employment. However, 'wage slavery' in modern economic society is associated with a whole pattern of living that creates a system of imposed demands on individuals associated with "wage earnings". Thus, an independent professional artist, for example, who has substantive control of his or her immediate working conditions, operates in a distinctive regime of work in a functional context. However, that independent artist may have to work eighteen hours a day just to keep up with the living expenses related to basic subsistence.

The demands of living expenses in the market-based society are driven by a milieu in which the ownership structures of institutions seek opportunities to maximise their monetary profit wherever possible. Measures by government to protect the 'public interest' of individuals from predatory market practices are viewed by orthodox market practitioners as "anti-competitive". With this in mind, an artist or other independent professional may, for example, have an apartment that is not subject to 'rent control standards'. As a result, their rent may rise continuously at an alarming rate, making it difficult to pay rent and buy the necessary food for survival. Their subsistence needs may also be deprived by demands from financial institutions to pay for student loans, incurred as a result of getting a basic college or university education. Wage slavery operates in such an economic system in which the individual is a "wage earner", primarily works as a response to the market commodification of access-opportunities. These sought access-opportunities are from education to basic housing to basic food needed for survival and in the United States to the commodification of a for-profit healthcare system. Wage slavery could be viewed to operate in a political economy which relegates the relationship of individuals to "economic society" to little more that "wage earners" with "purchasing power" in a market. The posited *New Economy* would affirm individuals as having vital economic rights in relationship to work specifically and "economic society" in general, supportive of a rejuvenated focus of human development. The currently prevailing framework of the so-called New Economy divests individuals from a system of economic rights in a manner that precipitates wage slavery.

———•———

The economic reality of survival in relationship to the market

Individuals in these Western industrialised societies have enjoyed certain recognised political rights, which include the right to vote, once every few years, to elect "representatives" to parliament and a system of political rights associated with the 'rule of law'. At least officially, these political rights include privacy protections and 'human rights'. However, after these individuals go to their workplaces, the political reality to which they are socialised may not be matched in the West by the economic reality of survival. Individuals are subject to an economic reality of having to access survival to the extent of their wage earning capability associated with the institution of work. Individuals with little or no purchasing power are denied relative access-opportunities for survival in societies that pursue orthodox "free market" principles.

An individual with little or no purchasing power is viewed as needing to seek work in the market economy in order to secure potentially emergency needed "wage earning", within an economic milieu of 'wage slavery'. An individual who is already employed may simply view further opportunities for job-relation promotion as a means to gain further "wage earning" capabilities in a commercial-oriented society.

Work and Human Development in a 'Renaissance Economy'

Societal redressing of "wage slavery" requires the renaissance of the institution of work from a principal function of "wage earning" to a principal function of human development. This notion is further critically contextualised and illuminated in the book entitled 'Work, the Economy and Human Development'. With this in mind, the human development paradigm is a context for an emancipatory framework of work. Within the context of this framework, conscious individuals have a natural right in a society to a high quality of living. In order to facilitate that high quality-of-living, an economic directorate needs to rely on an appropriate analytical framework. The ensuing analytical framework must be created around an appreciational context and a methodological system which is aimed at constructively and creatively facilitating human development. Quantum economics is posited as such an analytical context.

Work refers to an organised effort and time activity by individuals. In a posited 'New Economy' or "Renaissance Economy", work is an opportunity that is associated with creative self-expression. It is not simply an operation that is principally concerned with an individual's capability to secure 'wage earning' opportunities in a commercial society. The institution of work and aggregate economic development in modern capitalist society are oriented to respond to the vagaries of the "marketplace". 'Work' and aggregate economic development in a "Renaissance Economy" are envisioned to primarily response to high quality of survival of individuals consideration of human beings, rather than work as simply a wage earning operation in relationship to 'the market'. Work in a posited New Economy rather than being circumscribed by the demands of the "marketplace" is a creative process of individuality, professional independence reinforced by a system of 'economic rights'.

Economic rights ensure that the individual has an optimised economic security that frees the individual from coercive forces of the "market". The 'coercion of the market' refers to the extent to which contemporary market forces can conspire to force the individual into work as a 'wage earner' in a manner inconsistent with the individual's quality-of-life attainments, in response to income requirements for subsistence in a market economy. Wage slavery would be alleviated toward its prospective extrication in a posited New Economy. 'Wage Slavery' would be alleviated from the market commodification and rationing of access-opportunities that require purchasing power in critical areas of living from health to higher education. The posited New Economy would replace such purchasing power-oriented access to essential quality-of-living areas, in favour of a universal access in a public legitimated framework. One such model is found in the Canadian healthcare system. The extrication of 'wage slavery' in a posited rejuvenated New "Renaissance" Economy would also rely on a correspondent enhancement of economic rights that foster professional independence and the "*democratisation*" of the workplace.

CHAPTER 5

What is Capitalism?

∽

*"No man can serve two masters: for either he will hate
the one and love the other or else he will hold to the one
and despise the other. Ye cannot serve G-d and mammon
[wealth]."*

– Gospel of Matthew, 6: 24.

CAPITALISM HAS EVOLVED to become a perceived desirable and
necessary economic basis of a modern society. It is attributed
to be a sort of neutral and benign system that is identical to
democracy and individualism. Milton Friedman, a renowned
Nobel Laureate from the University of Chicago School, helped celebrate
this attributed feature in the book entitled *Capitalism and Freedom* (1962).
Capitalism has been embraced for its support to private enterprise as
being critical to attributed economic growth in the modern economic society... providing jobs and driving initiative towards 'boundless' opportunities. However, what is not discussed in public forum is the relationship
between 'capitalism' and 'capital'.

Capitalism is a political economic ideology which emphasises the market productivity of 'capital'. However, capitalism as a political economic
ideology pivots on the conception of 'economic society' that relies on an
intellectual conception of 'capital' as a venue or a forum in which property rights reside. It is that axiomatic political economic conception of
'capital' which has led to an ensuing political economic doctrinal system.

'Capital', in Western economic thinking, has traditionally been linked to a conception that the environment is useful only up to the extent to which its component features can be technically discerned and put to 'productive market uses'. Capital refers to a resource framework that can be used as chattel by an ownership structure. Capital includes money, financial equivalent property and other resources that can be used in a market of buyers and sellers. In 'capitalism', the paradigmatic focus of 'economic society' is on an environment where 'capital' is applied... all else is marginalised. Accordingly, capitalism is a political economic ideology which views the world as a bazaar, having items with attributable monetary value which can be acquired by agents and manipulated to deliver net market gain.

Capitalism, in its intellectual centripetal orientation around financial equivalent 'capital' in its modernised form, has also incorporated the concept of 'human capital' within its general scope of capital. The result has been that human beings have been viewed as simply another form of objectivised chattel within the monetised value-oriented 'resource framework' of capitalism. Essentially, capitalism, in its paradigmatic focus around capital, derogates from an alternative focus of economics, wherein the survival related needs of human beings would be the central paradigmatic focus of economics. What capitalism does is that it supports the institutionalisation of subordination and ensuing effective enslavement of individuals and communities to the proprietary interests of the owners of financial-equivalent capital that is in pursuit of attributable 'wealth'.

Capitalism has historically been, and still is to-date, a mechanism in which attributable 'wealth' is generated from the control, production and tacit domination of resources that have been conscripted towards the delivery of a marketable output. 'Capitalism' can take the form of 'private capitalism' as is currently practiced in the United States or 'state capitalism' as had been practiced in the former Soviet Union. Indeed, both 'private capitalism' and 'state capitalism' in the form of 'communism' currently coexist in the People's Republic of China.

Capitalism is an approach that societies apply to the universe in which this environment is reduced to a myriad of resources that can potentially be used to generate commerce that accompanies a context of 'Commercial Utilitarianism'. Indeed, capitalism as a political economic ideology advocates that the pursuit of existence among human beings is via empowerment through the commercial gains from the exploitation of conscripted resources. Within capitalism, commerce is not critically conceived of as a necessary means in a modern society to provide goods and services to individuals and communities. Rather, the prevailing conception of commerce construes its function as an activity that is the backdrop of a drive towards realisable profit at whatever human or general environmental costs. Here, the constitutional conception of the 'rule of law' provides little protection to "the masses" that are essentially disenfranchised by a legal and judicial system that favours the financially wealthy and powerful.

Having explored the relationship between 'capitalism' and 'capital', what is the relationship between 'capitalism' and democracy'? It is very obvious in representations that are usually made by various institutions of the Establishment internationally on behalf of globalisation that the term 'capitalism' has been and continues to be closely associated to 'democracy'. Spread capitalism is centred on the "free market" and you'll automatically help support the spread of democracy, so the official representation sounds straightforward enough. Unfortunately, this apparent alleged compatibility of 'capitalism' and 'democracy' has been inconsistent with a critical examination of history and ongoing political economy.

'Capitalism' and 'democracy' are almost as inherently conceptually linked as 'up' and 'down'. Democracy has developed from various evolutionary social movements and revolutionary upheaval that are concerned with the tenets which are associated with civil rights, equality, 'equity', fairness, social justice, representative and responsible government and social justice. Democracy is about empowering individuals as citizens in a community toward what the American constitutional founders referred to as a 'more perfect Union'... a society developed to serve the people, *à la* 'We the People...' as in the American Constitution.

While democracy pivots on the development of a society that serves citizens, 'capitalism' is oriented around the aggrandizement of 'capital'. 'Capitalism' strives to take away what democracy serves to affirm. Capitalism reduces the focus on individuals from citizens with rights to their being 'human capital' (as discussed in Chapter 10) that is to be managed by the proprietors of capital.

Democracy perceives "wealth" as the vitality and dynamism of a community in which people can pursue the civil rights and freedoms as social individuals in society. Capitalism, alternatively, perceives value and wealth in commercial financial-equivalent terms that foster capabilities which can be used to generate commercial outcomes that are related to the overall goal of profit. Capitalism does not in itself value civic constitutionalism which is associated to democracy. The historic and ongoing resistance of corporate entities to trade union activity testifies the demonstrable hostility of "capitalist enterprise" to the social empowerment of individuals.

Capitalism was stimulated by the rise of competing European empires which sought to conquer civilizations abroad. These colonial powers sought to use their resources acquired from conquests to fuel military expeditions and related campaigns. Various European empires in the name of so-called 'exploration', 'scientific discovery' and 'trade' would use capitalism to create dependency relationships.

Economic communities and particularly traditional economic systems that were organised communally, like the aboriginal peoples of the Americas, were seduced by Europeans into adopting a capitalist-oriented economic model. Similar promises of forthcoming prosperity are currently being used to try and seduce the so-called 'Third World'. The result of Portuguese, Spanish, British and French contact with aboriginal peoples was that they were subjected to campaigns of genocide, involving the use of technologically superior weapons and the intentional spread of diseases in an early form of biological warfare. These operations ended up taking away the land that was needed for livelihood of the encountered peoples. These operations were based upon cynical and exploitative transactions in the name of generating attributed 'wealth'. Indeed, when the so-called European "explorers" were searching for gold and other resources in the 'New World', the Middle East, Africa and India pillaging old civilisations for capital which was to eventually include slaves were the extent of the concern for the rights of the indigenous peoples.

Capitalism is in tandem with the drive for Empire, whether by the state or by private enterprise, rather than operationally being an instrument in support of the growth and institutionalisation of democracy. The co-existence of capitalism and democracy occurs in Western societies not because of an inherent compatibility, rather in a tenuous state. As the 'capitalistic' hegemony pivoting around the 'private capitalism' of corporate power increased, it has sought to displace democracy in order to secure capital for Empire.

The alleged relationship between 'capitalism' and 'democracy' was generated by Cold War rhetoric. Just When did the Chief Executive Officer (CEO) or the Board of Directors of any company that any individual ever worked for, on an on-going basis, use a voting by employees coupled with other mechanisms of democratic participation as a basis of supporting corporate development? Do gas stations co-operate with customers to evaluate fair quotations concerning gas pricing? Do they frequently appear to work to keep prices as high as possible? Would corporations spontaneously support the integration of women and visible minorities in management positions without policy leadership by government? Would corporations care as much about whether they pollute if there was not related public policy and related legislation by government?

The capitalistic enterprise, whether on behalf of private interests or on behalf of state 'collectivisation', is far from democratic. With that in mind, private-enterprise-directed social development pivotally spreads democracy, no more than does factories with smoke stacks help ensure clean air. Private enterprise directs the use of capital for its proprietors and its thrust is not in support of the commonwealth of citizenry with rights.

Capitalism and Freedom (1965) by the renowned University of Chicago Nobel Laureate, Milton Friedman, encompasses the usual clichés proselytised by current status quo economists and the Establishment. This cited title presents the mentality and ethos of the bloc of economists from the University of Chicago who is set out to create a sort of "civil religion" around capitalism and these advocates provide support via an intellectual system in the dogma of "positive economics".

Capitalism and Freedom (1965) could be viewed to be a sort of 'proto-Bible' that is used by the disciples of a 'New World Order' in support of the capitalist creed. During the 1960's, at the time of writing this title, the popular aspirations for universal brotherhood and sisterhood in society reached their height in Canada, the U.S. and Western Europe. Movements for civil rights, popular demonstration by highly informed and civically aware university students and other demonstrations against the Establishment experienced a genesis in America. People were exploring Eastern religions including Buddhism. Hippies, flower children and other citizens in society rebelled against materialism and opulence in general. The drive for insatiable profit advocated by constituencies within private enterprise cultures in the United States relied on the conditioning of people as consumers who will have a correspondingly insatiable drive for acquiring products.

The non-materialistic affirmations of a rebellious generation were viewed to be a threat to the continued attributed progress of "capitalism". In the view of a capitalist Praetorian guard, governments across Western Europe and Canada appeared to be overly influenced by these social movements. During that time, democracy was gaining ground; not only as a political concept, but it gained ground as an economic concept in the 1960's. However, in the view of the capitalist Praetorian guard, this type of development threatened to derail the aspirations for a 'New World Order' that was to be led by the self-ordained 'Apostles' of capitalism.

In the view of these 'Apostles', there was an apparent perceived need to "reign in democracy"... things were "getting out of control"... However, how could that emerging democracy be "reigned in" when democracy was the very basis of the revolutionary democracy which supported the French and American Revolutions, British Commonwealth societies (including the United Kingdom itself), Canada to the north of the USA and other old societies of Western Europe?

The emerging 1960's democracy would be reigned in by creating an elaborate intellectual subterfuge or propaganda which would be financed by a capitalist creed that would be aimed at bringing about their "New World Order" of the sort which would ensure continued influence of attributed 'wealth' and power. However, democracy which shared the communalism and essential non-materialist spirituality of the major world religions including Christianity, Islam, Hinduism, Judaism and Buddhism was too powerful to take head on. If "democracy" and social ethics that supported the idea the "man does not live by bread alone" (i.e. the pursuit of selfish financial opulence) could not be defeated by a direct attack and/or military confrontation that had been tried by Nazi Germany, why not try to subvert, co-opt and conquer democracy from within?

Chapter 6, 'Social Darwinism', presents the corporatisation of economics into a compatible intellectual system that would legitimate a cultivated milieu for private enterprise. With this in mind, the Apostles of a capitalist manifesto towards the accomplishment of the subversion and cooptation of democracy created a myth that was associated to what Milton Friedman in *Capitalism and Freedom* (1965) referred to as the "free man". Ingeniously, the Apostles of capitalism co-opted the romanticism that was associated with the cowboy and the American frontier and launched the myth that is associated with an attributed "free man". The romanticism of the American 'Wild West' was co-opted into an attributed "free man".

Such a modeled "free man", at its most basic level, was conceived to derive his freedom from not having any responsibilities... every man for himself, in the pursuit of, for example, gold and accompanying attributed "wealth"; living off the land, fashioning his own laws so-to-speak that were decided via weaponry at "show downs". This apparent model of the "free man" was the very milieu which was responsible for mass-eviction of aboriginal peoples from their land and corresponding genocide against "The Indians". To the Apostles of capitalism, as represented on page 2 of *Capitalism and Freedom* (1965) by Friedman, the concern of the "free man" was only "his own destiny". The "free man" was not a member of a community with basic social responsibilities to his/her fellow human beings. Society, to the Apostles of capitalism, must be concerned about conditioning an environment that is appropriately supportive of "private enterprise". Vested interest was merely a "collection of individuals" (also indicated on page 7 of the cited title). The "free man" was ostensibly a "financially successful capitalist" that was not caring for any attributed social responsibility.

Individuals, as conceived in this "free man" myth, were viewed not to have any basic social responsibility to each other. Similarly, government, as a corollary, was not to have any ensuing endowed social responsibility. Friedman, for example, attacked John F. Kennedy's representation that was associated with a 'national purpose' for America and implied a social responsibility among American citizenry. Indeed, an American "social purpose" might conflict with the vested interests of private enterprise. In order to avoid this potential conflict, the social purpose that was associated to constitutionalism and democracy in America and abroad had to be subverted. Accordingly, the "free man" was attributed to be supportive of "limited government". The democratic characteristic of government in America and abroad was to be subverted by the Apostles of "private enterprise" to a propagandised notion that government was inherently antidemocratic and anti-ethical to freedom.

The very outrageousness of such dogma can be easily exposed by a critical appreciation of history that indeed arose in World War II, about two decades before *Capitalism and Freedom* (1965) was written. It was not "limited government" that saved democracy at that time from prospective domination by Nazi Germany. "Limited government" also did not provide the necessary massive economic assistance that was needed by Europe in a recovery from the devastation by Nazi Germany and Fascist Italy. It was not limited government that freed the slaves in the American south from that region's "plantation economy". It was not limited government that alleviated verifiable discrimination against women and 'visible minorities' in the workplace. Indeed, it was not limited government that instituted the Civil Rights Act in the United States or supported the development of the critically acclaimed universal healthcare systems in Canada and Europe. It is not "limited government" that can effectively protect citizens from air pollution, acid rain and other excesses by private enterprise against the quality-of-life of citizens. Apostles of private enterprise capitalism were not really concerned about "freedom" of individuals to do more than to make profit-supporting purchases.

What these Apostles desired, with the proselytization of the "free man" myth, was a society in which individuals would view themselves no more than commercially disposed entities... that is, objects that are executing "private enterprise"; vested interests with the aim to derive attributed wealth, status and ensuing power. By limiting "government", the Apostles of capitalism could enervate a democratic civic spirit that would, in the view of these Apostles, threaten plans for a "New World Order" that is presided over by the capitalist creed. The "free man" was analogous to individuals that are being essentially alienated commercial entities that are divested from any social purpose other than to be manipulated implements managed by, and for, a capitalistocratic creed. "The "free man" operated in collectives as merely consumers of goods and services, who applied purchasing power in the paradigm of "positive economics".

Limiting democracy by the slogan of "Limited government" would help support plans for a "New World Order" by helping to quell popular challenges. The fascism of the State that was defeated by the victorious allies who fought against a "New World Order" that operated against democracy in World War II would be substituted in favour of a fascism by a corporate dominated private enterprise system, in which "the masses" would be seduced into a state of enslavement (as managed "human capital") by its capitalist 'proprietors'. Government, in the name of democracy, would no longer interfere with the aspirations of the members of a creed who desired the achievement of a "New World Order". No longer would there be a myriad of "undesirable' legislative protections" in support of outcomes such as the civil rights on behalf of citizenry that would interfere with the sought profit-oriented conscription of "natural resource capital" and "human capital".

The ideology of "selfish individualism" would be reinforced by the inculcation that the pursuit of material opulence is more important than human life and quality-of-living. That inculcation would be expected to provide a necessary basis of social control in support of the capitalist creed.

By disarming the democratic spirit, a more smooth evolution towards (corporate-managed) fascism could take place via private enterprise capitalism. Government would be converted from a representative institution, as for example, indicated in the American constitution, that would be in defence of "*We the People...*" to the position of "*We, Private Enterprise Owners and Major Shareholders...*" Ironically, the alleged paternalism that was decried by the Apostles of capitalism via *Capitalism and Freedom* (1965) was to be substituted with an apparent paternalistic guidance by an antidemocratic regime of private enterprise. The Apostles of private enterprise capitalism desired a "freedom of capital" to support ease of management by its proprietors rather than supporting freedom of potentially "rebellious" individuals in *responsive* and sovereign self-governing societies. That is what the formation of trading blocs like via the North American Free Trade Agreement (NAFTA), the planned Free Trade of the Americas (FTAA) and the European Union (EU) within the political economic context of 'globalisation', discussed in Chapter 11 is all about. Trading blocs in the form of so-called "Free Trade Areas" and "Common Markets" are designed to operate principally as "regimes of commerce" rather than as societies with people who have rights.

The Apostles of capitalism viewed government not as a creative agent of a democracy. Rather, as expressed on page 2, in *Capitalism and Freedom* (1965), "limited government" should confine itself to preserving "order" "to enforce private contracts" and to "foster competitive markets" and monetary policy. "Limited government", in other words, should only function as an agent, not of the diverse public but instead of commerce, for a capitalist creed, towards a "New World Order". The Apostles sought to create hysteria against the very institution of government via its demonization. These Apostles appeared to view responsible constitutional government as a "democratic threat" to a "New World Order".

The Apostles of private enterprise capitalism via the "free man" myth endeavoured to create an intellectual unity between the "ordinary citizen" and the "capitalist". It thereby sought to subvert the threat that the "ordinary citizen" through government via democracy posed against the plans for a "New World Order". The ascendance of a "New World Order" via the efforts of "Globalisers" has indeed brought with it a milieu in which protesters, for example, are not to be listened to as constituencies in a democracy. Rather, they are to be quelled in the sought evolution towards "International Fascism". To 'Globalizers', 'human capital' should be kept inline towards an envisioned "New World Order".

The Apostles of capitalism in advocacy of 'private enterprise' *à la* Friedman viewed an economy as having one of only two choices. Either an economy would be organised via "coercion" in the context of a "totalitarian state" as indicated on page 13 of *Capitalism and Freedom* (1965) or it would be alternatively organised via the "technique of the market place". However, this presentation appears to be supplementary intellectual subterfuge by the Apostles of capitalism that include Noble Laureates Milton Friedman, George Stigler, T. W. Schultz and Gary Becker. They aimed at obfuscating other viable choices for economic development that are neither 'capitalistic' nor 'totalitarian'.

"Stages of Capitalism"

What are the stages and attributions of the capitalistic development of society? The *first stage* of capitalistic expansion requires a 'cultural transformation to commercialism'. This stage has been apparent since early imperial expansion by European powers from the sixteenth century to current drives toward so-called "globalisation". Aboriginal peoples, in the America, for example, were exposed to this transformative pressure originally by European "voyages of discovery" during and after the sixteenth century. These initial steps were supplemented with reinforced economic socialisation pressures into the twenty-first century. African peoples have been exposed to this transformative pressure since the slave trade and it is also being reinforced via "economic globalisation" into the twenty-first century. Local and national economies, internationally, with noncapitalistic systems of economic development, are now being exposed to this transformative pressure through so-called 'globalisation'.

During a precursory stage of the transformative pressure, 'money' that may be already a part of the local economy becomes more than a "medium of exchange". Indeed, a society is 'capitalistic' as is commonly misunderstood, not simply because people and institutions use money to facilitate trade. Money, as 'currency', is a useful means to facilitate complex trade transactions in a modern society. In a "pre-industrialised" agrarian and artisan economic context, bartering has been used as a general means of exchange. Notably, in this precursory transformative stage to the capitalistic society, 'money' becomes a means to achieve attributed 'material success', *à la* 'materialism', which is over and above any human interpersonal, communal-related spiritual considerations such as social justice that is associated to the transcendental.

The ensuing and *complementary stage* towards 'capitalistic' development involves 'economic colonialism'. During this phase so-to-speak, commercial institutions often from foreign countries, with acquired superior purchasing power, "invade" local, regional or entire national economies. These commercial institutions mount a campaign to gain control of these 'new markets', not using the military force but using an acquired "economic force". This "force" utilises an already existing facility of money in an economy to mount an effort to buy-it-out. Control is sought-out by these commercial institutions in this phase. The control is executed by acquiring property which has what is conceived by a capitalist creed as having 'natural' capital, like petroleum and trees and **human capital**. Within this milieu, 'capital' is to be managed so as to achieve maximised profit to enable more waves of colonisation. Land is purchased for a relative pittance of monetary compensation or is seized outright through commercially induced local government corruption. This corruption is seduced by promises of attributed wealth to local politicians and bureaucrats with decision-making power.

In these circumstances, previous relative economic capability that was critically linked to equitable access by citizens to food, shelter and clothing and managed and supported by noncapitalistic public institutional innovations is attacked for being hostile to the promise of 'economic wealth' led by private enterprise. What is apparent, instead, in a stage of 'economic colonialism' are promises of wealth to very few (if any) of the citizens of the local economy. What usually occurs is economic disenfranchisement. This occurs as citizens are essentially evicted from their land, denying them of the ability to grow and raise food for their families. The local economy in general is usually eviscerated. As food becomes more scare in the local economy after the taking-over of food agricultural areas cultivated by local farmers by transnational commercial enterprises that favour non-food related "cash crops", food prices rise. Other prices of goods and services also rise with the distortive effects of infused and concentrated purchasing power. Prices for goods and services for the relative small constituency of a wealthy capitalist creed usually rise tremendously, but are affordable to this group. Meanwhile, dispossessed of their land and livelihood, "the masses" are forced to work as 'wage slaves' in the frequently harsh working conditions of colonising commercial enterprises in an economic environment where disparity is "elevated" to normalcy by capitalistic ideological pressure. A previously nurturing society is transformed into a capitalist state of the *'survival of the fittest'*. The nature of work is enveloped into a state of subservience to an undemocratic commercial management framework rather than a participatory economic framework.

The complementing *third phase* involves what the Apostles of capitalism referred to as a 'limited government'. The concept of limited government is used by the Apostles of capitalism and their disciples as a pseudonym for an apparent desire to 'limit democracy'. Thus, in a third associated phase in support of **'limited government** *in order to* **limit democracy'**, the capitalist creed seeks to quell popular social movements that are associated with transcendental or non-commercial conceptions of community. On commencement of a process of colonising the electorate into 'consumers' within the overall management of capital, there is also a process to colonise government to reinforce further systemic colonisation. This phase involves accelerated privatisation of previous public utilities/agencies that are associated with protection of a conception of the public interest.

'Corporatisation' is a *further complementing stage* of overall political economic consolidation that is led by a network of 'transnational enterprises'. This *fourth stage* consists of a decline of an economy that is made up principally of small businesses, *à la* "competitive capitalism", towards a society of increasingly large concentrations of economic power in the hands of "owners of large blocks of capital". This corporatisation process is critically assisted by an international banking system that operates to support the raising of borrowed financial capital as a backup to any shortfalls in purchasing power needed to accomplish "corporate imperial expansion". Institutions associated with 'free speech' including competitive mass-media along with other local businesses are bought-out and taken-over by industrial elite.

Mass-media institutions that pose a perceived potential democratic challenge to public policy pressures on behalf of corporatisation are bought out and manipulated by the promoters of this capitalist creed – news programmes become dominated more by propaganda designed to inflict political economic social control. Such a milieu operates against "progressive social policies" that are designed to support quality-of-living attainments. Progressive social policies are, in turn, viewed as anti-ethical to a capitalist profit-ethos. In this stage, corporations which recognise their new found pre-eminent economic power continue to grow in size as a result of various legislatively allowed predatory corporate takeovers and they seek to have an enhanced influence on government via powerful lobbyist pressures and large political campaign contributions. 'Democracy' begins to function in name only. Free elections may continue as a trapping of 'democracy'. However, slowly, elected representatives find themselves needing to bow to "Big Business" pressure, by passing favourable legislation or alternatively they become diselected at election time, in the face of huge financial campaign contributions to "more favourable and sympathetic electoral candidates". Democracy and/or other indigenous systems that are noncapitalistic in orientation or context continue to be pressured by corporatisation efforts.

'**Capitalistocracy**' is a percussive "*endstage*" to an essentially **fascistic political economy** that is sought by the capitalist creed. A 'theocracy' is, for example, "government by the leadership of churches, priests or some form of religious order". An 'aristocracy' is "government by aristocrats" as in nobility. 'Democracy' is "government by, of and for the people, where society via responsible government serves the diverse public and is protective of equality, human rights and constitutionally further elaborated and affirmed civil rights that are backed by the force of an elected legislature and law." In a democracy, government strives to achieve equitable and consensual approval and confirmation of the diverse public.

Government in a democracy is the civic institutional expression of a dynamic and pluralistic society. In contrast, the capitalist creed seeks to subvert, enervate, co-opt and conquer the institutions of democratic government that are viewed to undermine an idealised "unfettered" rapacious state of capitalism that is free of legal and other restraints in achieving sought attributed "profit". The capitalist creed seeks, indeed, what could be described as a 'capitalistocracy'. This sought 'capitalistocracy' refers to "government that is under the direct rule of, and that is in principal service to, the owners of large blocks of capital". A capitalistic society is concerned about furthering the interests of 'capital' and it conceives people as little more than an additionally manipulable capital instrument in its market operations. In such circumstances, "governance" is divested from parliamentary institutions to effectively reside within the financially wealthiest shadowing ruling elite with ensuing status and power to control and direct the society within the framework of managed capital.

To the capitalist creed as supported by the Apostles of capitalism, national boundaries and divergent national systems undermine the ability of the 'owners of capital' to pursue maximised profit with ensuing status and power from the management of capital. Nations are viewed as continuing to provide reinforcement to any remaining social movements within societies that may continue to resist the onslaught of 'capitalistocracy'. Their great histories remind embattled citizens of these societies of a prehistory (so-to-speak), before **'capitalistic cultural transformation'**, **'economic colonialism'** and ensuing stages.

The total obliteration of national boundaries is a precursor to an envisioned final idealised stage under capitalistocratic 'international fascism'. The obliteration of national boundaries is an attempt to complete the consolidation of an international capitalistocratic management framework that is articulated under globalised 'corporate imperial' domination.

While the Apostles and disciples of a capitalist creed indulge in intellectual subterfuge that is associated with the concept of the "free man", the apparent 'modus operandi' of the capitalist creed is a 'New World Order'. This 'New World Order' is sought to be executed via an internationalised capitalistocratic-driven fascism that is based on achieving maximised control over the individual because this creed is concerned about individuals, only to the extent that they respectively and collectively can be 'socially controlled' and "managed" to support maximised corporate market profit and to support ensuing maximised status and power via self-aggrandisement of financial capabilities.

CHAPTER 6

ECONOMIC COLONIALISM

୧ஜ৶

"As soon as claims to the newly discovered parts of the world had been staked, the claimants made a mad rush to get what economic benefits they could from their finds. Not only was there a desire to recoup the heavy costs of exploration, but there was almost an unnatural lust in the haste with which the pioneers expected to get rich. Here was an interesting commentary both on the motives behind exploration and on the prevailing ideologies of the Western world."

Shepard B. Clough, "The Formation and Early Exploration of Overseas Empires", *European Economic History: The Economic Development of Western Civilization*, p. 136, 1968.

E CONOMIC COLONIALISM is the process in which capitalistic oriented institutions seek to takeover and redirect a society towards its own institutional commercial objectives. 'Economic colonialism' continues to be pivotal to 'modern capitalism'. The recognition of this ascendancy is critical because of the preoccupation of a culture that is socialised by 'modern capitalism', with the need to achieve 'growth' that is associated with the drive to achieve insatiable profit. This drive is arguably most visibly portrayed within the modern stock market and how the mass-media reports on it. Principal shareholders look forward to increased corporate earnings and rising profit. Each report of profit drives up interest in acquiring the stock of that corporation and raises the price of the stock, thereby furthers ensuing calls for more corporate earnings and profit. Relatively long-term considerations, for example, to conserve 'resources' to ensure 'sustainable development' and perhaps longer term earnings are often disregarded so as to satisfy immediate demands for short term earnings and profit in a culture of 'instant gratification'. The culture of 'monetary profit' relies on accelerating and maximising the use of available resources towards the creation of marketable goods and services. In other words, 'modern capitalism' ostensibly concentrates on the definition of economics as the 'management of scarce resources', but is concerned about management in favour of profiteering.

This described culture of short-term profit maximisation is the vehicle of a culture of colonialism within capitalism. One should expect that a society that is based on an economic system which relies on the 'management of scarcity' as axiomatic to its economic development would critically be concerned about the long-term implications of its economic development activities. In the process, one would expect that 'resources' that are required in envisioned economic development activities would be part of some sort of a formulated implicit conservation strategy. However, this is not the resource management culture that has evolved into the modern capitalism that is associated with so-called 'globalisation'. Indeed, in the prevailing context, advocates of conservation have been viewed to be antagonists and frustrators of desired "job creation" and "economic growth" by Big Businesses and their reactionary allies within government. Notably, the jobs that are created from such strategies are also correspondingly for the short-term as corporations simply layoff or cut jobs outright after the depletion of resources. They then seek new market to move into in order to repeat the process all over again, but with hopefully diminished capital-costs associated to labour.

The short-term economic development prioritisation that has been galvanised with capitalism leads to the use of resources at rates that tend to far exceed the "ecological carrying potential" of the immediate environment in which capitalism is practiced. Whole forests are cut-down, lakes and other bodies of water become fished-out, and drinking water and tracts of land become degraded and over-polluted by the dysfunctional developmental activities of corporations. Wildlife destruction and negative impacts on agriculture are some of the other results and the list goes on. The Big Businesses that engage themselves in these activities do not want to "change their ways" (so-to-speak) in a manner that might affect their envisioned immediate profit margins. These Big Businesses cry out against the advocates of conservation and responsible development who want government to legislate fines and regulations to penalise the irresponsible activities of corporations that result in undermining the quality-of-living attainment interests of citizens in a democracy.

To help channel and control public opinion, these Businesses also seek to use their purchasing power to buyout mass-media including TV, radio, newspapers and internet news media. This tactic has indeed been a trend, particularly in Canada, the U.S. and other Western industrialised societies. In so-called Third World, media is frequently owned directly by state-government interests that have, in turn, been co-opted by monies of Transnational Corporate Enterprises. That co-opting is usually executed via various so-called international economic development projects. Big Businesses also look to use political and/or other contributions to subvert the integrity of various governments that may seek to represent their diverse publics.

What Big Businesses desire with instrumental support from governments is to seek "new markets" once the resources of the market(s) that these corporate enterprises already exist in appear to be near a point of exhaustion that threatens the ability to maintain the levels of short-term profit that had already been achieved to-date. The axiomatic drive of so-called 'globalisation' is to gain control of 'markets' that have been so far "underexploited" to-date, in support of the rapacious interests of Trans National Corporate Enterprises for their short-term profit horizons. 'Economic colonialism' is thus institutionalised within capitalism, towards supporting its short-term developmental and profit horizon which is contrary to long term 'management of scarcity'. The focus of capitalism requires new markets to 'invade and conquer' besides supporting a commercially centred pattern of economic development. Without new markets to invade and conquer, this short-term oriented economic system would basically collapse from the systematised overexploitation and destruction of the scarce resources that are needed to support human survival.

Raymond Samuels

Capitalism visàvis democracy within a context of economic colonialism

Capitalism can be viewed as being oriented around an ideology that is associated with the accumulation and the use of financial-equivalent capital as the driving force of economic development. Democracy, on the other hand, is concerned about the civil rights and freedoms of citizens and it is associated with a context of human rights and government as a creative institutional agent of a diverse public via a process of elected representation from that diverse public. However, capitalism is concerned about 'resources' as implements of "capitalistic development" and democracy is concerned about people in association to a context of "human development". Capitalism marginalises people in its developmental paradigm, while in the democracy people are the prime and central focus within its developmental paradigm. Capitalism's priority as the "accumulation" of capital has historically marginalised the human costs that are associated with its development horizons and its preoccupation with seeking to exploit new markets.

The European empires of Spain, Portugal, Britain, France and Holland that sought to explore the world from the 1500's were interested in acquiring new "raw materials" to fuel the expansion of their competing polities. There was little, if any, concern for the indigenous peoples of the "New World", Africa, Australia and Asia that were being subjugated having their civilizations pillaged and destroyed in the process of this sought expansion. The colonial "emissaries" of empire were to acquire raw materials which extended from spices to precious metals at whatever costs to the exploited society.

Technological knowledge of the use of metals in the creation of weaponry, together with treachery and theft, was used by the European powers to conquer various indigenous human civilizations and perfect the 'art of war'. The European powers maintained large tracts of official 'colonial possessions' into the early 1960's.

Businesses in the form of corporations grew in size during the twentieth century. Britain, as an Empire and Superpower, was in a steady decline after World War II which was an exhausting effort against the imperialist ambitions of Nazi Germany. In the place a Britain, a new empire was rising as a military and industrial power to take its place. The United States was becoming a society driven by a business culture and was becoming increasingly dominated by Big Businesses which were fuelled by the entrepreneurial spirit of American society.

The entrepreneurial spirit was in fact in itself fuelled by a democratic culture which was associated with the American constitution that had been designed to protect individual rights and correspondingly to foster a society in which citizens, sharing ownership of that society, contributed to the its vitality. What Big Businesses in America did was to successfully attribute this entrepreneurial spirit NOT to democracy itself, but instead to the private enterprise pursuits of the "owners of capital" or to the industrial elites of Big Businesses. Big Businesses fuelled by a growing culture of industrial elites were set out to hijack the evolution of American democracy.

By successfully proselytizing that it was the industrial elites rather than democracy itself, which drove American society, these elites were able to help support favourable governmental support to the expansion of American corporations into foreign "markets". As the United States grew as the largest domestic market economy and other countries sought to do business with the United States, the vested interests of American Big Businesses became linked to the attributed interests of globalising economic development interests. American and American-inspired Big Businesses' efforts to break down national barriers that were erected by various governments to protect themselves from the economic colonization efforts, via so-called "free trade", reached their apex via creation of "free trade initiatives like the Free Trade Area of the Americas (FTAA), "European Union" and so-called "globalisation".

From the imperial conquests of the European powers into the twenty-first century, the capitalistic interest in "expanding into new markets" has not substantively supported 'democracy'. The latest enunciations in support of 'democracy', in relationship to so-called globalisation efforts, amount to little more than public relations statements. The popular and evocative appeal of 'democracy' is merely being used as a convenient marketing tool to support the economic colonisation efforts of transnational corporate enterprises. If the rulers of an authoritarian, totalitarian or autocratic regime can be bought-out by direct financial contribution to their Estates and by promises of private material prosperity they and become friendly to the economic colonization efforts of these large corporations, there is little critical concern about the adoption of 'democracy' within these regimes. It is generally only when the rulers of these authoritarian, totalitarian or autocratic regime resist the threat to their power or to social support systems within their societies that the 'need for democracy' is touted by the supporters of the capitalist creed, in their attempts to overthrow these 'unfriendly' rulers in favour of a system that can potentially be co-opted as has been accomplished in America.

Capitalism: creation of wealth or the institutionalisation of deprivation

The conventional wisdoms of private enterprise capitalism is that through the organisational context of the 'free market', wealth is created by the independent pursuits of households and firms that participate in the buying and selling of goods and services. In these circumstances, poverty is implicitly viewed to exist where the market has not penetrated. Wealth is viewed, within the capitalist context, as evolving from the pursuit of the "making of money" and the drive for profit. Those groups in society who have been able to obtain profit via private enterprise are construed as reinvesting in the market towards the creation of additional wealth, thereby creating more ensuing commercial activity with more money changing hands and leading to additional wealth.

However, modern capitalism does not present a solution for the critical alleviation and redress of poverty. Indeed, modern capitalism exploits, capitalises and furthermore institutionalises poverty. Modern capitalism embraces poverty because of its "positive" potential on the drive for profit. The existence of people who are both poor economically and politically disenfranchised provided a base where private enterprise can exploit and capitalise as a result of ensuing depressed wages. The more political and economic rights, within a context of democracy, that people in a society have to ensure that wages adequately reflect their participation via work, the less organised managerial groups will be able to yield a "profit" for their corporate activities. The full fruition of a constitutional democracy in a society is anti-ethical to the drive of private enterprise interests for insatiable profit irrespective of human and ecological costs.

The following analogy might provide a basis for appreciating the problem of an alleged inextricable relationship between capitalism and wealth. Who is wealthier: Someone in an un-trafficked part of a desert, who is left there, with no means of out communication, with only the clothes on his or her back and with a trunk that has several millions of dollars in it as compared to someone who is left in a traditional village (with housing/shelter) with no money, but who is in a community that is adjacent to traditional farms, with bountiful crops providing food and clean water and where there is also clean air?

Money in itself does not make persons 'wealthy'. Indeed, within the context of this preceding analogy, the millionaire in the desert without access to communication, shelter to food as critical bases for survival is essentially very poor as compared to the 'wealthy' person without money. Unfortunately, the propaganda of modern capitalism is that persons with greater amounts of money are inherently 'wealthier' than persons with 'no money'.

Based on such sophistry, private enterprise society approaches societies where people have access to little or no money but they have a sense of generalised security in their access to food, shelter and clothing promising these societies "wealth". Modern capitalism constitutes an invasion force to such societies, essentially subverting the quality-of-living attainments by citizen-participants in the society. Through the "private enterprise" efforts of large Big Businesses from capitalistocracies like the United States, previously autonomous government institutions that were accountable to their citizens are co-opted to adapt to the cash-centred political economy of the "market economy".

Any remaining previous restrictions to foreign ownership or other legislation designed to protect citizens from exploitation by Big Business are chastised as "anticompetitive" and must therefore be withdrawn. With its superior purchasing power, private enterprise interests buy large tracts of lands from corrupted government officials, therewith disenfranchising whole populations from their land, farms and homes. This practice has occurred in parts of Africa. People are forced to work to try to eke out a living and pay taxes which the governments impose, but are paid little and at the same time face rising prices which are established by corporate market collusion with corrupted government officials for food and water, under the banner of what the International Monetary Fund refers to as "cost recovery".

Private enterprise interests pursuant to modern capitalism do not seek to "spread wealth". These interests, in the case of societies under authoritarian rule which is "friendly to corporations", seek to exploit the existing human suffering, socioeconomic malaise and any permissive laws that allow unchecked environmental degradation via pollution to maximise profit. Where there exist traditional, communal and democratic societies which are oriented around support for the quality-of-living attainments of citizen-participants, with complementary laws that help support personal security within society, private enterprise seeks to establish existential impoverishment as it accumulates its market profit.

Modern capitalism creates great riches for its practitioners by strategies that include dispossessing people of their farms, homes, access to food, access to clean air and access to any freely available healthcare. In other words, modern capitalism creates financial-equivalent profit by formulating strategies to take away operative social wealth. Modern capital engages 'households' and 'firms' in a state of "non-military warfare" with each other. In this state of non-military warfare and the operation of global markets, the capitalist victors accumulate "great financial-equivalent riches" through attrition among the resistors of their corrupting onslaught.

———•———

The Social Psychology of Capitalism vis-à-vis Constitutional Democracy

Though a constitutional democracy embraces all peoples as citizen-participants of a pluralistic society and cosmopolitan community, capitalism condemns whole communities, nations and even continents such as Africa and much of Asia. A democracy, in a spirit of equality and in support of related tenets of human rights, brings people to work co-operatively together in a constructive manner. Within capitalism, a state of "non-military warfare" creates an environment of social divisiveness as households and firms fight with each other in the market in a struggle for operational affirmation. In a democracy, treachery and criminal conduct that subverts inviolable human rights are deplored. Within capitalism, treachery and forms of essentially criminal conduct are embraced when they can be deployed in a relatively discreet manner that can serve the profit-making interests of capitalism.

Within traditional and democratic societies, family, friendship and other communal social structures contribute to strong allegiances that transcend money and other materialistic interests. These societies tend to view wealth in broad terms that relate to a social-civic vitality. However, within capitalism, as social structures are weakened from pressures to succeed financially, persons are conditioned relatively-speaking to contemplate treachery and function as "operatives" such that forms of criminal conduct against "friends" and family are executed if there are envisioned ensuing financial-equivalent economic rewards.

CHAPTER 7

SOCIAL DARWINISM

༄

"Fair employment practice commissions that have the task of preventing 'discrimination' in employment by reason of race, colour or religion have been established in a number of states. Such legislation clearly involves interference with the freedom of individuals to enter into voluntary contracts with one another. It subjects any such contract to approval by the state... considering a situation in which there are grocery stores serving a neighbourhood inhabited by people who have a strong aversion to be waited on by "Negro" clerks. Suppose one of the grocery stores has a vacancy for a clerk and the first applicant qualified in other respects happens to be a "Negro". Let us suppose that as a result of the law the store is required to hire him. The effect of this action will be to reduce the business done by this store and impose losses on the owner. If the preference for the community is strong enough, it may even cause the store to close. When the owner of the store hires white clerks in preference to Negroes in the absence of the law, he may not be expressing any preference or prejudice or taste of his own. He may simply be transmitting the tastes of the community... As a general rule, any minority that counts on specific majority action to defend its interests is short-sighted to the extreme."

Milton Friedman, *Capitalism and Freedom*, pp. 112-114, 1965.

Raymond Samuels

U NLIKE LIBERAL and other supporters of democracy, the Apostles of capitalism do not conceive 'freedom' within the context of human rights. The Apostles of capitalism conceive a 'freedom' that is based on relative purchasing power. Indeed, to this capitalist creed, an economy that is constructed around monetary policy is exclusively conceived of as being comprised of 'households' and 'firms' with relative purchasing power. In such a milieu, prices react to the tastes of consumers and the productive capabilities of firms to offer and deliver for sale, goods and services that have been demanded by consumers. Economic society, to the capitalist creed, embraces a conception of freedom that is analogous to an ocean with sharks, big fishes, small fishes and even smaller fishes. Economic agents that are analogous to the shark and the big fishes at the top of the "economic food chain", with relatively higher purchasing power having achieved the "greatest wealth", will have relative freedom over the small fishes and even smaller fishes which are more vulnerable to predation. To the capitalist creed, the "survival of the fittest" is a desired and "natural" economic order. Indeed, the capitalist creed limits "freedom" to a commercial concept that is associated to 'buyers' and 'sellers' who are exercising voluntary attributed "free" choice that is associated to commercial contracts. References to 'community' by "the Apostles" are correspondingly limited to the conceived participants as 'human capital' and commercial entities who have statistically verifiable consumption patterns. At times, there is also the 'community of interest' of Big Businesses.

To the capitalist creed, humans are not social beings, rather they are appreciated as being little more than barbarians who prey on each other to gain all the resources that can be acquired to support material power. To the capitalist creed, humans are little more than a primitive species of animals, with the difference that this species has acquired the technological capabilities through its intelligence to gain much greater access to control its domain than a lion for example. To the capitalist creed, the humans that can use their intelligence and cunning to gain and pillage the most resources and are able to work with others with attributed "superior intellect" that share a community of interest with the intent to advance commercial ends are the rightful "inheritors of the Earth". In the appar-

148

ent view of the Apostles of capitalism, the only desirable human value in a political economy is "the pursuit of commerce" within a context of the 'survival of the fittest', where values that are associated with social justice have properly been eradicated.

The nature of work, within the context of the "survival of the fittest", is transformed into conditioned economic strife that tolerates and gives rise to 'wage slavery'. The Apostles of capitalism conceive a dissembled conception of a "freedom" that is strictly commercial and is primarily associated with the opportunities of the principal owners of capital, who can enjoy the fruits (so-to-speak) of their superior purchasing power. Wage slavery refers to a condition where people via work must engage in activities for a personal income with which they may secure their basic survival needs, dispossessed of their choice potential as human beings with rights. To the Apostles of capitalism, 'wage slavery' is as "necessary" to the desired 'capitalistic growth' as was the old institution of 'slavery' in the plantation economy of the American south. Though those who did the work in the 'old institution' of slavery were not compensated with wages, the contemporary institution of 'wage slavery' provides monetary payment in the context where the denial of a human rights conception of freedom has been executed in a more sophisticated form.

In a "free capitalistic society", no one is "forced" to work in conditions that are in violation of their conceived human rights. It is not a concern to the capitalist creed if the only work that is potentially available is work in horrendous conditions including working conditions that pose an immediate threat to health and if such conditions have been made necessary to cut down on costs and maximize profit. While the 'old institution' of slavery was based on explicitly coerced labour under the presence of the military of imperial power, 'wage slavery' has become a comparatively "volunteered" condition of enslavement that is implicitly coerced by a private enterprise capitalist system rather than via military conquest and decree. Slavery was viewed to be a necessary part of capitalistic expansion that was ill concerned with human rights. The same basic idea of some form of slavery exists in the culture of "capitalist society" where it is treated as a "necessary evil" of the march towards the "economic progress". The mentality of the capitalist creed where "slavery" was executed as a valued institution in support of the evolution of commercial society exists.

Its operation has merely changed form to accommodate what is perceived as "undesirable social pressure" from supporters of human rights and such social movements which the capitalist creed seeks to destroy once and for all via its 'globalisation' efforts.

To the capitalist creed, there are the "rulers" and the "ruled". To the supporters of that creed, those who rule ought not rightfully to be the diverse public as a whole via the institution of government and its cadre of persons who, in the view of the capitalist creed, entail the "weak" and "minorities" of the society. To the capitalist creed, there should be a recognised constituency of rulers that is based on a pecking order which is comprised of individuals who have achieved the "greatest financial wealth" or assets from the ownership of capital. To the supporters of the creed, the rulers ought to be comprised of principally of executives in the oil industry and international finance. The capitalist creed is also an environment of prevailing culture of institutionalised racism which was apparent in the quotation from the Milton Friedman book, *Capitalism and Freedom* (1965) which was presented at the beginning of this Chapter. Also, although in the 21st century, the Apostles and disciples of capitalism are less strident in making such comments, the fruits of their attitude remain in the prevailing culture of modern capitalism. This apparent institutionalised racism within the culture of capitalism is an intellectual residual of the imperial expansion of the European powers. This expansion later rationalised a 'Social Darwinism' that viewed an attributed pecking order of races, in which whites were viewed to be "superior" by virtue of the ability of European powers to wage military conquest on other peoples, while other 'races' with particular reference to African peoples were to be viewed as inferior. The conceptual thrust of modern capitalism that is based on a Social Darwinistic intellectual foundation is that the natural order is a constituency of whites from the attributed "superior race" who are ruling over "less gifted" whites as well as attributed inferior races, the ruled. The ruled is supposed to serve the rulers in whatever enslaved capacity that is economically required of them. Society "should be at the sufferance of the owners of capital from the white majority racial groups.

"Contemporary Economics as successfully proselytised by the Apostles of capitalism

'Contemporary economics' supported by 'free market' capitalism and 'positive economics' is based on the computational assessment of data that are related to money and price-commodity relationships. Its axioms are... Let the market, not the state, set wages and prices. Indeed, Milton Friedman, on p. 35 of *Capitalism and Freedom* (1965), in the spirit of the disciples of American capitalism that was extended by its Apostles, rejected "legal minimum wage rates". For these Apostles, there is no such thing really as exploitation in the general intellectual system of capitalism. Instead, there is what Friedman referred to as "voluntary contracts". An owner of capital as an envisioned "free man" ought to be able to pay $1.00 per hour wage to his workers if he is able to find workers who are willing to work for $1.00 per hour or less. Accordingly, let the market determine earnings (by human capital) based on what the freedom loving capitalist is prepared to pay in wages and what attributed "human capital" is prepared to earn in the competitive pressures of the prevailing labour market, where the prevailing government is prepared to protect the financial-equivalent assets of the capitalists. If the freedom loving capitalist finds that $1.00 per hour is undermining potentially even higher profit earnings, this capitalist should be able to go abroad and seek workers (child labour or otherwise) who may be willing to earn 20 cents a day, if attainable, in whatever conditions, horrendous or otherwise, in support of profit by the capitalist creed.

The argument of the creed is that government has no business to intervene into what is an attributed "voluntary contract". This idealised state that is associated to work as a voluntary contract regards as an imposition legislative interventions that aim to safeguard quality-of-living attainments and has argued conditions that have become the basis of antiunionisation related legislation. Accordingly, the view is that government ought to not intervene in the efforts of a capitalist creed to obtain profit in an attributed "free market".

Within this type of operating economic background, 'wage slavery' is the outcome of economy in which people are not honoured as sentient social individuals, but rather as auxiliary resources of private enterprise that has evolved into a 'globalised' transnational corporate "superstructure".

An implied 'Social Darwinism' is apparent within the context which glorifies an economy that pivots on public acquiescence to an apparent Americanised frontier 'survival of the fittest' market context. Via a 'Social Darwinistic' milieu, the capitalist creed seeks to achieve in its efforts a 'cultural transformation to commercialism' and an accompanying economic colonisation by its centres of market dominance.

———•———

Backgrounder to the "Free Market"

The 'contemporary economics' that is "appropriately" based on a 'free market' axiom conceives the "progress" of human civilisation as occurring via driving "self-interest" and trade. In respect of 'trade' in a "free market", in all voluntary exchanges, where accurate information is known, both the buyer and seller achieve their targets. Therefore, in an increase in trade between individuals, groups or nations, benefits accrue to both parties to the trade. The capitalist imputation is that tariffs and other barriers to trade should be eliminated. A further argument is that given the universal existence of limited resources and unlimited wants, the market competition for resources and outputs exists in all societies and cannot be abolished by any economy-linked government edict.

A further argument is that since most individuals are not self-sufficient and almost all natural resources must be transformed in order to become usable as "commercial products", individuals – labourers, landlords, capitalists and entrepreneurs – must work together to produce valuable goods and services. It is also argued that historically the division of labour and the accompanying features of comparative advantage that accompany prevailing resource endowments contribute to the circumstances that vary in talent, intelligence, knowledge and technical capabilities that lead to specialisation and the exploitation of accompanying comparative advantage by respective individuals, firms and nations. Information about market behaviour is also diverse. Profit and loss are market mechanisms that operate as the guide to what should and should not be produced over the long run towards the attributed progress of civilization. The market is therefore accordingly viewed as being "infinitely wise" (so-to-speak).

"Given the limitations of time and resources, there are always trade-offs in life. If one wants to do something, one must give up other things that one may wish to do. Within the context of 'opportunity cost', the price that one pays to engage in a particular activity must be balanced against the potential gains from other activities that one has forgone... "Normally, prices are determined by the subjective valuations of buyers (demand) and the asking prices of sellers (supply) and not necessarily by any objective out of pocket cost of production. For any current budget, the higher the price, the smaller the quantity purchasers will be willing to buy. At the same time, the higher the likely price, the larger the quantity sellers will be willing to offer for sale. With this in mind, for every set of conditions, there are associated causes and effects. Actions taken by individuals, firms and governments have an impact on other actors in the economy that may be predictable although the level of predictability depends on the complexity of the actions that are involved.

There is always a degree of risk and uncertainty about the future because people are often re-evaluating, learning from their mistakes and changing their minds, thus making it difficult to predict their behaviour in the future. The result is that in the matter of 'government controls', "price-rent-wage controls may benefit some individuals and groups, but not necessarily society as a whole. Ultimately, such controls tend to create shortages, black markets and a deterioration of the quality of services that are offered.

The capitalist creed champions the idea that there is no such thing as a free lunch to rationalise its vision of a commercial society. As far as public management is concerned, in order to maintain a high degree of desired efficiency and good management for the Apostles of capitalism towards a

"New World Order", market principles should be adopted whenever possible." Accordingly, government to these Apostles and disciples "should try to do only what private enterprise cannot do and government should not engage in businesses that private enterprise can do better". The imputation is that government should live within its means... know its place in the "great scheme" of an attributed "natural economic order".

Another feature which is argued is that ensuing "fiscally responsible" economics should also rely, in general, on cost-benefit analysis, where net incremental benefits should exceed net incremental costs, and also on an accountability principle in which those who benefit from a service should pay for the service. According to this principle, people who are without money, for whatever the reason which is not really the concern for those who subscribe to the capitalist creed, are not entitled to any services in a "Brave New World". If someone has to work for the entire day in horrendous working conditions that violate the human rights of the individual, without even a minimum wage, merely to earn $5.00 for a meal, and who needs to live on the street, not having money for housing, that is of no substantive concern to the holders of the capitalist creed. In the view of the holders of the capitalist creed who are seeking to achieve a "Brave New World", let the strong inclusive of the attributed "racially superior" inherit the Earth. Let the "weak" perish.

———•———

"Free Market" modern capitalism

While not specifically advocating 'Social Darwinism', the preceding outlined axioms of an operating "modern capitalism" are based on an intellectual reliance on "positive economics". The thrust, which was devised by the Apostles of capitalism, is consistent with a computational and conceptual framework which is implicitly supportive of a Social Darwinistic economic "world view". Modern "free market" capitalism strives for the critical economic primacy of 'private enterprise' in an attributed "properly functioning" economy. In the "free market" conceptualisation that dominates a "Pax America"centred Western Industrialised economic paradigmatic framework, increasing corporate profits are regarded as a positive sign of "economic growth" and 'prosperity', while the prevailing demands of workers in unions, as an example, for an equitable share of that "prosperity" are viewed with great anxiety as a threat to continued so-called "economic growth" and 'prosperity'.

If the price (so-to-speak) of increasing profits is domestic layoffs, hostile labour laws and correspondent depressed wages and poor working conditions or areas that tolerate child labour and forced labour, so be it... Just keep it out of the spotlight of unnecessary bad press through the mass-media. In fact, why not acquire mass-media organisations to help manage the public opinion in a "consumer society"? Indeed, the massive purchases of newspapers, TV, radio and more recently internet mass-media related business that offer "news and information" in Canada, the U.S. and Europe are now a critical strategy in convincing a "consumer society" of the alleged "benefits" of attributed "globalisation". Such concentrated acquisition of the information sources will enable private enterprise cope up with the business of market competition and increasing profit towards a "New Economic Order".

———•———

The Genesis of a Social Philosophy of the American Business Culture

During the Cold War from the 1950's into the 1980's, to help appease groups contemplating "communism ", which is actually based on "state capitalism" in itself, capitalism was required to share the economic public policy focus with approaches that were all lumped together by the supporters of the capitalist creed as "socialist". The decline of the Soviet Union as a communist and military "Superpower" was supposed to signify the final triumph of private enterprise capitalism. The United States became the only remaining Superpower. This political development opened up the flood gates for its prevailing capitalist model to claim the Earth itself as the spoils of victory. Its economic system could spread without the military and ideological challenge that was earlier posed by the Soviet Empire. The evolution of a Social Darwinistic milieu in the American political economy had formed the intellectual origin of Americanised capitalism that would form the basis of free-market-driven globalisation efforts of the American Empire.

As discussed by a history professor from the University of Wisconsin, in an article entitled *"The Social Philosophy of American Businessmen"*, Stanley K. Schultz, (2000) intimated that "in the years leading up to and immediately after the turn of the century, corporations and the businessmen who were their recognisable heads came under increasing attack. "Laissez-faire", once identical to individual freedom, now signified corporations, trusts and an unprecedented loss of individual freedom." With critical concerns that were voiced in the American public about the threat to American democratic values that was posed by corporate capitalism, "American businessmen found themselves resorting to new ideologies and "scientific" terminology to defend themselves from those angry Americans who felt that the trusts were destroying their way of life."

> *"We hold these truths to be self-evident that all men are created equal that they are endowed by their Creator with certain unalienable rights that among these are Life, Liberty and the Pursuit of Happiness..."*
>
> (Declaration of Independence, 1776)

As further elaborated in this cited article, when Thomas Jefferson substituted "Pursuit of Happiness" for the original term "Property, " he may have foreseen the controversy over the meaning of freedom that would come to dominate the Gilded Age of politics. "With this in mind" two contrasting ideals of freedom clashed during this period. A heavyweight intellectual/political boxing match ensued with the ideal of "Pursuit of Happiness" represented by a great number of Americans who were fighting the ideal of "Pursuit of Property" which was supported by men like Andrew Carnegie and John D. Rockefeller. Both sides had logical justifications for their positions. However, the leading intellectual currents of the late 19th century eventually provided the "Pursuit of Property" heavyweights with knock-out punches like "Social Darwinism" and 'Laissez-faire'.

"Corporations as an originally perceived threat to American individualistic "Pursuit of Happiness'

The above cited article by Stanley K. Schultz, further inquires "Why did so many Americans view the new corporations and trusts as evil entities that destroyed the American dream of the "Pursuit of Happiness?" Though many answers can be given to such a question, there are important points that can help us understand the logic of those who despised the corporations":

———◆———

The perceived threat against freedom from a conspiracy between financial commercial and legislative power

Thomas Jefferson assumed that America would become a land of independent yeoman farmers when he wrote the Declaration of Independence. His view was that hard work and simple life would keep the nation as well as the individual strong. This individualist ethic had permeated the American social climate since the days of the Pilgrims. One conspicuous symbol of the American attachment to romantic individualism is the "American Cowboy" and the images of the "Wild West". Before the revolution that accompanied the legal accommodation to corporate reality, the American economy was founded on individual achievement and a Protestant work ethic. After the organisational revolution to the corporate reality, many Americans faced difficulties in adjusting to the concept of a new form of economic organisation that seemed to de-emphasise the human element.

To many Americans, corporations were essentially a potentially conspiratorial arrangement between legislators and businessmen. Subsequently, America indeed has evolved into a popular culture that continues to mistrust lawyers, legislators, "contractual arrangements" and "special interests" with a prevailing association to commerce and attributed linkages to "big businesses". Thus, it is not surprising that many Americans disapproved a legislative process that allowed a group of investors to create, with the backing of the state, a potentially powerful moneymaking device that would be impersonalised and unaccountable and would, with the backing of the state, be potentially powerful.

Corporations and trusts were viewed as entities that potentially threatened to destroy the age-old concept of free trade and healthy competition. Capitalism as an economic model certainly had its faults. However, one of its greatest attributed advantages is that healthy market competition can often benefit consumers and producers alike. As trusts and corporations grew larger and more monopolistic during the Gilded Age, people rightfully feared that free competition would soon be stamped out."

Some Americans, of course, believed that the "Pursuit of Happiness" and the "Pursuit of Property" could easily go hand in hand. For instance, Abram S. Hewitt, a well-respected businessman, philanthropist, public official and political leader, maintained that corporations were merely a more efficient means of producing the age-old "American Dream:"

> *"It is curious that the mass of the people of this country should fail to recognise that their best friends are the corporations because corporations have been the only barrier between the despotisms of ignorance and the invasion of the rights of property. Doubtless they abuse their privileges at times but they alone have the ability and the courage to*

resist attack and they are doing the work which was done
by Jefferson and Madison in the early days of the Republic."

Abram S. Hewitt

Abram S. Hewitt, as excerpted from the article *"The Social Philosophy of American Businessmen"* (2000), was represented as "honest man with a good public record. Even though he rationalised the actions of corporations, he nevertheless worked under the assumption that the "Pursuit of Happiness" was the ultimate goal of the American people. Others, however, tended to believe that "Pursuit of Property" was in fact the only justification that was needed for the corporation revolution".

"Pursuit of Property" and the "Pursuit of Happiness"

Attempts to reconcile the "Pursuit of Happiness" with the "Pursuit of Property" were unpersuasive to most Americans. Though men like Hewitt could claim that corporations were, in fact, beneficial to individual happiness, Americans could plainly see that this was not the case. Thus, businessmen had to resort to another tactic to persuade Americans that corporations were natural and the most effective method of doing business. Three main themes of late 19thcentury thought provided American businessmen a set of terms and ideologies to justify their activities as "Robber Barons:" These are 'Social Darwinism' in association with the 'self-adjusting economy' and 'profit incentive' represented as the principal 'human motive'.

Charles Darwin and 'On the Origin of the Species

In 1859, a humble, mild-mannered Englishman Charles Darwin changed the intellectual climate of the world forever when he introduced his book ***On the Origin of the Species***. Although theories of evolution had existed for centuries in European thought, Darwin's introduction of the idea of "natural selection" was a legitimate scientific hypothesis that obtained attention. Darwin had no intention of interpreting his work as a means of constructing society. In fact, Darwin purposely avoided discussing humans or human society in the context of "natural selection." Later intellectuals, however, treated Darwin's ideas as the basis of a far-reaching social theory that was known as "Social Darwinism.

——————

"Herbert Spencer and "Social Darwinism"

Spencer, another Englishman, took Darwin's theories out of the realm of biology and reworked them into a social theory. It was Spencer, not Darwin, who coined the phrase "survival of the fittest." To Spencer, human society should ideally be modelled on "Nature." As such, humans should never intentionally interfere with the processes of "Nature" which selects only the fittest human beings for survival into the next generation. Handouts to the poor, state schooling and systematised health care were considered dangerous by Spencer; they could only interfere with "Nature" by helping 'weak' humans to survive, thereby damaging the "purity" of the rest of the human race. Of course, Spencer was never able to clearly define what he meant by "Nature" nor he was able to clearly explain just which human actions could be considered "natural" and which were not. However, over 400, 000 copies of Spencer's publications were sold in the United States alone and he was one of the most influential thinkers of the late 19th century.

——————

William Graham Sumner and "Social Darwinism" in America

Sumner was Spencer's American counterpart. "In his economic and social outlook, Sumner was a Social Darwinist holding that distinctions of wealth and status among men were the direct result of inherently different capacities. This stratifying tendency worked for the good of society by eliminating weaker and encouraging stronger strains as natural selection does among animals and plants. Also, this tendency should not be interfered by sentimental, unintelligent attempts to hedge the free play of economic forces and personal abilities. In lectures and written works with titles such as "The Absurd Attempt to Make the World Over" and "What Social Classes Owe Each Other" (1883), Sumner championed *Laissez-faire* within a Social Darwinistic context as the only true principle of both economics and government. He decried all the movements that pointed to a welfare state (ref. Webster's American Biographies, G.& C. Merriam, 1975).

American businessmen were too happy to adopt the ideology of Social Darwinism in order to defend their business practices. James J. Hill, a leading "Robber Baron" of the railroadbuilding era, saw the chance to justify his actions with "scientific" terminology:

> "The fortunes of railroad companies are determined by the law of the survival of the fittest."
>
> James J. Hill

There were, of course, influential Americans who did not feel that Darwin's theories could be applied to social matters. One such individual was the historian Henry Adams, who said,

> "The progress of evolution from President Washington to President Grant is alone evidence enough to upset Darwin."
>
> Henry Adams

Raymond Samuels

Social Darwinism was an application of Darwin's ideas of natural selection and biological evolution to human societies. Its proponents were bent towards naturalising the social conditions of the period, particularly those conditions which aroused the greatest controversy and conflict – the rapid growth of an impoverished working class, the huge gulf that had opened up between rich and poor and the often horrendous conditions in the burgeoning industrial cities. Social Darwinists like Sumner argued that social existence was a competitive struggle among individuals possessing diverse natural capacities and traits. Overall, those with better traits succeeded, becoming wealthy and powerful, while those lacking in inner discipline or intelligence sank into poverty. Thus, the very conditions that reformers decried were to Sumner indications that society was functioning analogous to the "empiricism" of 'positive economics' as it should. Therefore, he argued that government must not interfere with ameliorate conditions because this would only result in the preservation of bad traits, even while penalising those who possessed good ones. Thus, social evolution was best served by an attributed "minimal" state. The context of Social Darwinism eliminated from advocated public policy any critical civic sense of moral obligation to the poor.

An apparent world view by the intellectual champions of 'positive economics', consistent with 'Social Darwinisitc' doctrine, is evident in co-rationalised support for the 'minimal state' in addition to a corresponding reactionary and selfish conception of a "free man" together with the rejection of social responsibility in an enlightened approach to economics.

The minimal state: Traditional liberal doctrine held that citizens were sovereign and the state existed to serve specific purposes for citizens. Sumner in responding to early pressure for social reforms by the state essentially reaffirms a fiduciary obligation context of the state to citizens in his Social Darwinisic theory. However, his argument was that the entire state owes anybody "peace, order and the guarantees of rights" (Sumner, 342: Joseph Boland lecture, 1995). He later makes clear that "rights" refer chiefly to property rights and a very limited notion of equal opportunity. It seems safe to say that "peace" and "order" refer to the state's responsibility to guard against foreign attacks, domestic insurrections and violations of the law; particularly violations of "the property of men and the honour of women" (Sumner 349). Beyond this, his position was that "it is not the function of the state to make men happy" (Sumner, 346). Sumner views social reform as little more than the use of the state to steal from "the rich, comfortable, prosperous, virtuous, respectable, educated and healthy" (Sumner, 341) in order to give to "classes of people who have not been able to satisfy their own desires . . . [and who] do not take their achievements as a fair measure of their [property] rights" (Sumner, 343).

Sumner's position is more consistent than those who strongly opposed social welfare and industrial regulation but made enormous exceptions when it came to subsidies and benefits for industry. Under the rubric of "jobbery", Sumner condemns "any scheme which aims to gain not by the legitimate fruits of industry and enterprise but by extorting from somebody a part of his product under guise of some pretended industrial undertaking" (Sumner, 354). He had in mind state development projects – buildings, internal improvements, investment credits etc., along with the "greatest" bit of jobbery of all, the protective tariff (Sumner, 354).

The "Free man": Sumner accepted without question that material success is indicative of virtue, specifically it evidences one's superior capacity for "labour and self-denial". These are the virtues ordained by "Gd and Nature", which have also determined "the chances and conditions of life on earth once for all" (Sumner, 343). The parallel between this biological predetermination and the Calvinist belief in predestination is only one of many parallels between Sumner and Calvinism. He thus argued that the one duty of "every man and woman" is "to take care of his or her own self" (Sumner, 351). In fulfilling this private duty, one at the same time fulfills one's social duty (Sumner, 352) and no man can do more than taking care of himself and possibly his family.

Given these premises, Sumner applauds the existence of large fortunes. Within his creed, the acquisition of wealth is identical to portraying one's level of virtue and wealthy individuals are the biological future of the species because they possess the best traits. Therefore, the state should not interfere with the accumulation of wealth because wealth comes through labour and self-denial and men would not strive to accumulate it if it did not secure advantages of higher order. Moreover, "the possession of capital is... an indispensable pre requisite [for the delivery] of educational, scientific and moral goods" (Sumner, 348). This assertion, especially the "moral goods" phrase, makes sense only if one lives in Sumner's moral universe. It is diametrically opposed to Thoreau's moral philosophy. In any case, it allows Sumner to conclude that private capital accumulation is co-extensive with the development of civilisation.

Sumner's denigration of workers is only the flip side of this argument. In it, those who are exploited have themselves to blame for their exploitation. By being spendthrift and indulging in "vulgar enjoyments", they lay themselves open to exploitation. And by increasing their numbers, they compete with each other for food and wages, thereby driving up the cost of the former and lowering the latter. His argument was that the few prudent thereby "suffer the folly of the rest" (Sumner, 348). This last observation actually clashes with Sumner's emphasis on social evolution as the outcome of competition among individuals since we see that a structural dynamic – the supposed promiscuous breeding of the underclass – actually prevents the meritorious members of this class from succeeding.

Repudiation of economic social responsibility: Sumner's doctrine can be perceived as a re-engineered liberalism that has been purged of almost all its links with social and civic constitutional responsibility. Civic virtue an active concern for the common good, a willingness to sacrifice if necessary for it and an understanding that public action is a vital mode of personal fulfillment is regarded by Sumner as mere meddling in other people's business. To him, popular sovereignty is undesirable given "the vices and passions of human nature". "If political power were to be given to the masses who have not hitherto had it, nothing will stop them from abusing it, but laws and institutions" (Sumner, 346). From his perspective, democratic government was not an unalloyed blessing since it also included representation of the attributed weak and inferior of the society.

———•———

The "Self-Adjusting Economy"

This doctrine of the self-adjusting economy that was so vigorously supported by 19thcentury businessmen traces its origin to the notion of the "invisible hand" that was postulated by Adam Smith. That writer published one of the most important books in the history of economics in 1776, in the midst of the American Revolutionary War era, – the year that Jefferson wrote the Declaration of Independence.

The book's full title is *An Inquiry Into the Nature and Causes of the Wealth of Nations*. This book is usually referred as *The Wealth of Nations*. Smith wrote the book, allegedly, "after discussing Laissez-faire beliefs with some of the physiocrats". Smith's book has been attributed to supporting an argument in favour of allowing people to engage in trade, manufacturing or other economic activity without unnecessary control or interference from government.

The attributed main arguments in *The Wealth of Nations* (1776) that are on the basis of free market capitalism doctrine might be stated rather simply: People are naturally selfish. When they engage in manufacturing or trade, they do so in order to gain wealth and/or power. This process should not be interfered with because despite the self-interest of these individuals, their activity typically generates good for of the entire society. The more goods they make or trade, the more goods people will have. The more people who manufacture do trade, the greater the competition. Competition among manufacturers and merchants helps all people by providing even more goods that frequently become available at lower prices. This collection of activities creates jobs and spreads wealth."

Following Adam Smith's attributed lead, an evolving community of interest in the nineteenth century, consistent with a nascent business community born from the American frontier milieu and with an evolving business-oriented American constituency of economists, there emerged a generally agreed upon four principal points of political economy. These imputed that 'political economy' which was the terminology that was used to speak about economics at that time is ruled by "unchanging, everlasting laws which can be equated with laws of Nature or G-d". Another point also imputed the presence of "self-interest as the only motive for human action and it is not only natural but is also beneficial." The third argument is that a "free competition is a permanent and necessary law of an effectively functioning market economy". The fourth imputation was that "government is an inefficient economic agency and should not be involved in operations that could just as well be conducted by private individuals in the market".

American businessmen were entirely grateful to hear economists and influential thinkers like William Graham Sumner justifying the actions of the corporations and trusts. With the intellectual support of the "science" of economics, late 19thcentury businessmen could feel that unethical but profitable actions were actually beneficial to the nation as a whole.

---·---

Profit motive as the only reliable incentive for action

Businessmen rely on the widespread belief that the profit motive rules the life of man. Businessmen, politicians and market economists widely agreed that if humans were explicitly asked to do good things for society, they never would. The argument was that only by creating wealth for themselves, businessmen would be able to help others; by creating jobs and encouraging investment in the nation's industrial centers. Andrew Carnegie, one of the least selfish of the early industrialists, claimed that even the most ridiculous spending habits of the wealthy were beneficial to the rest of the nation:

> "Millionaires are the bees that make the most honey and contribute most to the hive even after they have gorged themselves full."
>
> Andrew Carnegie

Businessmen of the late 19th century often used and abused ideologies in an attempt to rationalise their illicit practices. This period was filled with economic and social turmoil "and even honest businessmen often found themselves experiencing early versions of work-related stress". The "boom-and-bust" cycle of depressions and recoveries from 1873 to the turn of the century made investing precarious and market competition was fierce as companies struggled to survive. However, for all the difficulties that company directors faced in this period, the common workers underneath them often faced situations which were much worse. As business leaders became wealthier and more powerful, the men and women (and even children) who formed America's industrial backbone began to demand their piece of the American industrial pie.

———•———

"...and the weak shall perish."

"Free market" positive economics, indeed, appears to be based upon an implied conception of the "survival of the fittest". Its correspondent paradigmatic acceptance appears to legitimate a status quo assignment of relative power and relative weakness via the relative access of individuals to scarce resources and relative purchasing power within a system of market pricing. Furthermore, this paradigmatic context accommodates an implied Social Darwinistic process of 'natural' selection as the norm of a "properly functioning economy" that is based on a "normal" pursuit of a "selfishized" self-interest. In that milieu, the thesis is that the weak shall perish as an operation in the pursuit of the "public interest" as the "good of the strong" operate pursuant to an implied natural universal order.

———•———

Raymond Samuels

More on Sumner, Social Darwinism and private enterprise capitalism

In *What Social Classes owe to each Other* (1883), Sumner further elaborated Social Darwinistic political economic philosophy consistent with the mentality of a modern capitalist creed. According to Sumner, "certain ills belong to the hardships of human life. They are natural and part of the struggle with Nature for existence". Sumner, in further consistency with the mentality of the capitalist creed, indicated that "we cannot blame our fellow-men for our share of these. My neighbour and I are both struggling to free ourselves from these ills. The fact that my neighbour has succeeded in this struggle better than me constitutes no grievance for me." Sumner, in support of societal exclusion of the poor, also indicated that "a pauper is a person who cannot earn his living, whose producing powers have fallen positively below his necessary consumption and cannot pay his way." With this in mind "a human society needs the active cooperation and productive energy of every person in it. A man, who is present as a consumer, but he does not contribute either by land, labour or capital to the work of society, is a burden. On no sound political theory, such a person ought to share the political power of the state." The poor "must be cancelled from the ranks of the rulers"

According to Sumner, consistent with a modern capitalist creed, "it may be said that those whom humanitarians and philanthropists call the weak are the ones through whom the productive forces of society are wasted. They constantly neutralise and destroy the finest efforts of the wise and industrious and are a dead-weight on the society in all its struggles to realise better things." Furthermore, "whether the people who mean no harm, but are weak in the essential powers necessary to the performance of one's duties in life or those who are malicious and vicious, do the more mischief" is of no consequence on their exclusion from a society for the "strong". Sumner added that "under the names of the poor and the weak, the negligent, shiftless, inefficient, silly and imprudent are fastened upon the industrious and prudent as a responsibility and a duty. The terms are extended to cover the idle, intemperate and vicious who by the combination gain credit which they do not deserve and could not get if they stood alone."

———•———

Economics warfare in the pursuit of "self-interest" and "private enterprise"

"Free market" positive economics supports the existence of striving in a "rationalised state" of affairs, in which 'households' and 'firms' are engaged in a perpetuated state of "economic warfare" with each other, vying for dominance and conquest. However, the context also argues that the ensuing effects logically ensure the optimal 'management of scarce resources'. Buying into this doctrine of the intellectual champions of the 'positive economics' would require an acceptance of the premise that the parties *à la* 'households' and 'firms', though engaged in warfare and an endemic state of strife and upheaval form a more productive state of economic relations.

———•———

Economics on behalf of and by a Community of Interests in support of Rule by Big Business

"Contemporary economics" can be critically appreciated by coming to an understanding of who, from group has been successful intellectual champion, and what (if anything) did these intellectual champions have the potential to gain and for what purpose. The "contemporary economics" that relies on 'positive economics' that was championed by the University of Chicago School was not intended to be an "economics for everyone". The intellectual champions of those who were among the most financially affluent of a majority culture of a society and also had disdain for the financially underprivileged, racial minorities and other disenfranchised persons in society would not necessarily be expected to be empathetic about adopting an economic paradigm that is supportive of constructive "interventionism" by government in support of these latter groups. Indeed, intellectual champions of positive economics would look upon such interventionism as potentially undermining of the economic hegemony, even though these intellectual champions may have themselves become elite by such public policy complicity.

————◆————

'Positive economics' and the perpetuation of dominance

"Contemporary economics" that relies on 'positive economics' can be viewed as a "game" that relies on scientific methodologies to support the design of a logical internally consistent system that can be used to manipulate data so as to service the targets and the perceived vested interests of its intellectual champions. Contemporary economics that relies on "positive economics" complements the perpetuation of relative dominance. "Positive economics" rationalises a context which condones the pursuit of greed in the name of a dissembled conception of self-interest. It uses naive imputations in misattributions of statements by Adam Smith in the *Wealth of Nations* (1776) and overlooks the presence of constellations of adversarial power in the rationalisation of an empirically-based non-communal interpretation of human economic reality. Essentially, competing financial empires that are striving for increasing levels of profit at the expense of their employees who are subjected to ongoing threats of outright firings or mass-layoffs can draw on the positivist approach to economics in order to repress any demands for better work conditions or increasing wages.

Positive economics, as a rationalised system of 'Social Darwinism', "elevates" human civilisation to not much further than that of "savages" or alternatively that of the Lions, Wild Dogs, Vultures and prey on the Savannah that possesses the technology to perpetrate the self-annihilation of human civilisation. "Positive economics" can be viewed to be rules of engagement for "economic warfare" in which 'every man is for himself and every woman for herself' form the ground rules. The alternative idea that "man does not live by bread alone" is apparently irrelevant to the intellectual champions of "contemporary economics".

———•———

The Dynamics of 'Wage Slavery': Background to the evolution of the Labour Movement in America

The 'contemporary economics' that relies on positive economics for its intellectual rationalisation is driven by the premise that there exists an insatiable desire to acquire profit with its accompanying interest in driving down labour costs as well as other costs that may be generated by virtue of sustaining healthily conditions at the workplace. The largest businesses seek areas domestically as well as abroad that can best support depressed levels to wages and work-place-related cost conditions in a manner that may undermine human health. Large shareholding interests and owners of private enterprise that are concerned about the prices of a stock that arises from the actions of stock market speculators constitute a culture that, in its insatiable demands for more and more profit, harbour correspondent oversights of the human and the environmental costs of their neo-mercantilist preoccupations. Driven by an induced state of economic warfare and in defence of their own status and dominance, their apparent mindset is to construe forthcoming outcomes as either their ascendance or as a demolition of the ascendance of their competitors.

Wage slavery is a circumstance in which individuals, in order to obtain their subsistence, are required to participate in income-earning operations with which they otherwise do not identify or which they do not condone and which is against their free economic will. Wage slavery in America had specifically been identified by various union activists with a process in which the firm, within a purchase of an employee's work in exchange for a wage, executes a fair exchange which the employee can then convert into food, shelter and clothing. However, when a firm sets out to extract its profit largely from the labour of its workers and lowers the wages of the employee below the market exchange value of the outputs of its labour power, that output was seen as exercising "wage slavery".

———•———

"An Illuminating Historical Context

Thomas Jefferson had warned of the evils of an industrialised society where wealth separated men. He and his supporters hoped that America would remain a rural agricultural society where equality and a man's dignity could be maintained by tying men to the land. In his view, an industrial class system would erode democracy and equality. The Jeffersonians lost this struggle to retain their vision of America in the face of industrialisation. Yet there were some who sought to blend these competing interests. A fine example of this is the experiment at Lowell, Massachusetts in the United States. The founders of the Lowell experiment endeavoured to preserve America's agricultural base by employing rural women who would supplement the income on the farm. The experiment failed and soon Jefferson's vision would be relegated to the history books or curricula.

The early to mid-nineteenth century was a significant period of reforms in American history. Emerson and Thoreau were contemplating the essentials of life and William Lloyd Garrison founded the abolition movement. Out of this climate came the ten-hour movement. The movement achieved legislative success for the ten-hour day in several states. However, these laws contained one loophole which employers used. All these laws allowed employees to contract for longer hours if they wanted. Employers manipulated this feature to apply it to all workers and those who refused were fired and/or blacklisted. The presence of an eager labour pool caused by immigration weakened employee's bargaining power on this and other issues.

The "peculiar institution" of slavery was obviously a major cause of the Civil War. Yet, it was not solely a moral issue. Northern workers did not want to compete against slave labour. How could they? As Northern workers sought to increase their share of the wealth, their brethren workers in the South laboured without compensation. Northern labour leaders and industrialists thought that the South was trying to destroy capitalism and spread its slave power aristocracy on the nation. Unfortunately, there was no solution except war, but with the North's victory and passage of the 13th Amendment, the "peculiar institution" of slavery was abolished. However, for blacks, the struggle was not over. A long road towards freedom was ahead as it was for all workers.

The industrial labour force nearly tripled to about 8 million between 1880 and 1910. Large factories which had previously existed only in the textile industry before the Civil War increasingly became more common in a variety of industries. Labour was in high demand to run these new industries. Workers continued to organise and resist when their way of life and health were threatened. An economic study of this period should therefore also focus on the struggles of labour to secure safe working conditions as well as reasonable compensation. Notably, by 1910, approximately 25 percent of all American children were employed full-time in the nation's factories.

The mobilisation for World War I brought thousands of women and minorities into industrial plants in order to replace the men who went off to war. The Clayton Act, which was passed in 1914, set limits on the use of injunctions in labour disputes. In addition, the Ludlow Massacre occurred in Colorado. The wives and children of striking miners were set aflame when National Guardsmen attacked their tent colony during a strike against the Colorado Fuel and Iron Company. Following an unsuccessful strike by the United Mine Workers, the American President appointed the Colorado Coal Commission to investigate the Ludlow Massacre and labour conditions in the mines. Correspondingly, in 1916, an 8 hour day for railroad workers was created with the passage of the Adamson Act and that had the effect of averting a nationwide strike. A Federal child labour law was enacted in 1916 but it was later declared unconstitutional.

Another example of a historic labour related economic circumstance in the United States was The Industrial Workers of the World (IWW) strike in the Bisbee, Arizona copper mines in 1917. It ended with the deportation of 1200 miners to the desert by the local sheriff.

In the United States, The Wagner Act, 1935 (National Labour Relations Act) finally established its first national labour policy of protecting the right of workers to organise and elect their representatives for collective bargaining. During that era, The Guffey Act was passed with the intent to stabilise the coal industry and improve labour conditions. However, it was later declared unconstitutional (1936).

———•———

Urban Working Class Work Day, Wages and the evolving American Business Culture

A commonly-held and long-standing belief in American society is that hard work is good for the soul (See: Horatio Alger's Ragged Dick). In the 1830s40s, textile mill workers averaged 1618 hours per day. By 1865, the average workday was reduced to 1112 hours per day. The early 1880s saw a movement to reduce the workday to 10 hours and in a few cities such as Chicago, there was agitation for the now standard 8 hour day. A few businessmen and managers agreed to such reforms. However, most businessmen and managers continued to believe that workers benefited morally from the longer work day.

Employers believed that workers should not earn much more than a subsistence income. Why?

1. High wages hurt profits that were needed to open more factories and hire more workers.
2. Moral reasons: subsistence wages "kept the working class from wasting their money on booze, gambling and prostitutes."

——————

From the Wagner Act 1935 to implied anti-Unionism in contemporary American Economics

The Wagner Act (National Labour Relations Act) established the first national labour policy of protecting the right of workers to organise and elect their representatives for collective bargaining. The ethic of that Act was in support of alleviating the conditions of wage slavery in America, even though it can be argued that its thrust is being eroded in contemporary American society. Essentially, the current doctrine is supported by the adherents to and by the intellectual champions of "positive economics" who essentially impute that "unions" unnecessarily interfere against a free market and the profit-making interests of business in its function as the attributed best guarantee to individualism and freedom.

——————

Raymond Samuels

Distribution in the matter of the `scarce-management of resources' by purchasing power only

The contemporary economics that relies on "free market" as supported by positive economics as its intellectual centrepiece emphasises the greater "appropriateness" of the distribution of resources via purchasing power. Households with relatively little money for basic survival are relegated to the vagaries of the so-called free market where their fate may include homelessness, from not having access to affordable housing. Persons with no money and ensuing purchasing power are outside of the economic paradigm of contemporary economics which essentially harbours an indifference to their ensuing fate that is associated to poverty. The positive economics model is indeed a paradigm of social Darwinism. By supporting and condoning economic disparity that is based on relative access to purchasing power, positive economics is essentially indifferent to the fundamental concerns of economic welfare that had initially guided the classical economists who had construed the discipline as the 'management of scarce resources' to that end. World Bank and International Monetary Fund (IMF) policies towards economic development, in association with so-called 'globalisation' that strives to achieve a puritanical and doctrinal positive economic approach, testify the horrendous effects of positive economics on humanity and on management of scarce resources globally. The later globalisation chapter here provides a context to the overall dysfunctionality of the positive economics paradigm.

The macroeconomic application of positive economics condones exploitative human interpersonal relationships that are based on the pursuit of greed that is supportive of vested commercial interests. "Free market" capitalism conditions a culture in which human agents are relegated to the struggle for survival and are forced into wage slavery and the potential for total deprivation from access to basic survival needs; food, clothing and shelter.

Positive economics is based around a correspondent (and largely overlooked) intellectual axiom that people serve the economy. It is therefore consistent for positive economists to accept the proposition that the survival of individuals should be dependent on their relative access to purchasing power. The positive economics focus does not conceive an economy being there to serve the needs of people on behalf of their quality of life. As a result, positive economics has relied on legitimate denial of universal access to highest standards of healthcare available and legitimate condemning areas of cities, whole countries, continents, socioeconomic dislocation, crime, the spread of diseases, famine and starvation and the human rights violations that are associated with transnational corporations that are in the pursuit of their profit margins. Accordingly, in his 1992 Nobel Prize acceptance lecture, the positivist economist Gary Becker of the University of Chicago, in order to rationalise the callousness of positive economics, stated that "the welfare of people cannot be improved in a utopia in which everyone's needs are fully satisfied".

Privatisation: the Social Darwinization of Society

A modern capitalism that embraces so-called "free market" principles that are associated with *laissez faire* also embraces 'privatisation' within an economy. Privatisation refers to public sector/government owned enterprises that are being sold to private, profit-seeking (generally Big Business) enterprises. Community ownership in a cooperative or civic-oriented not-for-profit corporation and/or government-owned enterprises that execute responsible management of scarcity on behalf of citizens of a constitutional democracy can theoretically ensure more readily the achievement of quality-of-life attainments than can be achieved by privatisation.

The norm of an Americanized Big Business culture is an adversarial context among human beings as competing economic agents. Consistent with 'management rights', those who are classified as employees are expected to do what they are told. There is often little, if any, 'grassroots' consultation and direct involvement by these employees in the running of a business enterprise in which they are employees. Capitalism operates under private enterprise or under the state capitalism that is associated to 'communism'. Both operations subordinate decisions to the interests of 'capital' and its proprietorial ownership and in the process marginalise the interests of individuals as human beings, who are essentially dependent on the health of their environment to achieve quality-of-life attainments.

While ethical public administration via community ownership or government in a constitutional democracy can help ensure that public accountability safeguards the management of 'scarcity' in the environment, Big Business provides no such direct accountability. In numerous examples, in order to achieve maximized petty opportunistic relatively short-term profit, Big Business has demonstrated itself as being prepared to pillage and destroy the environment on which people depend for achieving quality-of-life attainments Its operating culture is inherently antidemocratic in its hostility to the inclusion of employees as responsible co-participants in its organisation and development. The often secretive nature of corporate governance, "insider deal-making" and ensuing decision-making, under the directive of principal shareholders with greatest amount of purchased shares, make the large corporation a troublesome owner of "resources" towards the "scarcity management" on which the public depends for achieving access to a high quality-of-life.

Elevated "privatisation" within a society brings with it the elevation of the dysfunctionality that Big Business brings into the public sphere. The "survival of the fittest" orientation of a private enterprise business culture under societal privatisation displaces the proceeding of a community-oriented culture of organisations in a manner that simultaneously subverts the possibility of achieving quality-of-life attainments. However, "Public enterprise" organisation that is corrupt is also not likely to serve quality-of-life attainments. Yet, at least, a "public enterprise" model provides an organisational framework that can provide the constructive basis for quality-of-life attainments if it is responsible, constitutional and democratic in its orientation.

How can Big Businesses with little critical concern for the quality-of-life within the workplace of their employees relative to achieving maximised profit provide a credible model for achieving quality-of-living attainments within the broader institutional context of society? Big Business in its business model of profit, at whatever human or environmental costs, does not provide a constructive lead-model in support of quality-of-life attainments.

The use of privatisation to displace civic community and government leadership in the development of strategic "public enterprises" in areas, in which the "profit ethic" would be harmful to the quality-of-life within a civil rights context, is analogous to a bank capitulating to thieves. Indeed, privatisation supports the legalised theft of what is essentially natural and public endowments and donating them to a relative handful of self-serving barbarians and speculators.

Within the context of 'commercial utilitarianism' (which is explored in the next chapter), Big Business endeavours to assign a financial/market value to any perceived component of nature. It looks upon these components as 'natural resources' that it ought to be able to use its purchasing power to acquire, pillage and/or destroy and then move on to similarly behave. However, there is a place for Big Business in society within achieving the quality-of-living attainments, but only as an engine of trading that is excluded from owning strategic environmental domains, in which the profit ethic would only destroy the environment to detriment the diverse public.

It is vital for Big Business to be circumscribed by overall quality-of-living public policies, including vigilant regulations concerning meaningful human rights protections for employees and also strict anti-pollution standards. The ongoing "survival of the fittest" culture within the political economy of a business culture is usually associated with the abuse of employees, human and civil rights, 'equality rights' and working conditions. These features are usually abused and ignored in the search for achieving the maximised profit. These tendencies with an economy that becomes more and more driven by a Big Business culture undermine societal interests in achieving the quality-of-living.

———•———

Raymond Samuels

Consequences on human interpersonal relationships: Strife, social alienation and criminality

Typically, modern capitalism institutionalises a civilization of inter-personal exploitation that frequently generates ensuing social strife. In it, governments are pressured to diminish or cancel completely various programmes that are developed to alleviate the atrocious hardships that are associated with disparities in financial wealth and purchasing power. Those households which have access to increased privatised financial power and have more disposable income available to them are the data sets that form the incentive to profiteering opportunities on which various corporations that provide goods and services draw. Housing, for example, becomes no more than a profit centre. Corporations simultaneously pursue mass-layoffs of personnel that become substituted by technology such as automation in the insatiable pursuit of profit. The people who are suddenly without jobs must scramble to pay mounting incoming bills. The persons who are unable to earn are more often becoming homeless, without the support of social programmes from welfare to even unemployment insurance, because of governmental unwillingness to focus on access to quality-of-life issues.

Constituencies in the diverse public, who continue to be frustrated by the callousness of Social Darwinization via modern capitalism, may become desperate. Although conditions become harsher in a society where social justice has been extricated from public policy, the drive for human survival continues. If strife continues and becomes more acute, the result has often been a society of rapidly increasing crime with the correspondent decline in human civility that accompanies social darwinization via modern capitalism. The rapid forced social transformations that are being induced into so-called 'Third World' countries via economic privatisation austerity policies, on behalf of so-called 'globalisation' that has been sponsored by the International Monetary Fund (IMF), have indeed often precipitated acute levels of crime in societies which had previously experienced comparatively little, if any, violent crime. Parts of South African, for example, have become the crime 'capital of the world', under an imposed regime of acute economic disparity prescribed by the social Darwinism within modern capitalism.

Modern capitalism's political economic orientation towards privatised wealth over societal quality-of-life attainments degrades a previously nurturing society, where people are caring and are secure in their survival needs inclusive of food, shelter and clothing. Instead, it seeks to transform such societies into an Americanised frontier society of "cowboys and Indians" who are shooting each other out in strategies to achieve 'wealth' and dominance and thereby achieve power.

Privatisation within the context of modern capitalism does not support the 'economic progress' of civilisation. On the contrary, 'privatisation', within the general context of modern capitalism, dissipates into a dysfunctional socioeconomic context of strife that is antithetical to 'human development', the creative output of a dynamic society.

Privatisation specifically enables the undermining of the representative capacity of a democracy via government to protect the basic human rights that are associated with human survival needs and a general defence of the public interest from interests that operate via private greed. Privatisation essentially represents the transfer of government owned or supervised public assets and resources to ownership/management by private corporations. Privatisation is a culture in which government, having transferred previous public accountability in resource management to private corporations, is supposed to ignore the pursuit of greed by these corporation as that greed is executed via irresponsible social activities in their drive for short-term profit. These activities may include reckless air and water pollution emissions, ensuing environmental degradation, and callous 'human resources' policies that include mass layoffs.

CHAPTER 8

COMMERCIAL UTILITARIANISM

"The minds of men will be completely occupied in acquiring wealth, and wealth will be spent solely on selfish gratification. Men will fix their desires upon riches even though dishonestly acquired."

Vishnu Purana

PRIVATE ENTERPRISE capitalism via "positive economics" builds upon a rudimentary definition of 'economics' as the 'management of scarce resources' and transforms the imputation into a supplementary interpretation where 'economics' is construed as an empirical analysis of the commercial utilitarian management of scarce resources, in association with money and related price-commodity relationships.

Positive economics relies on a 'utilitarian' conception of the universe. It regards something as having 'value' to the extent that it can be used as a commodity, assigned a price and then marketed for the commercial ends. Positive economics is 'economics' that is axiomatically concerned about computations which are associated with the supply of money, movement of money, relative value of money i.e. exchange rates and price-commodity relationships. Within its emphasis, people are not viewed within a scarcity management context where they aim to live with nature. Instead, they are viewed as "tamers" of "raw materials" that are living-off nature. The complexity of the human condition and human experience within a dynamic and vital environment beyond commercial considerations that humans rely on for their well-being are substantively marginalised if not virtually ignored as far as the prevailing positive economic paradigm of private enterprise capitalism is concerned. This chapter presents an exploration of the extent to which ongoing commercial utilitarian approaches associated to 'modern capitalism' complement 'wage slavery' and undermine 'quality-of-living' attainments.

Positive economics is preoccupied with fashioning an internally consistent management system for servicing the needs of commerce and profit. Positive economics essentially provides a measurement framework for attributed growth in the market performance of the components that are manipulated by the principal 'owners of capital'. The successful commercial use of features that have been labelled as "human capital" and "natural capital" is then measured on statistical indices, in which the monetary valuation of capital via flows of currency and pricing towards profit are pivotal.

In positive economics, human beings are regarded as little more than 'commercial equivalent entities' who buy and consume goods and services and use resources to achieve measurable commercial ends. Consistent with this approach, government is not a creative agent of a democracy in support of the quality-of-living goals of society, but is an attributed 'neutral' medium to help regulate through the money supply and relations between commercial entities. The contemporary private enterprise focused economics that relies on positive economics uses mathematical equations that help merely rationalise a preconceived Social Darwinistic vision of economic society in order to give a sense of erudition to their paradigmatical context and bamboozle the "less learned" masses. As a result, contemporary economics via capitalism overly equates the spread of commercial practices with economic development.

———•———

Utilitarianism in General: Synoptic Background

The concept of "economic utility" evolved in association with the operation of what was labelled as "utilitarianism". In economics, utility was argued as a measure of the satisfaction that individuals gain from the consumption of a good or a service. The doctrine of utilitarianism saw facilitation of the opportunities of individuals to maximise utility as a moral criterion for the organisation of society. According to utilitarians, such as Jeremy Bentham (17481832) and John Stuart Mill (18061876), the society should aim to maximise the total utility of individuals. Therefore, the aim was 'the greatest happiness for the greatest number'.

Utility was originally viewed as a measurable quantity so that it would be possible to measure the utility of each individual in society and add the results together to give the total utility of all people in society. It was viewed that society could then aim to maximise the total or perhaps the average utility of all people in it. This conception of utility as a measurable quantity that could be aggregated across individuals is called 'cardinal utility'. Notwithstanding this, the concept of cardinal utility suffers from the lack of an objective and interpersonally applicable standard of measurement.

———•———

Commercial Utilitarianism: Defined

'Commercial utilitarianism' refers to the pivotal idea within capitalism that resources are useful only to the extent to which such resources can yield an immediate 'commercial benefit' for its proprietors. Modern capitalism conditions the human psyche to see the world only in terms of value in relationship to the pursuit of making money. The pursuit of money becomes both a means and an end in the operations of achieving more and more money that may be used to acquire more outputs. In the culture of modern capitalism, consideration that is associated to the community, family and social expression of self becomes marginalised in the emphasis of the drive for money. Indeed, this emphasis becomes a whole 'way-of-life' in of itself and its acquisition boosts the egos of individuals who have been seduced to pursue status and power over their fellow human beings.

Individuals and institutions within the community have often been and continue to be easily seduced by the promises of financial and equivalent handouts from prospective colonial masters and private enterprise corporations. The sacred lands of their ancestors, wildlife and the environment are among other vital areas critical to the quality-of-life locally, regionally, nationally and even internationally. They then become easily sold as property to these prospective colonial masters. Individuals and institutions that are seeking a lifestyle which is associated with a culture of capitalism, on having received handouts, seek even more bestowals. Eventually, in the presence of the capitalist creed, the only feature that is left as sacred/enduring is the drive for money and all that it can allow individuals to acquire as trappings of attributed commercial-equivalent success. All else becomes secondary or of no consequence in the accompanying maturation of the 'capitalist creed' towards the New World Order.

———•———

What is a 'resource'?

The meaning of the term 'resource' comes from its root which originally implied life. That root is the Latin verb, 'surgere', evoking the image of a spring continually rising from the ground. Like a spring, a 'resource' rises again and again, even if its capabilities have been repeatedly used and consumed. The word highlighted nature's power of self-regeneration and her prodigious creativity. Moreover, it implied an ancient idea about the relationship between humans and nature that the Earth bestows gifts on humans who, in turn, are well advised not to earn the enmity of nature. In early modern anthropological times, 'resources' therefore suggested reciprocity along with regeneration.

With the advent of industrialism and colonialism, 'natural resources' became the parts of nature that are required as inputs for industrial production and colonial trade. In 1870, John Yeates in his *Natural History of Commerce* offered the first definition of this new meaning: 'In speaking of the natural resources of any country, we refer to the ore in the mine the stone unquarried (etc.).'

Pursuant to this view, nature has been enervated of her creative power and turned into a container for raw materials that are in waiting to be transformed into inputs for commodity production. Resources become merely any materials or conditions that exist in nature which may have potential for appropriate 'economic exploitation'. Voided of a conception of an inherent regenerative capacity, the attitude of reciprocity has also lost ground: it is now viewed that it is simply human inventiveness and industry which 'impart value to nature'. The prevalent view is that natural resources must be developed and nature will only find her destiny once 'capital' and technology have been brought in. Nature, as vital and living, was transformed into non-vital and manipulable matter its capacity to renew itself and grow is essentially denied.

———•———

Implications of a 'resource' conception in the definition economics

Economics has been generally defined as the 'management of scarce resources'. Within this definition lies the central problem of economics in relationship to quality-of-living attainments and 'wage slavery'. The conception of 'resource', within this definition of economics, prescribes a context which views living species and other parts of the environment as simply a myriad of "raw materials" for a "higher economic purpose" (so-to-speak) as ranked by market outcomes. In that context, a resource implies some form of "raw material" from which value is derived via its capacity to be used as "raw material" that is used in a commercial product. The "resource" context that is associated with the definition of economics does not intellectually embrace the inherent value of living species and other parts of the environment which respectively contribute to ecosystems on which human beings depend for their survival and well-being. However, in the chapter that addresses the reality of 'Quantum Economics', an alternative context that accommodates this feature regarding ecosystems and construes a rejuvenated 'management of scarcity' rather than a commercial utilitarian context of economics will be elaborated.

The prevailing commercial utilitarian intellectual conception of 'resources' within the current general economics related paradigm has brought market economic development interests into conflict with environmentalists, members of the scientific community (including ecologists) and other members of the diverse public. Therefore, the current general economics paradigm emphasises an intellectual context in which the "raw materials" in the environment are useful to the extent that such "raw materials" have an instrumental commercial use that is associated with the buying and selling of goods and services. For example, a tree in a rainforest that is not owned as capital for the purpose of making it into lumber or as part land that is to be cleared and built on for some commercial development is not a 'resource' within the conception of the current general economic paradigm and is, therefore, not factored into current calculations concerning economic well-being. Nevertheless, scientific research has demonstrated the critical invaluable contributions that trees, for example, provide for the well-being of the human species and other living species on Earth. In other words, the "resource" context of economics that is at the basis of calculations concerning economic well-being in associated to economic development and "economic growth" is fundamentally misleading and deficient.

————•————

Privatisation and the Civic Alienation from the Environment

It has been argued that 'landowners' have little incentive to invest in long-term measures such as soil conservation if they do not have the right to sell or transfer their land to market centred interests so as to realise the capitalised commercial value of any improvements. This is patently erroneous sophistry since the best examples of soil conservation such as in the hill-terraces of the Himalaya have been realised for precisely the opposite reasons. Communities that are not threatened by alienation of resources and their benefits have the long-term possibility and interest to conserve them. Indiscriminate support to privatisation of areas of the environment from energy to education programmes and Big Business interests alienates citizens from shared civic responsibility and undermines a constitutional democracy.

————•————

The myth of "profit", economic development and growth-associated to natural resources exploitation

Governments under pressure from Big Business culture driven economy give permission to mass-produce "commercial commodities" for a market of buyers and sellers with the goal of facilitating the earning of "profit" that results in economic dysfunctionalities as the destruction of whole forests or "fishing-out" of lakes and oceans that humans depend upon for their survival and quality-of-life. While that is happening, the largely corporate-owned mass-media will legitimate these activities via the dissembled TV newscasts and the radio airwaves. At the same time, the newspaper headlines will, for example, robustly announce the number of jobs that such essentially destructive enterprises have created from the perpetration of their environmental pillaging activities. These activities support the instant self-gratification of the materialistic self-aggrandising of the ownership of these enterprises often to the detriment of human rights and the quality-of-life of individuals and communities in general. The disciples of the Apostles of the capitalists, as economists for the Establishment, will also gather statistical data that are associated to its "market" economics paradigm *to legitimate these actives as contributing to an attributed "economic growth"*.

The "profit" and "economic growth" are recorded from such activities is an apparent myth that is based on the ongoing statistical manipulation of data under the ongoing paradigm championed by the Apostles of private enterprise capitalism. While an apparent relatively immediate monetary profit may be recorded by Big Businesses in their balance sheets, society does not "profit" as a whole from the destruction of whole ecosystems that the diverse public of a society depends on for its continued well-being. The tendency of the capitalist creed is to NOT view fish, trees and other living organisms that must be respected and conserved (as supporting whole ecosystems that the human species vitally depends upon for survival), as part of a global environment of interdependent ecosystems. The tendency of the creed that is proselytised by capitalist economists is to view the environment as "offering" to 'capitalists' who have the purchasing power a myriad of "resources" that can be processed into a marketable commercial products in order to achieve attributed "profit".

While the Establishmentarian economists are quick to record the immediate impact on "derived monetary profits" that is associated with such commercial exploitation, these same economists also do not factor in the ensuing cataclysmic essential losses to a society that arise from the destruction of whole ecosystems. Some environmentalists have championed "sustainable development" as an alternative to a free enterprise oriented economic paradigm that legitimates such rapacious commercial exploitation of the environment. On a cursory review of the sustainable development approach, it does appear to offer an alternative approach to "commercial utilitarianism" that arises within the capitalist economic paradigm. However, it is apparent from a more critical review of "sustainable development" that this so-called alternative approach still essentially relies on a "commercial utilitarian" conception of "resources" and "economic development", because "sustainable development" provides a sensitisation context to "environmental resources" without critically offering a competing paradigm to "market exploitation" as a basis of economic development. Within the sustainable development approach, "natural resources" are still essentially viewed as a form of "capital" that is to be exploited at a slower rate, perhaps but nevertheless commercially exploited.

————◆————

Utilitarianism as a general conceptual theory of "economic good"

Utilitarianism is both a meta-ethical doctrine and a theory in normative ethics. Utilitarianism holds, in its simplest form, that the good is whatever yields the greatest utility. At the same time, meta-ethics is the branch of ethics which studies the nature of ethics itself. The central question is not "What choices are right?" but "What makes a choice right?" Historically, proponents of significant meta-ethical theories in addition to 'utilitarianism' also include Aristotle, Thomas Aquinas and Immanuel Kant. 'Utility' is generally understood to be roughly pleasure or happiness. As a meta-ethical doctrine, it holds that "whatever yields the greatest utility" is the meaning of the word "good", thus it is a naturalistic theory of meta-ethics. However, as a normative theory, it merely holds that "whatever yields the greatest utility" is, in fact, good whatever the meaning of the word "good" may be.

Utilitarianism was originally proposed in 18th century by Jeremy Bentham and others. However, the concept can be traced back to ancient Greek philosophers such as Epicurus. As originally formulated, utilitarianism holds that the good is whatever brings the greatest happiness to the greatest number of people.

Historically, the concept of utilitarianism suffers from a number of problems, one of which is the difficulty of comparing achieved levels of happiness between different people. Many of the early utilitarians believed that happiness could somehow be measured quantitatively and compared between people through some form of "felicific calculus". However, the computation has not so far been constructed in practice. In addition, it has since been argued that the happiness of different people is incommensurable, therefore a felicific calculus is impossible.

Utilitarianism has been opposed because it tends to lead to a number of conclusions that are contrary to common sense morality. For example, if one were given the choice of saving one's child or two strangers, a general approach to utilitarianism suggests saving the strangers instead of one's child, because two people will have more total future happiness than one. This imputation seems contrary to common sense practice, especially in light of the feelings of duty that individuals have towards those individuals who are close family members.

Daniel Dennett uses the example of Three Mile Island in the United States. Against that background, the following background question arises. Was the near-meltdown that occurred at this nuclear power plant a good or a bad thing (according to utilitarianism)? He points out that its long-term effects on nuclear policy would be considered beneficial by many (at least it wasn't a Chernobyl!). His conclusion is that it is still too early (20 years after the event) for utilitarianism to weigh all the evidence and reach a conclusion.

Methods to try and get around some of these cases have been formulated into proposals about different varieties of utilitarianism. The traditional form of utilitarianism is "act utilitarianism" which states that each act is to be evaluated individually. An alternative form that has been often proposed is "rule utilitarianism", where the principle of "whatever yields the greatest utility" is applied not to individual acts, but is applied to decide upon ethical rules. These ethical rules may then be applied to individual acts. Another variety of utilitarianism is "preference utilitarianism", where rather than maximising utility, the ethical objective is to try to satisfy everyone's preferences. Peter Singer is a proponent of preference utilitarianism who has been attributed to use it to derive some highly controversial conclusions.

John Stuart Mill wrote a famous (but short) book entitled *Utilitarianism*. It was about Utilitarianism as a concept and as a modus operandi. Although Mill was a utilitarian, he argued that not all forms of happiness are of equal value. He illustrated that using his famous saying; "It is better to be Socrates unsatisfied than a pig satisfied." Notwithstanding, this attributed representation of Utilitarianism that is associated to John Stuart Mill provides a potentially useful concept. It can be applied to evaluate the purpose of economic development as a method towards the achievement of the attributed "greatest happiness" from the management of scarcity within the environment. Should an economy seek to fulfill the "greatest happiness" associated with the speculative developmental pursuits of "owners of capital" or should an economy seek to fulfill the "greatest happiness" that may be associated with prioritisations that are not necessarily forthcoming from commercial operations?

Private "commercial utility" versus public utility in a democratic society

Utilitarianism was initially applied to a conception of the satisfaction of human wants of an individual in a general context that was not limited to a commercial-orientation. Utilitarianism declined from the principal focus of economics as problems in the quantification of utility became apparent. The satisfaction of the wants of diverse individuals could not be simply quantified and accumulated so as to give an aggregate outcome. The economics profession turned to market economics with its well-developed system of quantification of "economic growth" as aggregate economic equivalent data that are associated to a myriad of exchange transactions. However, utilitarianism remained a tacit intellectual premise of the market economics paradigm. What substantively remained as a tacit part of the market economic paradigm was, in fact, commercial in its orientation. Appreciation of the satisfaction of human wants was restricted to a posited concentration of individuals on marketable outputs or products in a consumer society. Indeed, the Apostles of capitalism in their formulation of market economics did not conceive as being empirically important in a positivist context the "satisfaction of human wants" that were outside of impacts that operate through commerce.

———•———

Modern Capitalism and Human Needs

Modern capitalism was not designed to support responsiveness to human needs in a democracy that prioritises quality-living attainments. Indeed, modern capitalism has revealed itself to be an ideology that does little more than a legitimated mechanism that is used by the most commercially powerful of society to maintain their economic hegemony or 'empire'. The apostles of capitalism turned to political propaganda in a Cold War era, declared victory with the fall of the Soviet empire and used that declaration to proclaim the alleged triumph of this economic system. While democracy articulates a representative context for all citizens in society that will also be in support of tenets of equality, equity, human and civil rights, modern capitalism has an emphasis only on financial-equivalent results. Modern capitalism conceives political economic management via a so-called market which legitimates effective strife and the unsustainable long-term exploitation of resources by the owners of capital. In a modern capitalist paradigm, society exists to serve the profit targets of the principal owners of capital rather than to serve the survival needs of a diverse public

———•———

"Total Depletion of Resources" Towards an 'Environmental Holocaust'

In a constitutional democracy where government is a representative and responsible agent of the diverse public, government intervenes to protect the interests of the diverse public. In Ontario, Canada, this protection involved the government acquisition of hydroelectricity as a public monopoly. In doing so, the public interest could be safeguarded from profiteering by private enterprise from electricity as an essential resource. Such profiteering would have a deleterious impact on both the public and businesses. Democracy via government intervention can help protect the health of ecosystem through environmental conservation-related legislation on behalf of high quality biological survival for all species. Constitutional democracy embraces the environment as a common-wealth for all citizens that requires vigilant protection from the excesses of profit-making interests of rapacious private enterprise.

Left alone by government, the only limit to the execution of the destructive capabilities of Big Business on the environment is its purchasing power capacity to acquire property and deploy its tools of destruction along with its self-conceived ability to turn out a profit from the fruits of its destruction. The capitalist creed does not respect the sanctity of human life or living species in the environment. All that the capitalist creed can see regarding the environment includes unexploited resources to enable the making of products and the provision of goods and services that facilitate corporate earnings, thereby to help propel stocks and commercial value which is associated with other capital investments. Indeed, left totally alone, all commercially exploitable forests, fisheries and other precious ecosystems would be totally destroyed with the correspondent rise of pollution and precipitation of further environmental degradation. If the remainder of the community continues to be seduced by the immediate apparent material benefit of a "consumer society" as the course of the destruction of the environment becomes evident and irreversible, it will be too late for high quality survival. Results such as catastrophic health problems that are associated with ozone depletion, apocalyptic changes in climate, global oxygen depletion from the mass destruction of the rain forests, forthcoming famine, poverty and the spread of diseases on a global scale and accompanying social upheaval are engendered by a Social Darwinistic market-oriented development paradigm. The orthodox response to the protection of the capitalist status quo from prevailing rampant crime and terrorism has not been to alleviate the socially iniquitous conditions of economic disparity that support such rampant crime and terrorism. Indeed a quality-of-life focus that encompasses human rights and social justice would redress rampant crime and terrorism often associated with endemic conditions of social malaise and the dehumanising alienation of poverty. The alternative response of a capitalist political economy, essentially antagonistic to democracy to rampant crime and terrorism, has been a drive to international fascism, hostile to redressing fundamental "market" economic induced causes of rampant crime and terrorism.

CHAPTER 9

HUMAN CAPITAL

⤫

"Fortunately, education is of considerable interest in its own right and a matter of much current concern: laymen, policymakers and researchers are all worrying about the role of education in promoting economic and cultural progress as well as the ways to improve the educational process".

Gary S. Becker, *Human Capital: A Theoretical and Empirical Analysis, with Special Reference to Education*, p. 69, 1964.

T O "FREE-MARKET"-ORIENTED modern capitalism, the diverse public as "the masses" is merely a resource pool for a 'commercial society', where wages are roughly determined by the needs of firms in the market in relation to the availability of skills that are offered and needed by the market. Wage slavery is the outcome of the subversion of a conception of the rights of free individuals, who are engaged in work even though these rights had been framed into the protected and inviolable civil rights that are associated with a parliamentary constitutional system. These rights include anti-discrimination laws, social justice, working conditions and the institution of work as being more than a market-manipulated resource. While wage slavery is the basis of the 'use of human resource' in a commercial society, a human development approach that rejects humans merely a form of capital is the basis of a rejuvenated 'renaissance economy'. The aim is to generate quality-of-living attainments for a diverse public in a pluralistic democratic society.

———•———

The Origin of 'Human Capital' Within the Market Economics Paradigm

The view of economic development that was disseminated by Theodore Schultz, who, like Friedman, was a member of the University of Chicago School, was grounded in the conviction that agricultural development is a precursor to industrialisation. In applying positivist economic analysis to agriculture in poor countries, Schultz proposed that human capabilities, as capital, could be applied and exploited in a correspondent manner that is commonly applied to mechanical capital. The result was a theory of investment where the productivity of human capital could function as the wellspring of development and a primary solution to the problem of poverty. Among his publications were *Agriculture in an Unstable Economy* (1945), *The Economic Value of Education* (1963), *Economic Growth and Agriculture* (1968), *Investment in Human Capital* (1971) and *Investing in People: The Economics of Population Quality* (1981). Schultz won the Nobel Peace Prize thanks to identification of human capital as a critical operating component that enabled market economies to challenge how the communist system saw human labour as being accommodated in the capitalist society.

———•———

Education as a means of intellectually launching Human Capital theory

Education had been critically viewed within public policy priorities as a means to support the basic literacy that was needed by individuals to support their own self-development priorities and interests within society. Education had also been seen, prior to institutionalisation of Chicago school orthodoxy, to be enhancing their ability to control their own lives through various occupational areas associated with work, such as labour, in an economy. In the Chicago School precipitated evolution of the modern theory of capitalism, education has been shifted from being a means that enabled the individual in a democracy to support his/her own intellectual-related personal objectives and envisioned personal growth towards the realisation of his/her own self-directed contributions to society. The shift was made to the conception of education, in which information-acquiring humans are viewed as making investments in their skills, such as 'capital', via schooling towards greater "income" and market output.

Human capital theory has been heralded as being conceptually pivotal in explaining the development of capitalistic society. It was argued that the focus presents an innovative approach to explaining how economic output is supported as individuals are motivated to invest in themselves so as to reap the promise of a future greater economic payoff for themselves and the society as a whole as a result of that investment.

———◆———

'Human capital' theory outlined

The theory of human capital conceptualises skills as the product of investments that have been made in the technical training of individuals via formal and informal education and schooling. The theory frames a generally-accepted economic model to the extent that it has been propounded by prestigious economists at prestigious schools and has been accepted by capitalists as being pertinent to their priorities. The achievements of the human capital school, according to its adherents, explain why people go to college; it predicts the increased earnings which are associated with additional schooling or training and it has redirected economic analysis of education and earnings to life cycle models and away from current wages.

Human capital theory represents the 'modern capitalist' approach to the economics of education and training. It highlights the attributed qualitative aspect of labour as an economic input: "... human capital refers to the productive capacities of human beings as income producing agents in the economy" (Rosen, 1987, p. 681). According to Schultz (1961), human capital consists of health, skills and knowledge which have economic value. Human capital theory has focused mainly on the market productive value of education and training. The relative neglect of health as a component of human capital reflects the fact that until recently neoclassical labour economics had been directed mainly towards developed countries, where returns to incremental health are low. However, in developing countries, increments in health may result in high productive value and substantially increase the returns to education and training (Gill and Khandker, 1991, p. 2).

The investment aspect is essential in the human capital theory. The acquisition of human capital through education and training is an investment in the sense that the individual foregoes current income for increased earnings potential in the future (McNabb, 1994, p. 3). "A sacrifice for the sake of learning today is rewarded tomorrow (Psacharopoulos, 1988).

The theory of human capital is used to analyse the effects of skills development on productivity and income generation at the microeconomic and macroeconomic level. At the microeconomic level, human capital theory maintains that good health, knowledge and skills raise labour productivity, which in turn influences economic activity and societal well-being. The acquisition of cognitive abilities, the formation of competence and the transfer of information are considered the major link between schooling/training and productivity (Bowman, 1980). The basic assumption of human capital theory, in general equilibrium theory, is that the wage rate is determined by the marginal productivity of the worker. Wage differentials between persons are explained in terms of their education and working experience. The income difference between workers is considered to be the return on investment in human capital provided the workers had the information-guided foresight to make optimal choice between industries.

At the macroeconomic level, new economic growth theories have formulated models to explain long-run growth of per-capita income by introducing human capital into the neoclassical growth model. The effect of human capital on growth is the enhancement of labour productivity. The increase in "effective labour" or labour in efficiency units provides permanent incentives to accumulate production factors, thereby stimulating long-term growth of per-capita income (Lucas, 1988).

The evolution of human capital to a human resources approach

The human resources context of economic development within 'modern capitalism' indeed evolved from the human capital conception critically initiated by Theodore Schultz and further embellished by Gary S. Becker, a protagonist of the University of Chicago School senior faculty like Schultz that operated as Apostles of modern capitalism. 'Human resources' included both the quantitative (size of population, age structure) and qualitative aspects of human beings. Schultz (1961, p.8) maintained that "Human resources obviously have both quantitative and qualitative dimensions. The number of people i.e. the proportion who enters into useful work and the hours worked are quantitative characteristics. I shall neglect these and consider only quality components such as skill, knowledge and similar attributes that affect particular human capabilities to do productive work."

To Smith, Mill, Bentham and List, "labour is distinguished into mere physical exertion and the skill and mental power displayed in the exercise of the bodily act (Bentham, quoted in Kiker, 1966, p. 487). In contrast, Walras, von Thönen and Fisher consider human beings as capital which reflects the notion of "human resources. Following Fisher's definition of capital, the skill of an individual is not capital in addition to the individual himself. It is the skilled individual, who should be placed in the category of capital (Fisher quoted in Kiker, 1966, p. 488).

While human capital theory considers knowledge and cognitive skills as the most important link to productivity, the human resource approach further took into account a variety of links between individuals' capabilities and their productivity. People are born with different talents and individual traits that may make them inherently more productive in certain occupations. The socialisation and 'correspondence' approaches (Colclough, 1982) stress the role of non-cognitive or affective as well as motivational and psychological dimensions of human resources in productivity. Education and training may have an important impact on a person's values, attitudes, norms (socialisation effect), motivation and expectations (psychological effects) and behaviour (McNabb, 1994, p. 6). These are factors that influence a human being's capacity as well as willingness to work effectively and are considered important elements in the formation of the economic capability of human resources.

Incorporating the general human capital conceptual framework, the human resource focus is oriented to the development as well as to the utilisation of humans *as resources/implements*. Human resource utilisation is the extent to which available technical capabilities of humans are deployed effectively or contribute to the maximum achievement of individual, collective, organisational or national goals and objectives. Effective human resource utilisation for development may involve human resource allocation, maintenance and further development (Kiggundu, 1989, p. 151). "Human resources... constitute the ultimate basis for the wealth of nations... The goals of development are the maximum possible utilisation of human beings in more productive activity and the fullest possible development of the skills, knowledge and capacities of the labour force ..." (Harbison, 1973, p. 3, 115). Furthermore, while human capital refers only to the productive value of people, the human resource approach evolved to refer to economic as well other instrumental uses. What was viewed as human resources evolved to incorporate human capital theory in the context of the development of capitalistic society.

———•———

Human Development': the basis of an alternative framework?

The concept of human development was supported by ideas of A. K. Sen, elaborated by Mahbubul Haq and promoted by the United Nations Development Programme (UNDP). Sen defined development in terms of functionings achieved. Therefore, he argued that "one of the functionings that may be thought to be particularly important in assessing the nature of development is the freedom to choose" (Sen, 1991, p.16). Human development is defined as enlarging people's choices, where the choices range from political, economic and social freedom to opportunities for being creative and productive and enjoying personal self-respect and human rights (UNDP, 1990, p.15).

The human development concept is based on essential ideas. Firstly, human development becomes the real end of activities. Therefore, it moves *people* (or essentially impacts on people) to the centre stage of development. Secondly, human development relates to the formation of human capabilities and the use the acquired capabilities of people. Thirdly, a distinction is made between ends and means. People are regarded as the ends. However, they are also means of development. Fourthly, the human development concept embraces of the entire society. The political, cultural and social factors are given as much attention as economic factors (Haq, 1995, p. 16).

Haq considers four essential components of human development and to each of them human resources are assigned an important role. The four pillars are equitable access to opportunities, sustainability of human opportunities, productivity and growth and empowerment of people, meaning that people are placed in a position to exercise their own choices (Haq, 1995, p. 16 20). The level achieved on each of these pillars indicates the extent of people's economic, social, political and cultural choices.

Practitioners of human capital theory have viewed the formation and utilisation of human resources as one important policy measure to enhance the levels of the various pillars. Human development is viewed as providing the intellectual basis for the removal of barriers that limit the access of women, minorities or other groups to key economic and political opportunities. Within the context of human capital theory, higher productivity and growth require investment in people and human capital. Capital empowerment among many other factors requires investing in education and health so that people can take advantage of market opportunities as well as social and political opportunities and are able to participate in those activities, events and processes that shape their lives (Haq, 1995, p. 20). Expanding people's choices within the human development context constitutes the ultimate objective of development where choices are related to economic, political and social variables. Hence, the abstract variable i.e. human development is defined by economic, social and political dimensions. It has been pointed out that the human resource approach also relates to economic, social and political development goals. However, the correspondent human resources-related approach views human beings as *implements* in relationship to commerce-centre institution of work *in contradistinction with 'human development'*.

Here, human development is emphasised as being an outcome of the opportunities for using their time that is available to socialised human economic agents.

———•———

Critique of human capital

The idea of 'human capital' is an attempt by the Economics Establishment to get people within society to link their time-investment priorities to the 'human resources' requirements that are desired by a commercially-centred Big-Business-dominated private enterprise-oriented economy. Human capital was initially developed by Theodore Schultz who was from the University of School and had won the Nobel Peace Prize thanks to his contribution to the recognition that in the execution of development, human capital existed as an effective substitute for machine capital.

Before the human capital approach became critically recognised by economic practitioners and accepted as the basis for economic development, the resource base of the economy was conceived to consist of 'land', 'labour' and 'capital'. This accepted economic triad was the basis of economic strife within society into the 1960's, between labour as the 'workforce' that had a conceived intrinsic separate identity relative to 'owners of capital' who held investment stakes in large corporate enterprises.

The 'human capital' approach essentially assimilated a conceptualisation of 'labour' into the intellectual framework that had already existed for the recognition of 'capital'. This re-engineering of 'labour' (the providers of skills), as merely another form of capital, was later reflected by corporations and other organisations that changed the name of the departments concerned with job recruitment/staffing from 'personnel' to 'human resources' departments.

———•———

Raymond Samuels

Social Re-engineering of society via the education system

When T.W. Schultz developed human capital theory as an econometric model using the agricultural sector as an entrée, it was heralded as an innovative approach that would provide a useful new economic paradigm for American farmers and government decision-makers that would contribute to the revitalisation of American financing of agriculture. Becker's human capital paradigm that was critically based on the initial contributions of Schultz concerning human capital was pivotally oriented around education. The use of the human capital emphasis was, indeed, consistent with the facilitation of the corporatisation of society via education.

Education, before the perspectives of the human capital approach, was primarily conceived as a means of social empowerment through self-directed intellectual development. However, the combination of a vibrant movement towards democracy, an individualistic society, with a correspondent critical and nonconformist approach to education proved to be explosive in America during the 1960's. An education system that is guided substantively by principles of constitutional democracy will produce 'freethinkers'.

Such 'freethinkers' are inherently nonconformist. Students, who become graduates of such an educational system, are socialised to be idealists. Sometimes, graduates of such an education system, in their idealism, assertive of the equality rights of others and their rights that might be ignored by the institutional landscape, and nonconformity, may be even outright rebellious.

The 1960's, which was the apex of the manifestation American constitutional democracy in education in general and higher education in particular, did not turn out the 'best workers' from the perspective of corporate America. These independent-minded people also embraced all sorts of social movements that included anti-War sentiment in relationship to Vietnam; sympathy for economic democracy via unions; correspondent rejection of corporate exploitation; civil rights; and other demands for equality; including radical feminism and vocalised rejections of crass materialism.

What corporate America wanted were not independent-minded people who would potentially challenge authoritarian control by management. Such graduates helped invigorate American society in the 1960's from its comparative rather pedestrian conservatism that was pervasive in 1950's and prior decades. However, the corporate culture values *workers* that it can control while asserting its dominance in the process.

The corporate culture in America is not interested in the operational invigoration of forthcoming American society that was guided by the Declaration of Independence and the American Constitution.

To corporate America, constitutional democracy is an impediment to achieving the sought control over their own business organisations in particular and society in general. Education, in its former orientation in America and elsewhere, undoubtedly contributed to a broadly conceived economic development. The problem, however, from the corporate perspective is that the graduates of this educational system not only produced an "undesirable" mix of prospective independent-minded employees that was a threat to capitalist management, but also produced political idealists that rose to public office by the support of a like-minded electorate.

These political idealists, perhaps best symbolised by the Robert Kennedy bid to become President of the United States in the 1960's, too often championed policies viewed as "anti-corporate". Such democratic idealists threatened to move society into an "undesired" social economic utopia, in their apparent over-enthusiasm for seeking to fulfill the promise of the American Dream. Therefore, to corporate America, efforts towards such a 'utopia' had to be checked.

The human capital context provided an approach that could be used to make the link between education and economic development as opposed to a more "abstract link" that came with broader social and cultural development within the context of a democracy. Via the human capital focus, the emphasis is that people should logically invest in schooling and general training that can most readily yield optimised longer term income benefits through employability. Becker's human capital theory was used to co-opt education from a conception of individuals acquiring

critical mental faculties and skills (in self-development, as critical participatory agents in democracy) to a conception of schooling as a means of
getting skills that are linked to getting a job.

The human capital paradigm is an approach that focuses on the technical capability that people can provide to the market economic interests
of corporate growth via schooling and training. As a result, relative to an
individual's choice for liberal education like art, philosophy and literature,
the human capital paradigm embraces vocational education as being
more of a rational choice for investment in education and/or training.
Therefore, the human capital approach is used to encourage individuals
to give-up educational and other pursuits in disciplinary areas that are
potentially intellectually challenging to the status quo in favour of more
vocational schooling that is influenced by corporate financial sponsorship, where the graduates will also be more easily assimilated in their
workforces. Educators are seduced to encourage students to give up their
"proactive" liberal education for the promise of timely instant materialistic
gratification that will be afforded by higher salaries in technical careers
that corporations require.

Through the successful proselytization of human capital focus, traditional safeguards by higher education, university and college system to
protect "academic freedom" in association to students and faculty from
corporate intrusion, have been broken down. Indeed, from the 1990's and
into the turn of the twenty-first century, most of prevailing secondary
and post-secondary education has become little more than essentially
vocational training for getting specific job(s) in a corporatized context,
divested from *Cosmopolitan Human Development*. Such a *cosmopolitan Developmental* context would focus on affirming an individual's
own driven self-actualised participatory economic contributions as a
citizen-participant in a dynamic pluralistic and synergistic community
supportive of civil and human rights. This would be an alternative to a
so-called 'human capital' focus of society where humans conform to
corporatized-commercial developmental priorities. The concept of 'cosmopolitan community' is further explored in the book entitled *National
Identity in Canada and Cosmopolitan Community*.

The 'human capital' emphasis wrestled education away from a constitutional democratic orientation to a capitalist orientation, in which

people could be much more easily controlled as "socialised technical implements". Through the perspective on individuals as human capital, people are to be socialised to forgo broader intellectual self-development in favour of the promise of achieving more immediate income benefits by assimilating and conforming their educational interest to the technical job-related 'human resources' demands of corporate America.

The human capital focus has legitimated massive corporate financial input and managerial influence into university/college systems that has served to co-opt former academic independent-mindedness of both students and faculty. This development has also served to critically reorient the offering of "higher" education courses away from critical questioning and towards producing like-minded prospective employees (as well as purchasers of *commercial-driven corporate outputs*) with the pool of skills that corporations can rely upon to support corporate expansion.

Relatively bereft of their creative potential as independent thinkers, the graduates of this human capital focused educational system, from citizens in the electorate to those who become politicians, are now from a new "educational" experience. These students are exposed to corporate-sponsored buildings, classrooms, bursaries, foundations, libraries, courses and all facilities that had been earlier banned up to the 1970's and into the 1980's in Canada and the U.S. Having been more "appropriately" conditioned by the prevailing human-capital focused "educational" system, ensuing graduates will more readily link the progress of private (commercial) enterprise with the conceived simultaneous progress of individual and the progress of societal economic well-being in general. The human capital emphasis provides a useful and apparently benign context for the execution of covertly "politicised", socially controllable economic development.

The human capital emphasis also provides the framework to support corporate intrusion in the education system from kindergarten and Grade 1 with the provision of free computers and internet access to school boards that (Trojan Horse) bypasses teachers and imprints the young impressionable kids to a corporate culture in a classroom setting. Furthermore, the attitude shaping towards the corporate culture will be continued all the way to college and university.

From the 1960's, in a culture of rebelliousness, even into the 1980's, the interests of students as far as their reasons for choosing higher education were more relatively intellectual. Frequently, when they were asked why they chose to go to university after graduating from high school, their reasons would generally pivot around an interest in simply furthering their education in areas that they wanted to explore in their intellectual self-development. These prospective university students would often indicate an interest in 'making a difference' in areas relative to the quality-of-living of their family and the society as a whole. These students were often altruistic in their educational pursuits, seeking to pursue interests which would hopefully propel themselves into positions of social, cultural and political leadership. Their vision of "economic progress" was inextricably intertwined and indivisible from the essential pursuit of quality-of-living attainments that motivated their interests in higher education.

The breaking down of the Berlin Wall, the decline of the Soviet empire and the thawing of Cold War tensions between 'East' and 'West' provided a critical breakthrough in the proselytization of modern private enterprise capitalism. During Cold War tensions between the two Superpowers(the United States and the Soviet Union), American private enterprise capitalism had to temper its stridence. Socialist systems sprang up and claimed to be offering an attractive compromise, so-to-speak, between these two extreme essentially capitalistic systems. Such systems were prevalent in Scandinavia, the Netherlands, Canada, the United Kingdom and other parts of the world that continued to embrace the tenets that are associated to the 'welfare state' that is decried by private enterprise capitalism.

The disintegration of the Soviet empire provided a basis to declaring the 'victory' of private enterprise capitalism and helped also subvert politically "anti-private enterprise" socialist systems and correspondingly provided a basis for supporting the 'human capital' paradigm in an insurgent capitalist-directed globalised corporate agenda.

Notably, the targets that the institution of education is required to meet are central to the health of a democratic society. By nurturing an ethos of constitutional democracy, an educational system (from primary school to higher education) will increase social/socio-economic value. Such a milieu stimulates the implementation of public policies that support nonconformist "freethinking" as well as the value of tenets of democracy. These include equality, human and civil rights, civic responsibility, individualism and social justice. Such an education system will value a milieu in which people can acquire the skills to control their own lives and can contribute to overall quality-of-living attainments through their envisioned constructive contribution to society.

When the human capital focus ends up subverting the institution of education in relationship to democracy, the whole society can be conquered without the use of the military. When the employment-centred focus is able to direct the teaching curricula that setting for education as well as the general milieu in which impressionable kids are taught and socialised, it enables the affected generations and the whole society to be eventually transformed into an image. Furthermore, currently the one that is being promoted is the image which complements the goals of the institutional body corporate.

In it, citizens in an erstwhile democratic society and citizens of traditional and other societies with varying social systems become "socialised or conditioned into being "market-investment seeking" commercial entities that are essentially "corporate approved".

In these circumstances, the educational priorities of citizens will have become adapted primarily to the priorities of the commercial investment targets of the vested interests of Big Business. Students will end up seeking to structure their educational pursuits to ensure the compatibility of these pursuits with the skills demands of corporations. Pressured by corporations, the public service in general and education within the public sector in particular become adapted to facilitate private enterprise market interests.

———•———

Raymond Samuels

From Personnel Departments to Human Resources Department

With the gradual and precipitous rise of the labour movement in Canada, the United States, and abroad, the drive by "owners of capital" for insatiable profit was frequently tempered by the demands of employees in the workforce. The bellicose and frequently uncompromising management style by "owners of capital" that presided over Big Business (in Canada, the Unites States and the United Kingdom), together with militant employees that were represented by unions, often led to work stoppages. During this era, the staffing needs by corporations were supported by 'departments of personnel'. Such personnel departments which continued into the 1980's operated on a continued recognition of people as sources of labour effort within the context of corporate organisational development.

With the triumph of capitalism in the post-Cold War era and the correspondent ascendancy of the human capital paradigm towards a sought 'New Economic World Order', 'Personnel Departments' were replaced or essentially renamed in favour of 'Human Resources Departments'. This development represented more than a fashionable change name and instead represented an entire de-evolution in philosophical orientation towards 'people'. The question was the extent to which people would be accommodated as a part of a socially responsive corporate management framework or would be treated as just another form of capital or implement from investment decisions.

People as 'human capital', within the drive for the 'New World Economic Order' into the 1990's, were viewed to be a 'commercial utilitarian resource'. Like trees, livestock, land, buildings and other corporate assets, people were to be correspondingly managed to ensure maximum market measured commercial-equivalent output that allowed rising profit opportunities.

————•————

The ushering in of the technological society

The rise of the information-driven technological society brings with it the promise of the delivery of output which is supportive of high quality-of-living attainments. Protagonists of the desirability of the rise of the technological society can highlight changes such as important medical breakthroughs, the ease of communication between people and institutions that have been aided by from cell phones to computers and other material comforts that have been made possible by technological innovation. Indeed, it was frequently argued that forthcoming technological development which receives public support should be mindful of the need to foster the tenets of quality-of-life attainments and constitutional democracy. When medical breakthroughs are not made accessible to all citizens equitably through a universal healthcare system, overall quality of life attainment is threatened. For example, in Canada, under pressure of American private enterprise interests, the conditions of equity that operate in the Canadian healthcare system are being threatened. Correspondingly, the redressing of poverty had been the announced goal within the 'Great Society' platforms of President Lyndon Johnson of the United States during the 1960's. However, that has not become a national priority with the aim to redress disparity and create access to opportunities that are associated within technological development. Notably, in the United States and elsewhere, since that time, as the technological society evolves, democracy has become little more than a public relations pronouncement that goes ignored behind essentially the 'human capital' subversion interests of modern capitalism.

The 'human resources' approach within the consolidating capitalist culture of corporate America has been used to institutionalise the context of 'wage slavery', where a culture uses education as an instrument of 'human capital' formation rather than an instrument to complement human development.

In addition, by successfully emphasising corporate-centred vocational education and a covert subverting of unions and governments as equalising forces in defence of the interests of employees in participatory economic development, the human capital focus promotes a dependency oriented culture of work.

The culture that is being entrenched is one in which the promoted benefits of vocational education and training that were promised by representatives of corporations in the classroom and at job fairs are replaced with eventual realisation of the cold and grim reality of a corporate environment within a consolidating 'New World Economic Order'. This is an environment where profit is extracted for the 'owners of capital' and the majority shareholders of corporate enterprise who enjoy lifestyles of material opulence, even though that lifestyle is propped up by a wage-depressed workforce of 'human capital'. Yet, that conditioned human capital oriented milieu is unlike the one which was 1960's environment, where an articulate public had been able to potentially rebel in the knowledge of their citizenship rights in a vital democracy that they had gleaned from a critical liberal education.

Currently, unlike the socialisation that had been associated with the intellectual rebelliousness of higher education that reached in apex in the 1960's and continued to be prevailing in 1980's, we now have a different context. Subsequent dispensed vocational education conditions students and graduates to think of themselves as little more than "unlucky pawns of marshalled capital."

———•———

The undermining of social structures

Constitutional democracy is aimed at social structures such as the vitality of family and the community. Constitutional democracy affirms itself via its support for social structures that enshrine respect for equality, individuality and the right of citizens to be able to participate in society as well as their opportunities to achieve broad quality-of-living attainments. In a true constitutional democracy, commercial interests are always secondary to the sanctity of the protection of the human rights and the quality-of-living attainments of a diverse public.

The 'human capital' paradigm of economic development, in contradistinction to the requirement of a constitutional democracy, subordinates profit supportive market schemes, social structures that include family, friendship, all the way to community in a pluralistic society. The human capital focus as alluded in the preceding representation institutionalises a context, where human beings view themselves principally as commercial seeking entities, which use self-investment to optimise net market equivalent gains via increased earnings expectation and material benefit through the expectation of ensuing higher purchasing power and market results. Such a cultivated attitude towards personal time and effort commitment, such as education, pivotally and dysfunctionally affects otherwise healthy and vital social interpersonal relationships. A poignant example is the changing attitudes towards marriage in respective Americanised Western industrial societies. In such circumstances, the former sanctity of marriage is replaced with an apparent view of marriage as some form of investment that can appreciate like a mutual fund or as annuity in which one partner can secure a *financial* payoff via a divorce.

The 'human capital' paradigm institutionalises a whole material cost/benefit centred way of life for persons who are conditioned to pursue its outlook. As persons are socialised within such an educational system and make effort commitment calculations which are based on market cost/benefit analysis, they are also socialised to make corresponding calculations in matters that are related to personal association. Social structures, including marriage, family and other social relationships, become screened within corresponding calculations about the apparent market profitability that is associated with the maintenance of ongoing relationships. Indeed, persons are easily seduced into making choices to engage in treachery against their fellow human beings and even into committing crime if that commitment can secure the immediate sought-after financial benefits to help secure other potentially profitable relationships.

The human capital focus fosters a milieu in which human beings become alienated from one another with the accompanying breakdown of complex communal interpersonal relationships as they are reduced to being competing technical implements that complement a corporate techno-structure. People find that they have less time for general living as corporations instil mass insecurity, with threats of layoffs and outright job cuts. The employer, not having to worry about vigilant unions, uses the insecurity of layoffs, job-cuts and likely ensuing divorce and social hardships to make excessive demands on their employees. Workers, particularly so-called 'visible minorities' and immigrants, face pervasive exploitation in what may very well be unsafe and horrendous working conditions. But after all, to the body corporate, these individuals are simply human capital that is among other invested capital which is at the disposal of employers in their drive for profit earning. There, the institution of work via 'human capital' becomes a process of wage slavery that is divested from quality-of-living attainments. People are seen to work not as an affirmation of sought and chosen living-centred economic participation within a constitutional democracy, but simply in fear of an even worse fate; total functional dislocation from their survival options.

CHAPTER 10

Limited Government: Limit Democracy

༄

Ideologies about the goals of economically rational policies convey the inevitability of a clash between human rights principles and corporate interests. On the one hand, the free flow of influences in the marketplace is regarded as providing the best conditions to do business. On the other hand, adherence to human rights requires governments to intervene to counteract the worst effects of market forces to protect the vulnerable individuals, including women, children and indigenous people, promote better labour conditions and protect the environment.

Stuart Rees and Shelley Wright, "Human Rights and usiness Controversies", in *Human Rights and Corporate Responsibility: A Dialogue*, p. 8, 2000.

A government which maintained law and order defined property rights, served as a means whereby we could modify property-rights and other rules of the economic game and adjudicate disputes about the interpretation of the rules, enforced contracts, promoted competition, provided a monetary framework, engaged in activities to counter technical monopolies and overcome neighbourhood effects widely regarded as sufficiently important to justify govern-

> *ment intervention and supplemented private charity and the private family.*
>
> Milton Friedman, "Government in a Free Society", *Capitalism and Freedom*, p. 34, 1965.

D OGMATIC POLITICAL proponents of the free market private enterprise ostensibly champion "limited government". These proponents evoke a romanticised American Wild West frontier society of "cowboys and Indians" living off the land and fighting each other within a context of the "survival of the fittest". To these proponents, this is what "freedom" is all about. A barbaric society with laws that are enforced in the interest of the most powerful of society has no substantive concern for the enforcement of human rights. These proponents of 'limited government' apparently seek to emulate an operation of freedom that corresponds to roaming barbarians that often have less respect for each other than doing some of the species of animals on savannah. It happens, therefore, that consistent with a 'human capital' paradigm and economic colonialism, 'owners of capital' via the execution of a 'New Economic World Order' are not as interested in 'smaller government' as they are with a government that can be coerced through political campaign financial support and otherwise. Their interest lies in a corporatized government.

The proponents of private enterprise capitalism within the Establishmentarian economic profession, together with their other corporate and political allies, can indeed claim victory over the once somewhat popular welfare state econometric model with its association to 'big government'. However, these same proponents tend to also support 'corporate welfare'. In other words, the premise of these groups is that government should not and has no responsibility to intervene in support of the quality-of-living attainments of a diverse public in a democracy. Instead, government should intervene on behalf of corporate power. Indeed, Milton Friedman, as the supreme 'Apostle' of modern 'private enterprise capitalism' in *Capitalism and Freedom* (1965), fully supported a government that executed a "law and order" agenda that is consistent with the official policies such as those that are supported by the current

(2002) U.S. Republican Party administration. The premise is that such an envisioned needed government ought to be able to freely intervene to defend the political economic interests of the 'owners of capital' that have 'property rights' and ownership neighbourhoods to protect and contracts to enforce via domestic courts or international trade-related tribunals like the World Trade Organisation (WTO).

The apparent desired quest of the capitalist creed is not "smaller government". Rather, their intent is to only use such rhetoric via "educational programmes" that aim to undermine a responsible constitutional democracy that can intervene on behalf of a diverse public. These groups want to ensure that governments do not support quality-of-living attainments, which they perceive as being likely to detract from their essentially relatively short-term profit horizons.

———•———

Corporate Welfare under American private enterprise capitalism

Corporate welfare has evolved in the United States with the growth of the political economic power of the corporate organisation of resources and enterprise. In colonial America, the Crown Corporations such as the Jamestown Company and the Massachusetts Bay Company were given exclusive rights to exploit designated territories. In Ohio, for example, the state legislature passed the Ohio Loan Law in 1837 -disparaged by citizens as the Plunder Law – which required the state to tax revenues to private canal, turnpike and railroad corporations while permitting them to charge tolls also. Ohio, like other states, passed "special legislation" to confer benefits on particular companies. Government land givea-ways also provided a basis for railroad monopolies against framers in the United States.

The expansion of the federal budget in relationship to the New Deal and World War II also provided new opportunities for give-aways and corporate handouts. Other corporate interests took advantage of "urban renewal" efforts into the 1950's and 1960's which often benefited developers and construction interests at the expense of low-income communities. The bailouts of Lockheed and Chrysler in the 1970's narrowed the separation between government and business. These paved the way for the sharp upsurge in corporate welfare that was further accelerated under the Reagan Republican administration in the 1980's and was followed by the corporate welfare enablements that the George W. Bush administration inaugurated in 2000.

The U.S. government doles out more than $167 billion annually in what critics dub "aid for dependent corporations". This corporate welfare includes: (1) cash payments by governments to businesses; (2) government provision of below-cost products and services, such as loans and insurance, to businesses; (3) tax breaks for businesses; (4) laws and changes in laws that help the business bottom line; and (5) government purchases of goods and services from businesses at inflated prices (though laws are supposed to prevent this).

U.S. aid for international investors, exporters and importers exceeds $32 billion annually including benefits to such "needy" recipients such as General Motors, Citibank, Archer Daniels Midland and Boeing. The Market Access Program (MAP), for example, uses taxpayer money to reimburse corporate foreign advertising costs. The Overseas Private Investment Corporation (OPIC), for example, supplies loans and insurance at below market rates to companies investing abroad.

The justification for much of this corporate welfare is that the U.S. government is creating jobs. James A. Harmon, President and Chairman of the Export-Import Bank of the United States, puts it this way: "American workers have higher quality and better-paying jobs thanks to Eximbank's financing." However, the recent numbers that are associated with the five biggest beneficiaries of the activities of the Export-Import Bank of the United States – AT & T, Betchel, Boeing, General Electric and McDonnell Douglas (a part of Boeing) – provide a divergent perspective. At these companies, which have accounted for about 40% of all loans, grants and long-term guarantees in the 1990's, overall employment fell by 38% as more than a third of a million jobs have been cut. Nortel, heavily subsidised by the Government of Canada, made radical cuts in its jobs that would help maintain the earnings to its owners and executives.

Most jobs in the United States have been created by small and medium-sized companies. FORTUNE 500 companies, on the other hand, have eliminated more jobs than they had created in the 1990's into the turn of the twentieth century; yet they are the biggest beneficiaries of corporate welfare. Billions of dollars of corporate welfare are provided to subsidise opulence by top shareholders, management executives, brokers, lobbyists and other agents of associated professional interests, like consultants, in the U.S. The U.S. is reputed to have the greatest domestic economic disparity in the world. In the United States, the rich are getting richer and the poor are getting poorer in the areas of economic despair in inner-cities that include Detroit, Watts in Los Angeles and Washington D.C. This is the model of capitalism which the U.S. captialistocracy would like to globalise.

CHAPTER 11

CAPITALISTOCRACY: CORPORATE GOVERNMENT

∽

The success of democratic institutions depends upon the ability of voters to choose legislators who will exercise their judgements to promote the welfare of the people. Likewise, it depends upon the responsiveness of legislators to the popular will and the ability of the people to recall from office representatives who fail to fulfill these responsibilities. However, the rise of great corporations and the concentration of economic power within these agencies have facilitated the mobilisation of financial resources and the instruments for controlling public opinion with the result that pressured may be put on the elected representative to obtain legislation favouring those who control the corporations. So well organised are the methods of 'reaching' the legislature and so easily are the desired responses obtained that businessmen often look upon this method as the normal legitimate and expected mode of governmental performance. Without comprehending what they do, frequently they look upon the legislature as their legislature whose function is to serve their interest. Popular government becomes government by pressure groups and legislation tends to serve special interests rather than the common good.

- D. Lynch, "Economic Power and Political Pressure", in *K. W, Rothschild, Power in Economics*, p. 158, 1971.

> *"The government is not a neutral arbiter in economic matters, but it tends to reflect the aims of those groups which are in the best position to influence government decisions. Few would deny that the policies of Canadian Governments since confederation have been predominately shaped by business men... Permanent lobbies in Ottawa, innumerable special delegations, the moulding of public opinion through newspapers and other media and contribution to party funds have yielded an abundant return."*
>
> - L. G. Reynolds, *The Control of Competition in Canada*, 1940, p. 272, E. Ronald Walker, "Beyond the Market", K. W, Rothschild, *Power in Economics*, p. 39, 1971.

W HAT IS A CAPITALISTOCRACY? Consider that a constitutional democracy is a society which embraces tenets of equality, human and civil rights and related freedoms, where a representative and responsible parliamentary government are elected by citizen-participants and are accountable to citizen-participants. In a capitalistocracy, "owners of capital" who are among the most financially wealthy are conceived de facto as "principal citizens" by virtue of their relative representational support in government public policy making, relative to less financially wealthy citizens. While a democracy is about defending the principle of one person one vote, a capitalistocracy pivots on the idea of one dollar one vote as far as the political economy of decision-making is concerned.

In a capitalistocracy, owners of capital begin to enjoy more than just general influence in matters like the passing of favourable legislation. In a democracy, on behalf of the diverse public, government fights against corporate excesses that threaten the quality of survival of citizens. In a democracy, government can vigilantly intervene on behalf of citizens in defence of quality-of-life attainments. On the other hand, in a capitalistocracy, the interests of big business and government become almost indistinguishable. As is poignantly manifested in the globalisation protests that occurred in Canada, the United States and abroad in 2001, coinciding with various meetings by government representatives to discuss and consolidate trade agreements, government via capitalistocracy becomes a greater and greater ally of big business interests and becomes more and more callous and hostile to political dissent. In a capitalistocracy, government decision-making becomes an extension of the corporate boardrooms.

In a capitalistocracy, the interests of Big Business and government become more and more indistinguishable. The health of the economy is measured on the calculated "economic performance" of the wealthiest "owners of capital" in society. In this type of society, public policies that are formulated and executed by government become totally oriented around those objectives that the "owners of capital" want and can best assure the maximisation of profit margins and overall corporate earnings. The needs of the diverse public become viewed to be a threat to sought "economic prosperity".

In a capitalistocracy, government is directed by a clique of elites, who propose and get policies executed to perpetuate their hegemony. Democracy is tolerated in a capitalistocracy as long as it poses no substantive perceived threat to a government and "owners of capital" as "principal citizens". Democracy continues to be tolerated in its severely limited form to the extent that it provides apparent legitimacy to an otherwise quasi-authoritarian society. Democracy becomes a public relations mechanism rather than a substantive operational context. In a capitalistocracy, people are more and more critically disenfranchised from participation in the framework of decision-making that affects their quality-of-living. Furthermore, having taken over government, "owners of capital" deploy the institutions of government to further agree to strategies in support of the earnings and power of "commercial empires".

———•———

Raymond Samuels

Disinformation and Corruption

In a "true constitutional democracy", the activities of government are fully transparent to the diverse public. These activities include the formulation and development of public policies in support of economic development. In a "true constitutional democracy", such public policies are devised to support individuals in reaching their full self-realised potential. In contradistinction, a capitalistocracy supports a milieu of rampant corruption and disinformation. Where the decision-making and related processes are done in a clandestine manner beyond any scrutiny that is associated with public accountability, corruption can adversely affect public policies that are related to economic government. Typically, the "owners of capital" in a capitalistocracy demand that the resources of government are to be used to support their private agenda for wealth, status and power. These thrusts include demands by political contributors to successful political campaigns for preferential treatment without any regard to ethics, lucrative contracts, grants and low-interest loans along with other personal or corporate related favours.

Corruption accelerates in a capitalistocracy with the purchase of the mass-media by capitalistocrats, who are protected from scrutiny by their friends in government such that they end up in control of respective mass-media Empires. In collusion with a 'corporatized government', the mass-media via the corporate press conferences and multimillion dollar marketing campaigns weave webs of 'disinformation' that are designed to isolate the public from potentially inflammatory information about the activities of capitalistocracts. The denied information includes damaging details about the actual horrendous scale of the conspiratorial and negligent activities by capitalistocrats that undermine the quality-of-life attainments of citizens that include corporate-sponsored environmental degradation. Having thus sabotaged the institutions of "free speech", disinformation is exploited to its fullest that enables capitalistocrats to engage, without fear of public knowledge, in all sorts of short-sighted activities including those activities that are harmful to public health.

———•———

Measurement indices of economic development

In a constitutional democracy, the devising of measurement indices of economic development will be critically concerned with quality-of-living attainments of the diverse public. Welfare economics was the apex of the attempt by socially progressive scholars of the economics profession in the 1950's and 1960's to ameliorate the "survival of the fittest" context of "market economics". In contrast, in a capitalistocracy, measurement indices are associated to economic development from a market perspective as portrayed by the stock market and Gross Domestic Product (GDP). These measurements are oriented around corporate earnings and expansion rather than the quality-of-living attainments of citizen-participants in society. In addition, having been corrupted by capitalistocracy, government policy priorities also tend to reflect a preoccupation with appeasing the demands of the "owners of capital". Therefore, development that is linked to corporations is attributed to be inextricably linked to societal economic development and ensuing "prosperity".

——•——

Undermining personal and civic responsibility concerning economic development

A constitutional democracy embraces personal and civic responsibility that shows up enhanced quality-of-living in a society. This emphasis evolves from a societal context in which people, as citizen-participants, operate as "co-owners" of the society. In such circumstances, government becomes the central institutional means to facilitate an essentially envisioned "public ownership" of society by the citizens of a democracy.

Together, they share the responsibility to continue the welfare of a cosmopolitan community.

In a society which has embraced high levels of participation in democratic institutions, societal evolution occurs synergistically. That evolution embraces the diverse contribution of individuals who are striving to achieve their self-realised potential.

In a capitalistocracy, a milieu of disinformation and corruption creates a milieu of mass-disenfranchisement, malaise and alienation. "Economic development", as manageable impact on the evolution of the society, is conserved to the goals of elite of capitalistocrats which leads to an environment of growing attained economic disparity between the "financially rich" and those persons who become forced below the poverty line. Furthermore, as attributed "economic growth" and the focus of economic development are conserved by primarily Big Business interests, who are financially bailed out via corporate welfare schemes, society as a whole stagnates. That stagnation is due to the exclusion of large public constituencies from *creative* political economic participation. The result is that individuals who could otherwise participate in public discourse that is supportive to quality-of-living attainments resign themselves to the often corrupt elite-driven and oriented decision-making processes within a capitalistocracy. Such an environment that has corresponded with the decline of social structures under the pressures of modern capitalism has created spiralling conditions of dysfunctional economic malaise and alienation as people lose hope in their ability to support their quality-of-living attainments.

CHAPTER 12

CAPITALISTOCRACY: GLOBALISATION

⚭

"The most reliable data available, predominantly from supporters of economic globalisation, demonstrate how economic globalisation has caused the most dramatic increase in global inequality and poverty in modern history. Furthermore, this outcome is intrinsic to the economic globalisation model. Arguments that economic globalisation allows "fragile democracies" to "overcome poverty and create opportunity, " as [United States] Trade Representative Robert Zoellick wrote in the Washington Post (2001), are seriously mistaken. If such policies are pursued, the world could find itself in even worse circumstances in the future than those we find ourselves in today.

The United Nations echoes these words in its 1999 Human Development Report as "The new rules of globalization... [and]. The process is concentrating power and marginalising the poor, both countries and people.... The current [globalisation] debate is too narrow ... neglecting broader human concerns such as persistent global poverty, growing inequality between and within countries, exclusion of poor people and countries and persistent human rights abuses."...

As Professor Robert Wade of the London School of Economics wrote in The Economist, "Global inequality is worsening rapidly.... Technological changes and financial liberalisation result in a disproportionately fast increase in the number of households at the extreme rich end, without shrinking the distribution at the poor end..."

- Antonia Juhasz (the project director of the International Forum on Globalisation), "Does Globalization Help thePoor?," a report by IFG available at www.ifg.org., *Tikkun Magazine*, internet reference: www.tikkun.org, 2002

A S AMERICA OF THE LATE TWENTIETH and early twenty-first century developed into the only Superpower in the post-Cold War era, it has sought to maximise (imperial-like) control both domestically and internationally. With this in mind, what is globalisation?

Globalisation has been a critical goal of organised power since the genesis of early empires. Globalisation is essentially the quest for 'Global Dominion'. It is essentially about the conquest of territory and now minds at a 'global scale'. It was an ambition of Ghengis Khan and his Mongolian Empire that swept across Asia and into Europe. It was the goal of the Roman Empire that spread across Europe, into Asia and Africa. It was also the goal of Napoleon Bonaparte who presided militarily over the French Empire. Hitler, the 'Fuhrer' of the Third Reich, also championed 'globalisation', which Britain and its Dominions together with the United States, in spite of initial sympathies for this so-called 'success story of Europe', eventually fought against in World War II. The Western Allies recognised at that time that Nazi ambitions for racist economic expansionism via 'globalisation', as a pseudonym for 'Global Dominion' or 'Empire', constituted an apocalyptical threat to democracy, freedom and individualism.

Globalisation, in its current form, is not substantively less of a threat than it ever was when it was espoused under the championship of various totalitarian, authoritarian and officially fascistic regimes. Globalisation is the current goal of 'organised commerce-centred private enterprise' that is manifested in the 'Transnational Corporation'. It is an effort for 'conquest', not by states, and does not make use of explicit government supported direction of the military to achieve the conquest of territory and its attendant 'human' and 'natural resources'. Instead, it is a mind-manipulating conquest, in which a capitalistocracy executes transnational vested commercial interests that include overpowering and where necessary emasculating local governments, democratic or otherwise. Conquest is achieved not by the military but instead by commercial and ideological means. Notwithstanding this, the conquest, whether by the military or commerce, has the ensuing effects of domination against democracy, freedom and individualism.

Toronto: 'World Class City'

Toronto is Canada's largest city. Toronto, with the largest urban Italian population outside of Rome, Italy, the largest Chinese population in North America and the largest Greek population in North America, has become the world's most multicultural city; more multicultural than New York City, London in the United Kingdom, Paris in France, Berlin in Germany, Singapore or Johannesburg in South Africa. Toronto, as a dynamic city with demographically hundreds of 'ethnic' backgrounds, is not only officially multicultural but also *de facto* multilingual.

The City of Toronto provides services in well-over 100 different languages. However, the evolving modernisation of Toronto, as a great Canadian international metropolis, testifies the promise of globalisation. Toronto's attractive skyline is dominated by large banking interests with many billions of dollars in assets. Toronto is at a looming crossroads. On the one side, the Canadian society is essentially characterised by a developing social conscientiousness. It has attracted people of diverse social and cultural backgrounds and has been at the forefront of Canada's international stature as a 'model society'. The evolution may be compared with an environment which accommodates the displacing and trespassing that is associated with 'Corporate colonialism', where increasing poverty, homelessness and ensuing declines in quality-of-life including air quality have become the so-called necessary outcomes of 'growth' and 'prosperity'.

———•———

The 'modus operandi' of Globalisation

Globalisation is promoted by the societal Establishment as a world that is characterised by greater and friendlier interactions among peoples and nations, where folks are happily trading with one another, exchanging ideas, sharing quaint customs, traveling to and fro, equally enjoying the boundless prosperity which comes from "lifting barriers" to free and full expression of human wants, human aspirations and the money flow. The Establishment (the capitalistocrats and their academic shills) want people to link "globalisation" with some vague ideas of constant progress, eradication of poverty and planetary justice" (POCLAD). However, globalisation has effectively been turning the world into 'Earth Incorporated', where humanity and the natural environment are respectively accommodated as expendable/manipulable 'resources' on behalf of the interests of the financially 'mighty and powerful' society to perpetrate their will as 'conquistadors'.

Essentially, globalisation is about the eradication of local and regional resistance, within the nations of the international community and subordination to an insatiable drive for profit at almost whatever costs, inclusive of the eventual human induced destruction of Earth, on behalf of commercial posterity targets.

Within the context of the current paradigm of market directed economic development and ensuing targeted growth, the approach is that 'as long as today's needs for conspicuous consumption are met, who cares about what our world will be like tomorrow'. Accordingly, various "free trade" agreements like the Free Trade Area of the Americas (FTAA) and the correspondent example of the European Union as a 'common market' have been championed by the Establishment. The idea of a 'Public Purpose' as elaborated by John Kenneth Galbraith, the famous Harvard University-based economist, where government intervenes in the economy to support social programmes and alleviate dysfunctional effects of the 'free market', has been represented as inappropriate intervention that should be eliminated wherever possible. According to the logic of this globalisation-oriented economic public policy, let the economy be totally dictated by the workings of the interests of self-aggrandizement, as people, the environment and the Earth, in general, are respectively used by capitalists as technical implements for their Empires. The imputation is that the world will be a better place through the ensuing trickle-down results of this beckoning prosperity.

———•———

Official Globalisation

Economic "globalisation" is argued as a historical process that has been the result of human innovation that has been managed to form technological progress. It refers to the increasing integration of economies around the world particularly through trade and financial flows. The term sometimes also refers to the movement of people (labour) and knowledge (technology) across international borders. There are also ensuing and broader cultural, political and environmental dimensions of the globalisation ethos. However, at its most basic, "there is nothing mysterious about globalisation". The term has come into common usage since the 1980s. It reflects technological advances that have made it easier and quicker to complete international transactions – in both product and financial flows. The term refers to an extension of production and trade co-ordination beyond national borders as a result of the same type of market forces that have historically operated for centuries at all levels of human economic activity -village markets, urban collectives in concert with pricing operations and financial arrangements.

Markets promote production efficiency through competition and the division of labour i.e. the specialisation which allows people and economies to focus on what they respectively do best. Global markets offer greater opportunity for traders to tap into more and larger markets around the world. The ensuing developments include access to more capital sources, technology, cheaper imports and larger export markets. However, the presence of markets does not necessarily ensure that the benefits of increased efficiency are shared by all. Countries must be prepared to embrace the public policies that are needed and they may even need to enter into programmes of the international co-operation in order to facilitate a flow of domestic benefits.

———•———

A regime of Free Trade or Globalised Corporate Welfare

So far, in order to support their cause, the proponents of globalisation have relied on the rhetoric of the advantages of free trade. However, in the current reality, while the globalisation ethos is disapproving the represented "unnecessary" legal and other forms of government interventions on behalf of citizenry and the natural environment, this ethos is far more tolerant of legislative intervention on behalf of the largest corporate enterprises which include passing of favourable laws and eventual government financial-equivalent subsidisation to these corporations. Essentially, these corporations have been allowed to develop a sort of "untouchable" status, beyond the questioning of domestic citizen, , political groups, , and the reprisal of international tribunals. Additionally, gross domestic product (GDP) represents an ambiguous indicator of what has been achieved.

———•———

Globalisation and its values

U.S. President Clinton, while in office, indicated that "as we enter the 21st century, the global economy requires us to seek opportunity not just at home but in all the markets of the world. We must shape this global economy not shrink from it [and must be] in support of the protagonists of globalisation".

But as this global economy takes shape, what are its values? Do they include human rights and democracy? And how do those values relate to free trade and economic growth?

Globalisation and human rights How does an interdependent global economy affect the rights of people? Can the pursuit of money and morality coexist? Those were questions in a PBSTV special that was moderated by C. Hunter-Gaultregarding 'globalisation'.

Ralph Nader had cogently articulated that the "essence of globalisation is a subordination of human rights, labour rights, consumer and environmental rights and democracy rights to the imperatives of global trade and investment... This is world government of the EXXONs by the General Motors for the DuPonts".

Other questions that were posed include: What will this new world order mean for human rights in social and economic terms in Asia's sweatshops among the growing ranks of child labourers for protecting the environment or dealing with Africa's tyrannical regimes? What can be done? What should be done?

The anthology of associated discussions had as reference meetings that were convened high in the Swiss Alps in the exclusive resort town of Davos. The World Economic Forum was holding its annual meeting to discuss global issues. At that convening, corporate logos of every stripe were on display alongside national flags. Summits that were once staged by and for heads of state are now also run for captains of industry, CEOs and the influential corps of economists who serve and advise them in an auxiliary role, one could say as their 'shills'.

Among the participants in Davos was GEORGE SOROS Chairman of Soros Fund Management the billionaire investor, speculator and philanthropist.

According to Soros, the Davos meeting is an enormous sort of cocktail party a lot of contacts, people meet. It is actually symptomatic of the age because you have presidents and prime ministers courting the financiers and the industrialists. Protesters that were heard are construed as the rumblings of the masses, against the "righteous organised power" of a 'New Economic Order'.

At that forum, another participant, ROBERT HORMATS, Vice Chairman of Goldman Sachs, stated, "I think there's been a lot of progress on human rights, but I don't think linking trade and human rights is a very productive process". He further indicated, "There are human rights interests but they ought to be part of a separate discussion with other governments... The great beauty of globalisation is that it is not controlled by any individual, any government and any institution. It provides people the ability to communicate across borders, trade across borders and raise capital across borders".

However, George Soros went on to indicate that he was not as certain as many of his colleagues that economic growth by itself will necessarily guarantee that human needs will be met. He indicated his fears of what he sees as the instability of what he termed the "capitalist threat". His imputation was that "the capitalist threat is that the system is unstable and liable to breakdown. That's one threat. And second, the system is very powerful. It's extremely successful. And due to its success, it penetrates into areas of life of society which it doesn't really belong to. There are other needs in society which cannot be fulfilled by the market and those needs are neglected. So, there is some market failure but much greater social failure – in fact a failure of the political process...

———•———

Globalisation and Intellectual Sophistry

The prevailing official pronouncements about globalisation are based on an apparent sophistry that the ongoing declines in the quality-of-life, with particular reference to the so-called developing countries, have not been further ossified or even accelerated by the intrinsic globalisation ethos itself. The imputation is that such negative results are the unfortunate outcome to these parts of the planet where substantive globalisation still needs to reach. Indeed, it is argued that although globalisation offers extensive opportunities for truly worldwide development, it is not progressing evenly. Some countries are becoming integrated into the global economy more quickly than others.

The argument is that countries that have been able to integrate are seeing faster growth and reduced poverty. The "outward-oriented" policies brought dynamism and greater prosperity to much of East Asia. With this in mind, proponents also argue that in contrast in the 1970s and 1980's when many countries in Latin America and Africa pursued "inward-oriented" policies, their economies stagnated or declined, poverty increased and high inflation became the norm. In many cases, especially Africa, adverse external developments made the problems worse. However, as these regions changed their policies, their incomes have begun to rise at least the incomes of a newly developing group that has used its intellectual skills to prosper accordingly. An important transformation is underway. Encouraging this trend, not reversing it, is the best course for promoting growth, development and poverty reduction.

Globalisation proponents "sympathise" that while crises in the emerging markets in the 1990s have made it quite evident that the opportunities of globalisation do not come without risks – risks arising from volatile capital movements and the risks of social, economic and environmental degradation created by poverty – that is not a cause for any indignation and should not be a reason to reverse direction. Instead, all concerned – in developing countries, advanced countries and of course investors – should embrace policy changes to build strong economies and a stronger world financial system that will produce more rapid growth which will automatically ensure that poverty is reduced. A little bit of pollution and cataclysmic effects on poor/non-wealthy people, who are like that because of "their own fault", are also principally made up of basically so-called unintelligent so-called inferior races anyway (like all those "niggers" in Africa), should not be allowed to stand in the way of the vagaries of a glorious international financial system, which the entire civilization relies upon, for the measure of the course of progress.

————————

Official Globalisation: Historical Overview

Globalisation is not just a recent economic phenomenon. Some analysts have argued that the world economy was just as globalised 100 years ago as it is today, but today commerce and financial services are far more developed and deeply integrated than they were at that time. The most striking aspect of this circumstance has been the integration of financial markets that has been made possible by modern electronic communication.

The 20th century saw unparalleled so-called economic growth with economic achievement as global *per capita* Gross Domestic Product (GDP) increasing almost fivefold. However, this growth was not steady;

the strongest expansion came during the second half of the century, a period of rapid trade expansion that was accompanied by trade and financial liberalisation.

In the inter-war era, the world turned its back to internationalism or globalisation and countries retreated into relatively closed economies with protectionism and pervasive capital controls. This structural pattern was an alleged major factor in the devastation of this period when per capita income growth fell to less than 1 percent, based on International Monetary Fund/World Bank statistical data, during 19131950. For the rest of the century, even though population grew at an unprecedented pace, recorded per capita income growth was over 2 percent, with the fastest pace of all coming during the post-World War II boom in the industrial countries.

Indeed, using those references, the story of the 20th century was of remarkable so-called average rate of growth in income, but it is also quite obvious that the progress, when so measured, was not evenly dispersed. The gaps between rich and poor countries and rich and poor people within countries have grown. The richest quarter of the world's population saw its per capita GDP increase nearly sixfold during the century while the poorest quarter experienced less than a threefold increase. In addition, income inequality has clearly increased.

———◆———

Official Globalisation and so-called Developing countries

Essentially, globalisation means that world trade and financial markets are becoming more integrated. But the question is how far developing countries have been involved in this integration? Their experience in catching up with the advanced economies has been mixed. IMF and

World Bank statistics show that since 1970, in some countries, especially in Asia, per capita incomes have been moving quickly towards levels in the industrial countries. However, a larger number of developing countries have made only slow progress or have lost ground. In particular, per capita incomes in Africa have declined relative to the industrial countries and in some countries have declined in absolute terms.

However, incomes do not tell the whole story; broader measures of welfare that take account of social conditions show that poorer countries have made considerable progress. For instance, some low-income countries, e.g. Sri Lanka, have quite impressive social indicators. One recent IMF Working Paper published in 2000, entitled 'Globalisation and Growth in the Twentieth Century', finds that if countries are compared using the UN's so-called Human Development Indicators (HDI), which take education and life expectancy into account, then the picture that emerges is quite different from that suggested by the income data alone.

Notably, the IMF helps champion the goals of the international *financial* system concerning economic development. Therefore, its priorities are not necessarily focused on the quality-of-life attainments of the typical human economic agent in a society that is undergoing commerce articulated economic development. Therefore, in executing its perception of its mandate, it presents the following features as critical components of the development packages that it seeks to complement:

- Macroeconomic stability to create the right conditions for investment and saving
- Outward oriented policies to promote efficiency through increased trade and investment
- Structural reforms to encourage domestic competition
- Strong institutions and an effective government to foster-good governance
- Education, training and research and development to promote productivity
- External debt management to ensure adequate resources for sustainable development

Pursuant to those targets, Chapter IV of its World Economic Outlook, May 2000, the IMF articulated that growth in living standards springs from the accumulation of physical capital (investment) and human capital (labour) and through advances in technology (what economists [traditional economists] call total factor productivity).

Many attributes are represented to either purportedly help or hinder these processes. The paradigmatic approach therefore argues that the experience of the countries that have increased output most rapidly shows the importance of creating conditions that are conducive to so-called long-run per capita income growth. So-called economic stability, institution building and [what it labels as] structural reforms are at least as important for long-term development as important are financial transfers. What matters, according to the IMF, is the whole package of policies, financial and technical assistance and debt relief if necessary.

----------•----------

An Advanced Country Perspective: Does Globalisation Harm Workers' Interests?

Anxiety about 'globalisation' also exists in so-called advanced economies. How real is the perceived threat that competition from "low-wage economies" displaces workers from high-wage jobs and decreases the demand for less skilled workers? Are the changes taking place in these economies and societies a direct result of so-called 'globalisation'?

Economies are continually evolving and 'globalisation' is one among several other continuing trends. One such trend is that as industrial economies mature, they are becoming more service-oriented to meet the changing demands of their respective populations. Another trend is the shift towards more highly skilled jobs. However, it is evident that these changes would be taking place – not necessarily at the same pace

– with or without globalisation. In fact, globalisation is actually making this process easier and less costly to the economy as a whole, by bringing the benefits of capital flows, technological innovations and lower import prices. In such circumstances, economic growth, employment and living standards end up usually being all higher than they would be in a closed economy.

But the gains are typically distributed unevenly among groups within countries and some groups may lose out. For instance, workers in declining older industries may not be able to make an easy transition to new industries.

What is the appropriate policy response? Should governments try to protect particular groups, like low-paid workers or old industries, by restricting trade or capital flows? Such an approach might help some individuals in the short-term, but ultimately it will be at the expense of the living standards of the population at large. Rather, the prevailing developmental paradigmatic perspective is that in these countries, governments should pursue policies that encourage integration into the global economy while putting in place measures to help those that have been adversely affected by the changes. In a commercially managed economy that as a whole embraces globalisation and the promotion of open economy, a government that squarely addresses the need to ensure that the benefits are widely shared can also foster positive trickle down effects to the bulk of the population, while at the same time encouraging investment that the very wealthy find financially attractive.

———•———

Economic Reforms, Globalization, Poverty and the Environment

At that Davos forum, a substantive summation of the effects of globalisation was articulated by David Reed, Macroeconomics Programme

Office (MPO), WWF and Herman Rosa, Programa Salvadoreo de Investigación Sobre Desarrollo y MedioAmbiente (PRISMA), who co-authored an article entitled "Economic Reforms, Globalisation, Poverty and the Environment, regarding 'globalisation'. They helped sum-up the general dysfunctionality of 'globalisation' in the argument that "while economic reforms and integration of the world economy have proceeded with unrelenting vigour during the past 20 years, policy makers continue to ignore the parallel social, environmental and institutional reforms [that are] required to generate sustainable and equitable improvements in the human condition." They also pointed out that "as presently prac-ticed, institutions and social structures, through which economic reform programmes are implemented and economic crises are managed, often exacerbate social inequities, reinforce the conditions that generate and re-produce poverty and [that] fuel the poverty-environmental-degradation relationship in developing countries." Furthermore, they also argued that "the ensuing concentration of wealth and environmental assets, coupled with the deepening poverty and environmental vulnerability of impov-erished groups, has reduced policy options for policy-makers, thereby sharpening the trade-offs between economic growth, social equity and environmental sustainability."

These effects have shown up in the following areas:

ENERGY SUPPLIES: Global energy use has increased by over 70% in the past 25 years and is expected to undergo 50% increase from 1993 to 2010 bringing with it increased greenhouse gas emissions from fossil fuel use and projected increase in global warming. However, while developing countries hold 80% of the world population, they only consume 33% of global energy supplies with expected increases in their share in the near future. Regional growth in energy use is likely to be significant in some regions. In China and South Asia, CO_2 emissions from coal will likely increase given the increase in quantity demanded.

WATER: Consumption will increase and shortages are likely "to become one of the most pressing resource issues of the 21st century". Projections indicate that up to two-thirds of the world's countries will undergo moderate to high water stress by 2025. The unequal distribution of water, combined with rapid increase in quantity demanded, and increased pollution will mean that there are likely to be serious shortages in much of the world. Some of the most affected parts of countries will be rural areas. They will likely experience scarce water supplies and high levels of poverty.

POLLUTION: Rapid industrial development has led to high levels of air, water and waste pollution in many countries. Several forms of pollution threaten both land and water. High levels of fertilizer use, combined with fossil fuel and biomass burning and land clearing, have led to significant releases of nitrogen that have, in turn, overburdened the absorptive capacity of natural systems. The majority of human-generated nitrogen releases result from fertilizer use (much of it concentrated in developed countries). Another source of degradation is acid rain (sulphur dioxide). In Asia, at current rates, harmful atmospheric emissions will triple in 20 years. These forms of degradation, combined with CO_2 and other forms of pollution, pose threats at the global level. Yet, when combined with other pollutants particularly in urban areas, they lead to high-levels of localised air pollution 1.4 billion urban residents are exposed to unsafe air. For example, in Latin America, about 25% of urban dwellers are exposed daily to high levels of air pollution, with the result annually of 65 million man days lost to illness. This has serious implications for human health, economic development and the environment. Water pollution is a serious problem in much of the world. It is estimated that 2.9 billion people lack access to adequate sanitation and 1.4 billion to safe drinking water despite investments of over $100 billion.

DEFORESTATION AND BIODIVERSITY: The world's forests continue to be under relentless pressure; between 1990 and 1995, annual forest loss in developing countries was estimated to be at least 13.7 million hectares. In the majority of countries surveyed by the FAO, forest loss, which may be attributable to increased access to previously remote lands, has increased. The primary pressures continue to be a combination of small-scale settlement and conversion for subsistence and large-scale government-supported conversion to other uses. In addition to forest loss, there is increasing concern over forest degradation caused by assaults from fire, drought, pollution and pests. As roads are constructed to open areas, these speed their conversion to other uses and result in forest fragmentation, which also leads to biodiversity loss. Only 20% of large contiguous forest blocks, known as frontier forests, remain intact worldwide. This forest fragmentation and loss, along with other factors, are closely associated with significant biodiversity losses worldwide. Aquatic biodiversity is threatened as well 58% of coral reefs are at risk and 27% are at high risk.

———◦———

Economic Change, Poverty and the Environment: The challenge of understanding complex relationships

Admittedly, the relationships among economic change, poverty/inequality and environmental degradation are poorly understood. The fact that favourable increases in global aggregate output and trade are coupled with the unfavourable deterioration in poverty indices and environmental degradation has prompted even traditional development institutions to review their approaches and assumptions about economic reforms and 'globalisation'.

Some World Bank studies admit that while so-called adjusting countries have performed better than so-called non-adjusting countries, as regards poverty alleviation, the overall gains in reducing poverty are far from the anticipated and promised results.

———◦———

Raymond Samuels

Globalisation: Has a new form of World War been declared?

In an episode of the original series of the science fiction television series *Star Trek* during the 1960's, the characters of the crew, Captain Kirk, his first and science officer Spock, and the doctor of the Starship Enterprise landed on a planet in the midst of an "interplanetary war" without the usual evidence of mass killings and destruction to infrastructure, but with a high rate of "casualties". This did not make any sense to the characters featured in this script. However, Gene Roddenbury, as the creator of *Star Trek*, helped present an envisioning of war on a planetary scale fought by non-conventional means in terms of war at least. In that *Star Trek* episode, "ruling groups" from previously warring planets who had previously used military methods, including "mass-bombings", were fed up with conventional war being such an uncontrollable "messy business" that threatened to kill off members of the "ruling group" itself and destroyed the very technology and overall infrastructure that helped perpetuate the power of the "ruling groups". To help solve this apparent dilemma, these "ruling groups" agreed to change the nature of war so that it would be "sanitised" in the view of the "ruling groups" in such a way as to spare their elite, with their technology and their infrastructure of social and ensuing economic control. The "ruling groups" decided to structure war into a containable process with the use of sophisticated technology. Computers would be employed to compute ensuing casualties of war in each domain of the "ruling groups". After each "hit", the computers of the ruling groups measured the wins and losses of each side. Numericized amounts of the populations of each domain of the "ruling groups" tallied by computers were rounded up in a clinical chamber and were then to be killed/exterminated by "vaporisation"... casualties of war by different means than conventional warfare, but nonetheless casualties.

With this in mind, 'globalisation' can be analogously viewed to be a warfare based on principles of Social Darwinism on a planetary scale. The casualties of this new form of World War are nonetheless casualties. Indeed, there have been more casualties of this war than the combined casualties of World War I and World War II. Millions and millions of people have become casualties. The directorship among these prospective conquerors, who wage their declared 'globalisation' planetary war, envision a "Brave New World" which is ruled by people who are similar to themselves and also envision the enslavement of the remainder of 'humankind' that has not been already sacrificed. This ruling group's first battlefield that it aims to control is the minds of "the masses". Once "the masses" can be seduced into viewing themselves as "human capital", they can be more easily subjugated to the will of the pursuit of the self-perceived utilitarian interests of the "ruling groups" as they proceed in the "management of capital". The "management of capital" is then regulated by the capitalistocratic state through globalised control of money, as currency in the efficient acquisitions of resources, and through the day-to-day concentration of people on themselves as "human capital" that is to be managed in concert with the will of a "corporate culture".

CHAPTER 13

Institutionalised Fascism

❧

"Who wields power is not important, provided that the hierarchical structure always remains the same."

— Nineteen Eighty-four, 218.

"In the past, the ruling groups of all countries, although they might recognise their common interests and limit the destructiveness of war, did fight against one another and the victors always plundered the vanquished. In our own day, they are not fighting against one another at all. The war is waged by each ruling group against its own subjects and the object of the war is not to make or prevent the conquests of territory, but to keep the structure of society intact."

— Ibid., 207

CAPITALISM SEDUCES people to give up their rights in favour of promised financial-material related prosperity. On having been seduced into giving up their rights, people are then dispossessed of their ability to control their lives and affirm and execute priority to their quality-of-life targets. Under such circumstances, economic disparity ensues that the rich get richer, while "middle-income" earners in industrialised societies lose ground in terms of well-offness as an ethos of "privatisation" and "market" rationalisation dispossess them of previous social and societal benefits that they had previously enjoyed.

In these circumstances, the poor get poorer. Within the context of economic disparity, social traumatisation manifests a context where crime increases as social structures decline. An environment of poverty, where human rights are overtly subverted, creates a milieu of despondence.

As inequity that is associated with repressiveness in a captialistocracy continues, extremist groups (from gangs to religious fundamentalists) may organise themselves and engage in forms of terrorism to strike the apparent oppressors in order to redress perceived economic inequities. Indeed, the supporters of the capitalist creed usually do not respond for promoting redress of inequities in society because that type of response would, in the view of the capitalist, potentially adversely affect short-term profit horizons. Accordingly, the threat of fascist encroachment does not come from armies, navies and air forces as in World War II, but rather creeps into the norms of society as a result of the (almost single minded) efforts of supporters of the capitalist creed to secure the sought flow of profits.

By the time people who have been seduced out of their rights realise that capitalism's promise of relative instant economic gratification of opportunities for great riches is somewhat misleading, their capacity to resist through social structures will have been undermined by the capitalistocrats. Furthermore, by then, their personal security and their environment will also have been destroyed.

On having sold out or on having been bought-out or even taken over by force (like African peoples and the aboriginal peoples in the "New World"), laws are created and their administration is presided over by "judges" in a capitalistocracy in a manner that preserves the new status quo. Police and the military are used to principally enforce and protect the property interests of elites from reprisal or rebellion by persons who have been repressed by elites of the capitalistocratic administration.

———•———

Co-optation of the legal systems and judges

Within a democracy, legislation is passed by parliaments and the laws are then formally created that affirm the inalienable civil rights of citizens. Any citizen, who perceives that his/her rights have been infringed at work through institutionalised racism, harassment or other such infringements, can rely on laws and the enforcement of laws by judges in courts in a supportive, fair and equitable manner. In democracies, trade unions that help protect employees as union members are recognised as providing a critical counter-veiling force against the potential for control excesses by the management. Included features are the protection of working conditions, wages and other rights. However, in a capitalistocracy, citizens can no longer rely on laws and the enforcement of laws by judges within courts in a fair and equitable manner. Indeed, where challenges are made by "the masses" through litigation that may be lodged against Big Business interests, judges begin to ignore the enforcement of laws that still exist within courts. In such circumstances, judges tend to become Praetorian guards of the status quo and preside over nominal "Kangaroo Courts". In that type of political economic milieu, justice is made into another purchasable commodity. There, the active defence of perceived infringement of rights also becomes less accessible to the diverse public in general as "overly-priced" lawyers principally work for Big Business interests and shy away from "insufficient paying" humanitarian causes that may be perceived to threaten their sought streams of corporate money. Additionally, in a capitalistocracy, corporations pressure legislatures to repeal any laws that they view to be unfavourable to Big Business. The unions are also viewed to be a threat to short-term profit horizons and overall management rights of the capitalistocracy and Big Business.

———•———

Raymond Samuels

The Division of Labour and Institutionalised racism

Constitutional democracy is critically based on tenets of equality. It embraces a pluralistic society. The measure of a democracy is its treatment with the minorities. A constitutional democracy is not based on a "simple majority" as a 'republic'. The United States that has traditionally embraced cultural assimilation with a "melting pot" philosophy has evolved from a 'republic' to a capitalistocracy. In Canada, a multicultural policy was developed officially to support domestic multiculturalism in relation to the development of Canada as a parliamentary democracy.

In the absence of prohibitionary laws and effective enforcement of them, institutionalised racism has always been an implicit but integral part of capitalism and has become more apparent in Canada with the retreat of democracy to its vices. Capitalism has evolved as a mechanism which European powers used to invade and conquer kingdoms and nations. Historically, they used their technology to create and wage/complement military crusades. The tactic has enslaved and was used to pillage otherwise advanced but less militaristic civilizations. In addition, as a part of their tactics of low cost control of access to resources, European civilizations have created ideological systems of 'White Supremacy' to reinforce their racist centred control. Once local resources have been distributed to representatives of the military victor, rights to use them were then legislated as being vested in commercial capabilities.

It is much easier to use idea of legitimating foreign corporatized rights of access to resources which the local population has been persuaded to hold rather than local standing armies to retain local control over an environment. In that coordinated manner, African peoples and the Aboriginal peoples in North America were dispossessed of their resources.

In the early technical stages of capitalism, a reserve of human labour power from the subjugated group was sufficient to keep the flow of raw material coming and to provide a market for products which the imperial power exported. However, as technological development progressed, new layers of attitude and resource control became necessary and the reinforcement of 'White Supremacy' took on subtle educational techniques.

Persons of European ancestries also began to experience disenfranchisement with the development of capitalistocracy. However, this is a disenfranchisement but it was without the added perniciousness of the institutionalized racism to which "visible minorities" are subjected. In the prevailing societies, "visible minorities" are kept out as much as possible from areas of critical political leadership and executive management that might open the "flood gates" to other minorities. Essentially, the quality-of-living attainments of persons is critically undermined by institutionalised racism as insecure "owners of capital" seek to maintain the traditional "whiteness" of their ranks by limiting the employment opportunities for minorities as much as possible to service and public relations in addition to lower-management jobs or jobs in highly public areas of responsibility but with little power.

——————•———————

"Open Air" "Concentration Camps"

Nazi Germany during World War II rounded up many millions of Jews, Gypsies and other people and took them by military force and exterminated them in heinous concentration camps. This was a horrific holocaust of inflicted genocide against what Nazi Germany perceived to be "inferior races". Modern capitalism deplores such "crude methods". Rather, with the evolution of capitalistocracy, human rights concerns become peripheralized to simply "making money". The capitalistic society via an ideology that is associated to "globalisation" does not threaten and wage war indiscriminately. The extermination of people and effective military conquest of territory to obtain more "natural" resources via military efforts, like Nazi Germany did, would squander political alliances. Instead, via the promotion of a market economy around purchasing power rather than around the promotion of quality-of-living and human rights, people who are without sufficient access to money find themselves condemned to what could be viewed as "Open-Air" concentration camps. They are (incorrectly) viewed as being less of a challenge to the claims of capitalistocrats for the natural resources of these societies.

The view of international capitalistocratic institutions such as the IMF is that notwithstanding the fact that such individuals have been cut away from their subsistence roots and forced into the money economy, government should shut down financial support to services that cannot be operated on a "user-pay" basis. The essentially myopic capitalistocratic economic development view is that the section of the population that has been marginalised into the 'Open Air Concentration Camp' will be without resources to even begin to think about making any challenge to the capitalistocratic prescription of their fate.

In contrast to that "user-pay" capitalistocratic development focus in a constitutional democracy, the capability to participate in freethinking consequent to critical education is valued. Such a societal milieu embraces the value that an educational system which cultivates critical capabilities brings to citizenry capability that can support citizen participation in debate on various local civic, national and international related issues (inclusive of support for the financially-challenged). In such a societal milieu, citizens are able to assess critically what strategies may be most effective in achieving desired results.

Modern capitalism on the other hand is comparatively threatened by the dissemination of critical education. The more an education milieu supplies learning on behalf of critical processing of information, the more citizens will be able to assert any rights they have to protect themselves against encroachment from the perceived excesses by "owners of capital". Indeed, Capitalistocracy, with its substantive antagonism toward democracy, encourages cult-like devotion to the view of "progress" as being indicated by the buoyancy of increases in the levels of market outputs.

————•————

Information and social control

A constitutional democracy embraces and is supportive of a highly independent communications media that can contribute to a more critically informed and aware public that can execute vital public participation in spirited debate. Such participation can lead to more representative public policies. Such circumstances result in informed decision-making.

However, a more informed and critically aware public is likely to pose a threat to the short-term profit horizons of owners of capital. For example, they can protest various excesses by the "owners of financial-equivalent capital". The drive of that group for short-term profit horizons may include the continued chopping-down of whole forests and mass-pollution of ground water. There are also numerous other destructive impacts on quality-of-living attainments of the diverse public. However, in order to reduce their awareness, Capitalistocracy calls upon various mind and attitude control techniques to mould and shape, in the media, statements of "public opinion" that do not substantively conflict with its private enterprise vested interests. The result is an ensuing growing culture which accompanies further control of the mass-media in the image of the "owners of capital' where the afflictions of quality-of-living discomfitures by capitalitistocrats (domestically and internationally) are ignored in the public media.

In Canada in 2002, newspapers, television, radio and internet news-related sites reflected the growing ownership concentration of a mass-media by a handful of owners that have allied themselves with a resurgent political economic domination to American vested interests. This development has been consistent with new right-wing party alignments in Canada that have grown with the destructive impacts of the American-dominated "Free Trade" agreement that has brought with it the growth of the fusion of American financial input into formerly sovereignty preserving institutions.

George Orwell in his book Nineteen Eight Four (first printed in 1949 and reprinted by Penguin Books in 1990) indicated that the "trick" so-to-speak is to provide an appropriately designed educational system. The one which is consistent with what he indicated and the one that has been adopted via "human capital" theory is designed to assimilate people to serve as automatons in certain needed functional jobs requirements of the "machinery" of society. The strategy is not to provide support to education in a way which would stimulate individuals in the polity to develop enlightened creative potential and critical intellectual mass introspection.

The prevailing state of such a de-evolution and stagnation of the education system is roughly illustrated in the 'Jay Walk' portion of America's prevailing NBC television "Tonight Show" which is hosted by Jay Leno. In that section of the programme, the university students who are interviewed can barely answer the most relatively basic questions.

> *They could only become dangerous if the progress of the industrial technique made it necessary to educate them more highly. Since military and commercial rivalries are no longer important, the level of popular education is actually declining.*
>
> George Orwell, *Nineteen-Eighty Four*: 219, 1990 reprint.

Information control is sought by capitalistocracy towards neofascism in order to support social control and other demands by capitaliostocracy, including immigration controls, to protect the society from "mew ideas" and perspectives that might be viewed to conflict with the status quo.

In a democracy, society serves people. Consistent with this target, technology is also developed and implemented to operate consistent with the promotion and the achievement of human rights as sacred and as a standard of ethics. Responsible citizens in a democracy (members of the scientific community, the business interests and government) are expected to refrain from the use of privacy-destroying surveillance systems. However, in the capitalistocracy that flirts with neo-fascisn, the people, as 'human capital', are conceived as entities that are expected to service society under the antidemocratic top-down direction of the capitalistocrats. Additionally, in this latter system, technology is developed to support both the desired short-term profit horizons of corporations and elevated levels of "commerce" even if the associated activities lead to environmental destruction (at accelerated rates).

However, if quality-of-life is to be a target of economic development, new management initiatives will be necessary. In particular, even if the market is to be used as a development technique, the production techniques that are chosen will need to accommodate the binding technical constraints (in respect of the impositions on the environment that require accommodation to its tolerances). Development policy will be required to unambiguously execute these constraint impositions to prevent service to (short term) market priorities from running amok and threatening the access of future generations to a high quality of survival.

CHAPTER 14

QUANTUM ECONOMICS: TOWARDS A REJUVENATED ECONOMICS PARADIGM

⌘

Q UANTUM ECONOMICS is a context of holistic aggregate economic development appraisal. It arises from the recognition that individuals are seeking mixes of 'technical' services and opportunities from their trade and exchange. The mixes will allow individuals to achieve survival that has preferred quality attributes. Quantum economics is cognisant that conscious individuals seek to participate in how their society evolves and they also seek to acquire mixes of technical services which will meet their needs in matters such as food, shelter and health and safety. Essentially, quantum economics recognises that individuals are seeking to enhance their quality-of-life.

The capitalist society places *NO* direct or indirect focus on ensuring that individuals have access to critical services on behalf of achieving a higher quality-of-life. In contrast, quantum economics imputes that the economic development institutions (in view of their co-ordinating responsibilities) which are associated with monetary programming (through banking regulations) and fiscal programming (through taxes, subsidies and "zoning" responsibilities) may not be seen as being separate from the ones out of which the access of individuals to a high quality-of-survival arises. In addition, the targets which governments see themselves as needing to execute on behalf of "economic security" are pivotally linked to the priorities which the particular government has in respect of the quality of survival of its citizens. There are also other mixes of "services", such as roads, transportation regulations, parks, harbours and electronic regulations, which governments will manage subject to the product flows which the particular government sees itself as having the responsibility to promote.

With its emphasis on the mixes of critical services which become available to individuals, the quantum economics focus challenges the administrative machinery of the prevailing economy to recognise that economic management achievement is indicated by the impacts on people rather than by the level of aggregate commerce that has been generated. Therefore, quantum economics challenges the aggregate policy and economic development programming directorates of governments in a monetised economy. The quantum focus challenges these economic directorates to look at the extent to which prevailing programmes allow those members of the society, who are without access to high financial earnings, inclusively to support the achievement of a threshold to a high quality-of-survival.

Members of the society are recognised as having rights to "a path in living" which they exercise via (considered strategies of) effort, time and resource commitments. Governments are therefore emphasised as having *responsibilities* to ensure that "coalitions" within the society are not allowed to conspire (either directly or indirectly) to deny other individuals or groups of them responsible access to "the path in living" which they seek. Accordingly, it is emphasised that the aggregate resource management targets must be aimed at complementing the efforts of conscious individuals who themselves are seeking to use their effort commitments to service the path in living at which they aim. This focus on servicing how individuals seek to go about their lives contrasts with the focus which construes governments as having the responsibility to prioritise and complement the resource management targets of 'capitalistocrats'.

In the process of servicing the immediate requirements of their path in living, individuals enter into trade and exchange of wares over which they have property rights and also into exchange of their time housed efforts. However, the trading environment in which they operate is facilitated by the instruments of governance in the society at hand. For example, there is the medium of exchange (money) which that system of governance provides and legitimates. Yet, the presence of this measure of market value must not be allowed to confuse the principle that it is to support technical services (wheat flour, steak, cars, aeroplanes, housing and song and dance material) on behalf of the quality-of-living that individuals are seeking to acquire. Therefore, even if markets are active, quantum economics does not have, as its primary focus, the rate of growth that has been occurring in financially augmented trade. Rather, it primarily addresses strategies which governments need to execute if they aim to facilitate the access of individuals to mixes of technical services on behalf of securing a high quality-of-survival.

Quantum economics is cognisant that economic management comprises of the *selections* of trades and effort commitments which individuals make as they go about utilising resources and time to execute a path in living. Furthermore, these trades and effort commitments emerge from an awareness-guided accommodation which individuals set out to make to the plethora of occurrences and events that they see as framing the reality in which they live. Quantum economics recognises explicitly how the awareness of individuals forms a critical component of the forthcoming pattern of economic reality.

Typically, individuals make the types of trades which are legitimated by the societies in which they live. However, quantum economics emphasises that in the living (as time-use-management) that individuals do, it is not necessarily the prospect of securing financial-*equivalent* 'profit' from a trade which guides "economising efficiencies". The quantum focus argues that the resource management operations which individuals select portray their attempts to execute a symbiosis between themselves (as conscious entities) and the material reality in which they live.

Over human evolution, the prospect of enhancing consciousness (rather than the objective of securing net financial-equivalent gains from trade) has complemented human resource manipulative adjustment to reality. Within the resource manipulative operations into which they enter, humans have recognised and have also construed a jointness between themselves (and their activities) and the remainder of their reality. As a result, conscious individuals tend to look upon reality as 'communality' that reveals itself to them as they participate. Although there may be financial equivalent prices/costs which can be placed on items, individuals are also considering how targets in living are served. Considerations in respect of living form additional "prices" and "costs" which pursuers of quality-of-life targets do not overlook. Therefore, what market data such as GDP show do not tell about economic development performance.

Quantum economics argues that in the light of their awareness, conscious individuals engage with each other so as to operate as inheritors of a commitment to survive. Additionally, as a part of their commitment to survive, conscious individuals (singly as well as in their groups) set out to design and execute strategies which will enable them to make efficient use of the survival-time that they secure. The human discovery of technology has therefore emerged in concert with the respective attempts of human economic agents to seek to be more effective managers of their time.

Quantum economics argues that as a result of their recognition that myriad technical linkages exist within and between the components of their reality, conscious individuals begin to seek to create an environment of survival which is portrayed by available mixes of technical services. The survival-centred outcomes, which quantum economics requires that governments must use their responsibilities, must be facilitated.

Against that background, the argument is that economic development is the outcome which is forthcoming from the prevailing *collection* of time, effort and resource management commitments that people (have the opportunity to) make in their collectives. Economic development achievement is therefore not merely about the level of commercial-equivalent value from competitive market equivalent activity. Rather, the measurement of aggregate economic development performance must communicate about the extent to which the ecology of that environment of survival, in which the trade data arise, is forthcoming or is being fostered.

Quantum economics examines the extent to which resource coordination is being executed on behalf of structuring an ecology of survival. Notably, the term economics (which has evolved into a particular disciplinary focus on reality) comes most directly from the Old French word "economie, " meaning "management of a household". The French adopted the term from the Latin word "oeconomia", which was in turn derived from the Greek word "oikonomia". Oikonomia came from the word "oikonomos", which separates into "oikos", meaning house, and "nomos" meaning managing.

In contrast, in quantum economics, the "household" which is being managed is the forthcoming environment which nurtures the survival that is accessible to conscious humans. The management question is the mix of technical impositions on that reality which a governance system elects to tolerate. Therefore, the management question that quantum economics addresses is the extent to which *responsible* individuals, whatever the level of their financial income is, will be able to access in the environment at hand the mixes of features which enable them to secure a high quality-of-survival.

Quantum economics is analytically cognisant of the survival which individuals secure. This context comprises of the opportunities which they have to choose in *their time-housed effort* and in association with other resources (as they fit themselves into the "household" which is formed by the plethora of events that comprise/sustain their reality).

The oldest recognised written work in the field of economics is *Oeconomicus*, a book on farming and household management that was written by the Greek philosopher Xenophon (430?355? B.C.). Yet, despite the Greek origins of the term, 'economics' was not an important field of study for the ancient Greeks, who, in spite of occasional references to economic matters, were more interested in philosophy and ethics.

However, so far, in Western society, "traditional economics" is oriented around the operation of the "market" where items are traded at financial-equivalent prices. That type of economic focus is NOT concerned about the quality of the opportunities which humans have to manage their survival-time.

The Western market economic context is indifferent as to whether human economic agents either seek or have the opportunity to use their resource allocated efforts so as to integrate their survival with the unfolding of the ecology of reality. Instead, traditional economics (as the propaganda arm of the capitalist *political* philosophy) incorporates and promotes an awareness fostering paradigm of economic development where humans are socialised to be selfish, greed-oriented pursuers of financial-equivalent gain. The result is that the "analytical" context of traditional economics ends up embracing (and essentially arguing priority accommodation to operators who pursue *private*) short-term financial-equivalent profit horizons (even though that pursuit may be detriment to long-term survival-centred considerations).

"Traditional economics", via its market paradigm, concentrates on the promotion of a private self-centred financial-equivalent emphasis and focus. In addition, it also provides an associated well-developed appraisal framework for managing reality in terms of assigned trading-related financial value. In it, the banking system in the society is guided to manage money in the support of the targets of the "private owners of capital" that also offer these resources as "security" to loans which the banks provide.

From its ideological base within the *political* context of modern capitalism, "traditional economics" views human beings in the functional roles that they perform in financially-centred market operations. It therefore primarily views individuals as sources of (hireable) skills. They are also seen as potential customers who must be inveigled or seduced into making profit-generating purchases of wares, which capitalist corporate entities are selling in their strategies of securing additional financial profit.

In contrast, 'quantum economics' appreciates individuals as seeking to manage their effort commitments so as to symbolize with evolving reality (as a prevailing eco-system). Therefore, the quantum focus emphasises that although individuals make use of components which have financial-equivalent prices, achieving survival that has a targeted quality is the symbiosis technique that individuals are pursuing.

Quantum economics therefore requires a complementing system of governance to aggregate economic development programming. Aggregate economic development programming within 'quantum economics' relies on the monitoring of resource utilisation that complements high quality of survival. The focus is not econometrically engineered to promote the financial prosperity of principal owners of capital. Neither does it promote the ascendance of rank selfishness, self-centredness and materialism. Additionally, work is seen as an operation in the living-centred environment. Therefore, the institution of work is not allowed to exist as a form of 'wage slavery', in which persons work primarily in order to claim financial compensation, which will give them rights to the components in a survival "game"; (where the rules are devised and controlled by the "owners of capital". The aim of 'quantum economics' is to arrive at an environment of living as an evolved economy in contrast to the control that is postulated by Adam Smith's "invisible hand". In a *de facto* market context of an "invisible whip", on the one side, there is the threat of financial ruin and denial of rights to subsist by unsympathetic creditors that are ready to 'pounce on' the victims of the commercial "game" (who because of their "weakness" do not keep up).

The absence of a living-centred focus and an emphasis on relationships of financial convenience which arise within the capitalistocratic society include marriages. These have a tendency to break up when one spouse believes that the marriage has reached sufficient "maturity" (like a mutual fund). The break-up is precipitated when the expected flow from the "money tap" appears to present less promise of subsequent expected growth than his or her spouse had demonstrated previously.

Individuals in traditional market economies are also conditioned into the perception of need to maintain respective acquired "lifestyles" that are associated with acquisitions that are linked to materialistic displays. Individuals therefore become behaviourally imprisoned (within the status acquisition via commercial consumption of assuaging (profit generating) within a regime of 'wage slavery'.

Yet, "elucidative" analytical statements in the paradigm of traditional market economics state that facilitating the enhancement of "human satisfaction" is the objective that the economics discipline seeks to foster. However, it is the satisfaction of those who hold or develop the capacity to acquire money that forms the focus of the discipline. Traditional market economics emphasises money as the supreme property and techniques for acquiring or managing money become advanced pivotal gateway to (if not the limit on) the attainment of "satisfaction". Therefore, in the market economic paradigm, the acquisition of money functions as a means and as an end in itself.

In contrast, quantum economics recognises money as one of the created resources on which individuals draw. Therefore, it argues that while individuals may be seen managing money, they must first be recognised as entities that are operating (on behalf of their survival) under the influence of their consciousness. Hence, there is need to concentrate on an appreciation of individuals as seeking to apply techniques of time and resource management towards achieving a survival-centred symbiosis with their environment. That is why development achievement is indicated by available mixes of survival-supportive technical services. That is also why development achievement is indicated by the extent to which the accompanying environment of trading (which delivers services) complements a survival-centred eco-system.

Notwithstanding, over the past seventy to eighty years, capitalism (via the paradigm in market economics) has had the opportunity to execute a pervasive socialisation which does not have an emphasis on preserving the eco-system. Furthermore, Western Europe is now asking the formerly socialist societies in Eastern Europe to adopt the capitalist norm as a condition of membership in the European Union as an integrated Common Market. These formerly socialist societies are being required to condition their citizens to accept and operate within the premise that the complements to survival will only be forthcoming as purchased services at market prices. The citizens of these formerly 'socialist societies' are being asked to accept that very high social and environmental costs of the market regime have to be paid for "progress". These social costs include the destruction of social programme public policy infrastructures directly linked to areas of socio-economic security and the resulting socio-economic dislocations that include poverty, increased crime and social malaise in general. These alleged inevitable environmental costs to "progress" include pollution and other areas of environmental degradation. The accompanying market stipulation is that it is only by concentrating on acquiring money that these individuals (as members of their respective societies) will be able to have access to the prospects to achieve the technical complements of their survival.

The public policy which market economics advocates is trapped within the underlying focus on an economy as an environment which is made up of *traders among financial opportunities*; buyers and sellers. Forthcoming public policy is therefore not aimed at an environment where people *live*. Market economics therefore condemns persons who have no capability to access purchasing power (and thereby capability to impact on how available resources are managed) to a sort of economic "irrelevance" in resource-allocated decision-making matters.

The policy and programme implication is that in the society, persons who are without (or who have been unsuccessful in securing) purchasing power ought merely to be content with what 'crumbs' are trickled down to them or with charity and other bestowals that happen to arise as the targets of the principal capitalistocrats are administered).

However, when the forthcoming eco-system and the survival-centred environment at hand are seen as outputs of tolerated resource management operations, it does not follow that the generation of aggregate short-term market value is more important (among the participants in the society) than having access to clean water, clean air and other such vital areas.

Institutional support for a socialisation that promotes the drive to acquire the convenience of money focuses primarily on financial results overlooks and de-sensitises individuals to the environmental awareness out of which their survival (as conscious entities) has been forthcoming. The current market-focused economic paradigm of financial-equivalent "growth" and "development" has therefore become a context which aided by modern technology (of evolving sophistication) is proceeding towards the destruction of planet earth. The result is that when market economists offer statements about economic truth, the deductions and imputations which they make from statistical computations completely lack regard for aesthetic considerations about *how* sustained human survival and choices in resource management are linked.

Quantum economics (in face of the complexity of human consciousness and how it has influenced effort management over human evolution) construes the market-focused paradigm as comprising a highly myopic and primitive conception of "development" and "growth". In the market economic paradigm, humans are conceived as being little more than barbarians, essentially as "hunters and gatherers" that are pillaging and destroying in pursuit of "power" as the acquisition of control over "resources" and financial-equivalent wealth. In contrast, quantum economics lays emphasis on the environment which is delivered and leads to policy and programme implications regarding what will be tolerated in the pursuit of holistic aggregate economic development. For example, the quantum focus leads to the requirement that private producers who use production techniques that despoil the environment will be required to also bear privately the remedying costs of its environmental impositions on the society.

The rejuvenated economic paradigm which quantum economics presents emphasises that although humans acquire and use money, the resource management operations in which they engage are also aimed at executing an aesthetic. The quantum focus emphasises that aggregate economic development management also has a responsibility to complement that aesthetic which human economic agents are pursuing. That is especially so because an appreciation of the aesthetic, which human economic agents seek to pursue/secure in their living experience, is axiomatic to facilitating what individuals seek to do in prevailing ecosystems. As a result, the rejuvenated economic paradigm draws due attention to the fact that a prevailing aesthetic directs what humans do by motivating them to have and pursue a broad conception of quality-of-life.

The operating presence of consciousness in the effort selections into which human economic agents enter leads them beyond an execution of initiatives towards an enhancement of capacity to selfishly pursue material possessions although that is the focus out of which market economics evolves.

This quantum economics focus is presented in awareness of the context in which a quantum science operates. Normally, a quantum science recognises the infinite complexity of the make-up and the response of atoms as being approximately but not completely captured by conventional mathematical computational analysis.

Essentially, mathematics is used in quantum science to *guide* an overall composite understanding of atoms as the building blocks of the universe.

Within that understanding of quantum science norms, quantum economics views the *raison d'être* of the series of programme initiatives towards economic development as being on behalf of the quality-of-life of the involved human economic agents in the polity to which the development data apply. As a result, quantum economics does not construe economic development as portraying growth (that is secured/indicated) as achieved elevated levels of utilitarian exploitation of "resources" such that materialistic commercial advancement is forthcoming.

Quantum economics moves beyond the perception of human beings as barbarians who are in competition with one another to secure financial-equivalent "self-prowess" and "self-aggrandisement". Instead, it focuses on human beings as sentient entities who have quality-of-life attainments as the central focus of their resource manipulative endeavours.

Somewhat analogous to quantum science, an introduced "quantum economics" conceives the decision environment out of which human economic reality emerges. It recognises that decision environment as being an infinitely complex universe of interrelated data points which promise a survival path to individuals and to which they accommodate via the selection and the application of their time, effort and resource management combinations. Accordingly, the place of statistical computational analysis in that universe is to assist (that is to help to guide) programme and policy towards facilitating the achievement of quality-of-life attainments from resource management endeavours.

Quantum economics recognises that there are important variables in respect of human survival and quality-of-living (as the sought targets) that cannot be fully captured unless the prevailing concentration on commercial-equivalent market statistics is de-emphasised. Statistical evaluation will be able to tell the proportion of the population that is without adequate levels of purchasing power so that they can be active contributors to total market results. In quantum economics, the quality of the environment in which these people survive is recognised as one of the outputs from development. In quantum economic analysis with its focus on more than commercial-equivalent "economic progress", development-related statistical analysis of market data is not conceived as generating an irreducible and unassailable guide to development programming. Currently, the prevailing market-oriented paradigm attempts to represent economic development and "economic growth" within highly integrated commercial-equivalent market calculations that pivotally include "Gross Domestic Product" (GDP).

In the prevailing GDP-linked economic paradigm, anything which cannot be owned, packaged, marketed and sold in the process of commercial exploitation does not have economic value. However, in quantum economics, planet earth and its infinitely complex parts that human beings rely on for their survival inherently have value such that the effective beneficent operating systems in these parts must be husbanded if sustained human survival is to be secured.

The quantum appraisal context seeks to provide a focus for executing the necessary husbanding of the parts of these operating systems (of planet earth). At the same time, the members of the society make use of the technical advantages that are provided by monetisation in association with division of labour.

The 'quantum economics' focus gives prominence to consciousness as a management context to *how* human economic agents organise their reality. Therefore, the focus also conceives human beings as entities who are seeking to grow holistically as communal sentient beings in creative social synergy with each other and with the planet. The quantum economics focus therefore accommodates humans as being beyond barbarians and operating within the context of a qualitative expression of themselves. Its appraisal context accommodates value beyond commerce that includes aesthetic survival-centred considerations which cannot be casually discarded as has occurred in conjunction with the prevailing market economic paradigm.

The result is that the quantum economics focus concentrates on appraising how extensively the outputs from prevailing legitimated production and trade operations arise in eco-systems that are consistent with access to quality-of-life and the requirements for human survival. The quantum economics focus emphasises the (technical) mixes of (critical) services that are delivered as well as the eco-system in which the deliveries occur. As a result, the quantum focus goes beyond the appraisals of economic development that concentrate on what has happened to aggregate "commerce".

The quantum focus does not emphasise the use of skills development and training in development programming as strategies for enhancing the delivering of market operators in a 'consumer society' via activities that capitalistocracy depends upon to support its target of opulent self-aggrandisement. Therefore, quantum economics argues an appreciation of the responsibilities of *aggregate* economic development management that includes the impacts on people that are forthcoming from prevailing resource management operations. In that regard, the book *Work, The Economy and Human Development*, addresses the responsibility of the system of governance to the economy when it is the enhancement of human development rather than aggregate commercial output which is the indicator of performance.

———◆———

What is 'Quantum Economics'?

Quantum economics is a proposed rejuvenated approach which links the resource management that humans do to the aesthetic of targets in quality-of-living that they have. The approach aims to assist the management system which makes policy and executes programming on behalf of aggregate economic development i.e. the aggregate economic development directorates. It aims to provide a context which respective aggregate economic development directorates can use to monitor the extent to which the programmes and policies which they are pursuing are also facilitating the quality-of-living to which members of the society have access.

The quantum economics focus is on how people (irrespective of their level of financial income) are able to live in the light of the resources that are available in the society at hand. One of the peculiar features of the quantum economics focus is that it explicitly recognises that the consciousness which has evolved in concert with human survival over the eons has historically operated as a critical organiser and an orienteer of the time and effort management commitments which humans' economic agents make. The "Quantum Effect" therefore arises from the recognition that in spite of what market economists and the Apostles of Capitalism argue, the human interaction, as effort and resource managing agents, with the plethora of data points that form reality is substantively about more than commercial-equivalent results. Therefore, the quantum focus recognises individuals as manipulating (available) information, rationing their time commitments and managing resources towards securing a preferred sustainable pattern of survival.

The quantum economics focus therefore queries the 'social sciences' message that resides in the trade and exchange operations which are said to portray the "economic development" that is occurring.

The quantum focus also recognises that as they set out to acquire the technical components with which they will execute their plan of sustained survival, individuals make use of the convenience that a prevailing currency provides. The focus also recognises that towards maintaining

Raymond Samuels

the type of social environment to which it is committed, a society typically creates a number of directorates. These directorates are given the responsibility to monitor and evaluate towards public policy consideration and appropriateness. With this in mind, currency and a system to protect its integrity are some of those features that a society creates. A currency can do its job only when its quantity is regulated in the light of the number and the variety of different items that are to end up having a price at which trading takes place.

However, quantum economics is focused on the mix of items from the prevailing resource base to which individuals have access. It is also focused on the character of the opportunities that individuals have to impact on how their environment unfolds. In the light of the widened mix of "outputs" from resource management on which quantum economics focuses, it does not argue that it is the access of individuals to money which must be their "ticket" to their right to access components on behalf of a higher quality-of-living. However, quantum economics does present an appreciational context that acknowledges the importance of a political economic environment where the division of labour that accompanies the efficient use of time and effort to produce output is also linked to "fair" financial compensation for effort that has been provided. Additionally, since many of the critical ("environment" linked) outputs, such as public health and air and water quality, on which quantum economics focuses, are not traded items, there will be a number of compensatory issues that must also be factored accordingly. In contradistinction to "laissez-faire" "free market" economics, 'quantum economics' recognises that unions have provided a constructive countervailing force relative to management power in the political economies of the West.

The execution of a society that is guided by the awareness that quantum economics offers will therefore start with a political resolution regarding *'What are the achievements for its members (in respect of quality of living), within which a society aims to portray itself?'* There are also a number of issues regarding the rights of societal members on and off the job that are to be regarded as inviolable.

The quantum economics context *explicitly* recognises the components which are involved in the delivery of the complements of survival. These include private renewable resources, non-renewable resources, resources which the government holds and protects on behalf of the society (common property resources) and other government-provided institutional resources such as the courts and the instruments of internal and external security. Therefore, the background out of which manifest deliveries of sought services are forthcoming is very complex. However, amidst that complexity of ownership relationships, the quantum economics focus does not start from the appraisal premise that forthcoming mixes of available survival-supportive technical services will largely be those which are consistent with the targets/convenience of (capitalistocratic) profit seekers. As a result, the 'quantum economics' focus does not start from the analytical premise that society must be managed on the principle (to the effect) that individuals will be able to access mixes of technical items that they need to secure a high quality-of-survival, only if they can EARN enough money to make commercial deliveries of these services profitable.

Yet, notwithstanding its de-emphasis on the enhancement of commercial output (in favour of an emphasis on determining the extent to which mixes of outputs that are consistent with access to a high quality-of-living have been facilitated, the 'quantum economics' focus is also an alternative to the Marxist-Leninist approach that had been practiced in the disintegrated Soviet Empire during the Cold War. The management functioning had essentially been economics as 'state capitalism'.

The relative prices for respective services in a trading environment and the prevailing rates of interest are principal features, on which market economists focus. However, those two features do not form the overwhelming routes through which the institutional features impact on how an economy manifests itself. For example, unless a development directorate is politically committed to facilitating the access of individuals to enhancement in their quality-of-living/survival, its programme initiatives will be equally indifferent to that outcome. Accordingly, such directorates are UNLIKELY to take initiatives which foster the flows of the respective types of services which contribute to quality-of-life attainment. As a result, capitalistic governments that have such indifference tend to focus primarily on the market value that has been traded.

Notably, both systems of capitalism (state and private enterprise) have demonstrated themselves to be essentially repressive to human rights and also destructive to the environment. Both systems of capitalism effectively practiced marginalisation of the quality-of-living attainments of people in favour of pillaging resources for the priorities of respectively 'private' or for 'state' capitalistocrats.

Quantum economics argues that overall, the essential holistic aggregate "economic management" outcome is portrayed in the opportunities to "live" which individuals face. Therefore, features such as the mixes of opportunities of individuals to manage the commitment of their time and the capability of the prevailing eco-system to nurture the survival of individuals form the critical indicators of attainment. Therefore, an appraisal of performance which merely stops at the reviewing of the volume of trade is therefore woefully inadequate to tell of the extent to which quality-of-life attainment has been serviced. Instead, performance appraisal should examine the extent to which a holistic aggregate economic development directorate has executed or is executing its responsibility to coordinate environmental protection on behalf of securing a high quality of sustained human survival. The extent to which the development directorate has also been indifferent to the consumption opportunities of significant portions of the population must also be examined with a view to proposing remedial strategies in that regard which will be necessary.

The effective aggregate economic development management task of an economic development directorate which is committed to quality of life attainment is to budget the technical carrying capacity of the environment so as to foster time use management opportunities that are consistent with human development as the outcome. Accordingly, the analytical question is: What are the features which portray the access of individuals to a high quality-of-living and at what levels must these features be forthcoming to confirm the target has been achieved?

Quantum economics argues that towards the delivery of the complements to a high quality-of-living and thence to the achievement of human development, the aggregate economic development must commit itself to securing the needed critical information. Thereby it will be able to determine the initiatives that it will need to take so as to ensure that variations in access to or in the delivery of these technical components to quality-of-living are positive.

The accesses of individuals to respective outputs that meet the require-ments for food, shelter and healthcare are some of the features whose availabilities will make for enhanced quality-of-living/survival. However, there are additional choice/behavioural opportunities which will com-prise of technical components.

Each critical sought type of a particular service component or at-tribute together with its delivery level will be regarded as a "quantum component".

At the same time, it is true that money, as 'currency', can facilitate trade and exchange among the produced quantum components and many of the technical inputs and supportive features which are required to deliver the quantum components. However, when quality of human survival is also to be accommodated in matters of economic development, there is need for a more comprehensive focus on the role that money plays in the underlying organisation out of which the 'quality-of-living' attainments arise. For example, when the achievement of human development and its associated quality-of-life features is the holistic aggregate output target, a society need not make the financial administration and management capability of individuals or groups the pivotal concern whether the needs of such individuals will be serviced.The Quantum Effect emphasises that economic achievement is demonstrated by *the* opportunities which par-ticipating citizens secure to sustained access to the critical complements of survival as well as to fulfill their own self-realised human develop-ment. As a result, it does not start from the premise that all productive resources in the society should have an attached "for Sale" sign so that these resources can be acquired and then have their usage determined by capitalistocrats who will offer a plethora of traded items on behalf of a 'consumer society'. Instead, the quantum economic focus argues that regulations regarding the acquisition, usage and management of these re-sources must be formulated in recognition of the high quality of survival principle. That principle is based on the critical conservation of non-re-newable resources in a manner that complements the quality-of-life. That principle is also based on the ecologically sensitised use of renewable resources. The 'scarcity management' of resources in a 'quantum focused' economic milieu is towards the human development of the citizen-par-ticipants of society as conscious individuals with natural economic rights.

These natural economic rights are associated with the premise that the environment is a common endowment for humanity linked to the continued health of ecosystems in relationship to high quality of survival.

In the light of that focus regarding available resources, quantum economics emphasises wealth as the collection of instrumental (technical and institutional) features which the members of a society/polity create towards generating for themselves and their heirs a high quality-of-life/survival. The focus therefore sees wealth as being ultimately comprised of the level and mix technical components/features/capabilities on which a society can systematically draw. Furthermore, the quantum economics focus also emphasises that legitimated patterns of resource-use must be those that are consistent with survival-supportive equilibrium in the prevailing delicate environmental eco-systems.

In the quantum economics context, wealth, therefore, comprises of technical as well as management capability that is being co-ordinated on behalf of enhanced and sustained quality-of-survival. Items that are traded can therefore be wealth if their production and usage complement the eco-systems and the delivery of the quantum components out of which a high quality-of-survival will arise.

The quantum focus particularly recognises that these eco-systems effectively provide the basis for sustaining and nourishing life across regions, nations and the continents on planet Earth. Therefore, quantum economics requires that additions to wealth as a development outcome must be measured in terms of features which portray more than the forthcoming commercial-equivalent value additions to resources and outputs. As a result, the quantum economics system does not rank the outcomes from holistic aggregate resource allocation and management simply in the light of the reductionist aggregate commercial-equivalent results that have been forthcoming. Rather, the quantum economic system is concerned with the extent of relative equilibrium in ecological sub-systems. These form pivots to the delivery of the quantum components which are portrayed as access levels to preferred mixes of sought services. However, the accesses which individuals have to *patterns of time-use experience* which they respectively associate with the quality-of-living at which they aim are also quantum components whose delivery levels must be evaluated.

The quantum economics focus requires an aggregate economic development directorate to refuse to tolerate the generation of dis-commodity deliveries that are inimical to the historical commitment of the human species to sustained survival. Therefore, outcomes that are associated with the financial emphasis must also be appraised in terms of the extent to which these outcomes arise in concert with service to the sustained vitality of life as well as service to human survival of a high quality. The development directorate will therefore need to:

(a) Limit the delivery of outcomes that are counter-productive to the preservation of an environment/eco-system that complements human survival

(b) Attract the co-ordination of human understanding and human capabilities towards the structuring of a preferred environment of human survival.

A fundamental component to the quality-of-living focus which quantum economics argues is the proposition that the production activities of individuals as conscious human economic agents are aimed at their self-development as aware managers of their lives who are proceeding to fulfill what their understanding of human development consists of. The analytical approach of quantum economics is therefore interdisciplinary and holistic. Furthermore, the quantum economics focus recognises that the achievement of human development as the ultimate outcome is forthcoming from personal as well as aggregate economic (resource) management initiatives.

Quantum economics proposes the incorporation of a rejuvenated framework for an objective appraisal of 'development' that is executed/managed as the "social sciences of living".

Additionally, within the emphasis on "human development" as the outcome, persons are regarded as entities with the constitutional rights of sentient human beings who, by virtue of their political citizenship, also have rights on the extent to which the prevailing resource base of the society/economy operates to complement their survival.

Essentially, Quantum Economics embraces or construes macro-economic outcomes as being forthcoming from 'constitutional economic governance'. The economic functioning of the prevailing macroeconomic milieu will then be appraised in terms of the extent to which it operates as a co-ordinator of the forthcoming pattern of aggregate resource management results *to the service of a diverse public.*

However, the quantum economics focus also argues for the need for an execution of science-guided management strategies towards a more assured delivery of an environment of human ecology and civilization that is consistent with the sustained delivery of a high quality-of-survival. In the process, it sets out to bring a broad based survival-oriented technical focus to the plethora of data streams that accompany the private trade and exchange which a society legitimates in the name of commercial-equivalent economic development.

The quantum focus invites respective aggregate economic development directorates to include, in the evaluation of their economic development performance, additional ambient environment-centred technical data that are associated with the output deliveries at hand. For example, the 'quantum economics' focus questions what progress in resource allocation has humanity achieved by the destruction of the habitat that is necessary for human survival?

There are local environment-related elements that must be brought to bear on the choices of production techniques. However, on a global scale of reference, there are environmental issues such as ozone depletion, apparent "global warming", famine in certain parts of the world, species extinctions and the destruction of delicate ecosystems (and other potential ensuing cataclysms. The result is that 'quantum economics' requires appraising forthcoming mixes of deliveries of technical complements to survival relative to the delivery of sought quality-of-life levels minimising environmental threats to human survival.

At the same time, the quantum appraisal focuses on the combinations of economic quanta as these are portrayed in *patterns* of technical results to which individuals have access. It also calls attention to the patterns of environmental exploitation that the society tolerates. Therefore, it draws attention to the extent to which prevailing quantum shortfalls could be effectively remedied under the guidance of evaluative priorities which are consistent with environmental science with the wisdom within social sciences and their associated mathematical quantification of efficiency and the qualitative delivery requirements of participatory constitutional governance.

The quantum economics focus is on service to the quality-of-survival targets at which conscious self-directing human economic agents aim. It explicitly recognises that commercial activity has evolved to be a vital instrument in the co-ordination of the trade that accompanies division of labour. However, the quantum economics focus at the same time recognises that the health of the interdependent global ecosystems is also an inherently productive part of the economy of human survival. It recognises that there is a present threat, as annihilation of the human (and other) species, which accompanies the current performance measurement emphasis on the pursuit of the commercial short-term profit operations that get computed as contributions to GDP.

To help combat that potential annihilation outcome, the quantum economics context concentrates on economic development strategies which emphasises the forthcoming technical flows of critical services. In the process, it does not regard/accommodate human beings as auxiliary *instrumental* participants that are to be managed or can be seduced on behalf of the financially-centred profit margins on which commercial enterprises concentrate.

———•———

Quantum economics Methodology

'Conventional Science' views reality as an ordered system that may be potentially understood and thence manipulated to achieve targeted results. That prevailing 'world view' (so-to-speak) is also applied within the positivist scientifically based approaches of economics particularly as propounded by the University of Chicago School of economics).

That economics 'world view' construes of economic reality as the behavioural/organisational background that generates the (statistical) data which are revealed in operations that arise in association with prevailing levels of unfettered trade and commerce. The economic 'world view' of that school of protagonists then imputes that via systematic analysis of the statistical data that are associated with production, trade and exchange, humans can discover techniques which will allow them to achieve increasingly greater levels of control over associated (production and trade) matters.

That positivist economics focuses on how economic reality is to be approached based on a premise. It imputes that an understanding of the universe which is based on or derived from an axiomatic order also essentially provides the basis of an ensuing intellectual paradigm to the effect that the unfolding of reality is implicitly predictable.

By implication, 'traditional economics' (in that type of apparent Newtonian conceptualisation of reality, which it then imputes to the world of human responses) conceives a derivative axiom. It imputes that humans with more understanding and technology and who are better able to 'conjecture' and predict will be able to achieve higher levels and forms of managerial custodianship over the resource management operations which form their 'living space' in the universe.

Contrary to the Newtonian focus on which traditional economics has drawn, quantum science conceives reality as systems of juxtaposing apparent 'order' and 'disorder'. Quantum science, in somewhat contrast to 'conventional science', relies on an intellectual context of comparative humility.

A quantum focus on the universe is based on an approach to its study which realises that the universe is infinitely complex with levels of "disorderly" randomness and spontaneity that are beyond the scope of predictability. Accordingly, quantum science concentrates on (or essentially appreciates) the data that are associated to the observation of phenomena in the universe as being 'snapshots'. In addition, the quantum context does not assert that a greater composite of snapshots will reveal total prevailing reality and will lead to the discernment of an 'orderly system' towards 'predictability'.

The context of quantum economics proposes to embrace a corresponding approach to that which has been taken by quantum science. Thereby, quantum economics seeks to avoid arrogance in the universe of human to resource interfaces that could lead to an unforeseen 'catastrophic outcome' in human survival. Such unforeseen results can arise as a result of the unappreciated linkages that exist between human survival and respective selections of resource management strategies.

While recognising that laws of the universe exist and also embracing efforts to understand those apparent laws, quantum economics (in emulation of quantum science) conceives an infinite dynamism to the prevailing universe. The "Quantum" economic focus appreciates the prevailing economic universe as the interface which occurs when humans seek to achieve effectiveness and efficiency in the combinations of their time and effort with the remainder of the data points in prevailing reality. Therefore, quantum economics starts from the premise that the individual human interaction with others and "resources" comprises of an interface as well as operations in an irreducible order.

Quantum economics recognises that within the operations of that irreducible external order, the phenomena of consciousness and the vastness of the reality with which it seeks to cope lead individuals to form groups that will take *respectively* ordered approaches to the coping strategy.

For example, there are respective disciplinary (and skills) groups that concentrate on understanding and manipulating respective parts of reality. Within the experience that there are respective specialisations, the approach of quantum economics is to seek to foster a comprehensive order in respect of how aggregate trade and exchange operations are managed. Thereby, it aims to foster the achievement of an economic management order where the result is the efficient attainment of human development from the interfaces with reality that humans execute via their time and resource management commitments.

On recognising that a human development oriented ordering system is behind the resource allocated initiatives which human economic agents have pursued over their evolution, the Quantum Economics focus emphasises the following:

> An aggregate economic development directorate has *non-transferable* responsibilities for facilitating the execution of an ecology that complements the achievement of human development.

For example, government, as the authority figure in the aggregate economic development directorate, has responsibilities for budgeting the carrying capacity of the prevailing eco-system. It also has the responsibility to stipulate sanctions that will be executed for assaults that are made on the capability of the eco-system to support a sustained high quality-of-survival for the individuals who live in that environment.

Essentially, Quantum Economics is the policy planning and programme management evaluation tool of a society which is prepared to accept and execute its responsibility for carrying-capacity-budgeting in respect of the environment at hand. However, the society can execute that budgeting (as a development management operation) about the features which challenge the optimal expression of a high quality eco-system only if its economic development directorate also has access to technical information.

Government, as the authority figure in the economic development directorate, will therefore need to make threshold stipulations of technical results as impacts on the survival-centred and quality-of-life-oriented carrying capacity of the environment and the access of individuals to complements of survival that will/will not be tolerated.

However, at the same time, the methodology as well as the appreciational background, out of which quantum economics emerges, is mindful that to perpetuate the execution of organised power, typically the power holders seek to achieve maximised control of the existing political economic environment. The quantum economic focus is also mindful that these power holders rely on their discernment of order that can be analysed and, where possible, manipulated.

The quantum economics focus therefore recognises that in service to the objectives of the holders of power, 'traditional economics', as it evolved in concert with a conventional (Newtonian) conception of 'science', set out to discover in the human interface with reality which operates via trade what that disciplinary group could present as the irreducible order. The traditional economics focus then emphasised that the irreducible order in respect of trade matters operated as a desire of individuals to secure net financial-equivalent gain from their trade and exchange operations.

'Traditional economics' then set out to argue and identify the operating components and principles that could be instrumental tools of 'organised power' if it is to perpetuate itself and its interests in the environment where the trades are being executed. However, there also exist trade-linked operations that produce negative effects on survival, such as air and water pollution, justice and health care only at "purchased" prices, but the holders of organised power in the society prefer to overlook.

Quantum economics comprises of a new focus. It emphasises that even though financial management is an intermediate operation that "greases the wheels" of the operation of division of labour in the effort and time commitments of individuals, humans also aim at the achievement of impacts (interface outcomes). In particular, quantum economics argues that respective conscious humans aim at interface outcomes which are consistent with the achievement of human development. Therefore, they do not primarily aim at securing net financial-equivalent results.

In addition, quantum economics argues that protection of the supportive eco-system is a required ancillary technique to the delivery of human development. The quantum focus then stresses that impacts on the quality-of-life *achievements* of any responsible participating member of the body politic comprise of the salient computational indicators of development performance. Accordingly, the quantum appraisal focus does not emphasise the attainment targets at which a capitalistocracy and its agents aim.

Historically, conventional scientific methodologies have been used to creatively contribute to the enhancement of human knowledge. Instances of enhancement in knowledge have also tended to lead to insights on *how* reality functions. However, these insights (which the knowledge-enhancement, about the interface between humans and resources, tends to create) have frequently also been used to facilitate the execution of organised power as a need to dominate.

That type of facilitative function which new knowledge tends to generate has frequently also driven tri-ballistic warfare from antiquity up to the warfare that uses modern military technological arsenals.

Against that background of the need to dominate, which knowledge enhancement has historically been used to facilitate, the proposition of a prevailing inherent 'disorderliness' in the universe, which quantum science argues, can be viewed to be the enemy of 'conventional science'. Correspondingly, unlike the focus of traditional economics on net financial-equivalent result, as the indicator, the quantum economics imputation that living, which is consistent with human development and is the target of the human-to-resource interface, departs from the organised order.

Additionally, to emphasise that the mix of time and resource commitment opportunities, i.e. the substantive output, departs from the controlled output flow, about which market economics talks. Instead, the imputation is that as individuals go about the living that they do, they use their time and resource management operations to search out achievements which significantly extend beyond financial-equivalent outcomes. The substantive imputation is that human economic agents seek to deduce/achieve *a meaningful understanding of HOW they can efficiently budget their efforts to secure a sustained symbiotic relationship with how their environment evolves.*

However, the reality in which humans execute their time and effort management initiatives comprises of a mix of myriad directed as well as accidental interfaces. It is these interfaces of time, effort and resource allocated operations that essentially frame the living which individuals respectively do. In recognition of that background, the need for a "Quantum Effect" argues that in the effort commitments which individuals make, they set out to use their understanding (and where possible to enhance it) so as to create *patterns* of outcomes that (in turn) create the experience in living to which they aspire.

The quantum economic focus therefore imputes a universe which is comprised of the myriad interface experience between human time and effort commitments and the data-points in prevailing reality. The quantum economic focus further emphasises that the framing of the direction and the substance to living (which emerges at these interfaces of conscious humans with the data points of reality) is beyond the stipulation of scientific reporting. Therefore, unless individuals are conditioned (as they are in capitalist societies) to emphasise the utilitarian outcomes from their encounters, management of how they will respond is not likely to be within the definitive control of the holders of political economic power.

Quantum economics emphasises that the prevailing effort and time commitments which individuals make are the pivotal results of their consciousness and are used by individuals to execute fulfillment and content to/in the living that they do. Individuals are recognised as managing their effort and time commitments towards executing a meaningful association with the reality of which they are a part. However, the quantum economics focus also emphasises the presence of a holistic aggregate economic development directorate that is correspondingly committed to enhancing the quality-of-living opportunities to which individuals have access. Therefore, it recognises that the prevailing technical interface operations with the rest of reality, in which private individuals engage, are feasible by virtue of the prevailing and accompanying social support system of the community in which they live.

Substantively, the Quantum Economics focus seeks to better inform that social support system. In executing that information support task, the quantum economics focus points the directorate to the search of individuals for a synergy (as quality-of-life attainment) which functions as the common target which they seek to secure from their interface actions with reality. Quantum Economics therefore draws attention to environmental features (inclusive of ecological ones) *that must also be met* if a high quality-of-living is to be forthcoming to members of the society irrespective of their levels of financial income.

To service the access of individuals to the interfaces out of which a high quality-of-living will be generated, a holistic aggregate economic development directorate will need to take initiatives to facilitate the access of individuals to critically needed technical services. Therefore, notwithstanding the principle that many technical services can operate as varyingly close substitutes for each other, the analytical focus will be on the levels at which these technical mixes will be forthcoming and the eco-system in which these services arise.

———•———

Raymond Samuels

The Enlightenment in the Quantum Economic Renaissance

Quantum Economics substitutes human development as a living-centred attainment target for the commerce-centred one that has been framed into the systems of measurement of "traditional economics" (as currently applied). The market economics emphasis is on individuals as 'price takers' who are budgeting their *financial-equivalent* resources among alternative outputs that sellers of respective services are offering. That market economic focus pivots on a commerce-centred ideological orientation. In contrast, the basic premise of quantum economics starts with individuals as "budgeting" their time-for-living and living is emphasised as being aimed at securing human development as an experience.

The quantum economics outcome is forthcoming from societies that are prepared to execute their responsibility for budgeting the carrying capacity of the environment (or the eco-system) at hand towards protecting the opportunities for quality-of-life enhancement that are accessible to its members irrespective of their respective levels of financial income.

When the quantum economic focus emphasises that the budgeting which human economic agents do on behalf of the quality-of-living at which they aim recognises that when individuals enter into economic management operations, there are also survival-centred "prices" on which they draw as conscious individuals. Therefore, unlike traditional market economics, the quantum economic focus does not emphasise individuals as necessarily limiting their choices to results from financial or financial-equivalent computations when they make economic management decisions. Neither does the quantum economics focus emphasise the society as seeking to foster maximum financial-equivalent market growth.

The traditional economics presentation focuses on individuals as traders among commercial-equivalent opportunities rather than entities who are seeking to use mixes of outputs and resources to frame and structure their lives. That focus of traditional market economics has a number of unfortunate consequences. A particularly glaring one is that market economists typically develops an analytical indifference to the ongoing practice of assaults which are currently being executed on the (survival-supportive) health of natural eco-systems.

Indeed, traditional economics does not emphasise opportunities in living as one of the outcome sets from resource management. Therefore, the fact that assaults on the ecological carrying capacity environment are inimical to the long-term survival of humanity on planet Earth is *not* an outcome about which traditional economics concerns itself.

In contrast, quantum economics is particularly focused on resolving whether individuals who are without claim to high financial incomes in the society have access to a high quality-of-survival. The quantum economics focus therefore argues the proposition that the ecology which accompanies the management of scarcity is a critical economic development management outcome. Therefore, how that ecology has been affected must be appraised prior to making statements of forthcoming economic development achievement. As a result, 'quantum economics' also imperatively requires that the aggregate economic development directorate should be mindful that the execution of programme and policy operations which foster the access of members of the society to a sustained high quality-of-survival is its primary economic development management responsibility.

The quantum economics focus therefore requires the aggregate economic development directorate to foster the deliveries of critical survival-centred services. It must also at the same time initiate policies that budget the carrying capacity which the environment as an eco-system is required to bear.

The aim of the holistic aggregate economic development directorate must also ensure that its programmes and policies are such that the quality-of-survival of the respective humans who live in the environment at hand is not impaired. Therefore, it must also take initiatives to limit assaults on the carrying capacity of the natural environment so as to ensure that a high quality-of-survival will be forthcoming to members of the society and their heirs.

A society that is indifferent to the need to have in place, effective policing techniques that aim to protect the access of individuals (irrespective of their financial incomes) to opportunities for a high quality-of-survival and views aggregate resource management reality through the prism of financial budgets will seek to complement opportunities for private profit rather than to complement the ecology of human survival.

While fostering/complementing the survival of individuals as beings who are in communities is a societal priority, this target has consequences for the initiatives that an aggregate economic development directorate will need to execute Firstly, the directorate will need to be prepared to service the opportunities for access to the complements of survival that is secured by members of the society who are without high financial income. Therefore, even when individuals need to use the market to acquire services, the directorate will need to appraise and police the consistency with which the prevailing resource base is servicing the ecology of survival.

Clearly, 'Quantum Economics' does not argue an economic management process which relies on the postulated neutral beneficence of the impact of Adam Smith's 'invisible hand' as the assurance mechanism which will lead prevailing trade to operate on behalf of the mass of the people who share a society. Instead, the quantum economics focus is mindful that the pursuers of private profit have so far been largely allowed to ignore the environmental destructiveness of their initiatives. Therefore, the quantum economics focus argues for **the explicit need** for an approach to development co-ordination that seeks to restrain the negative impacts on human survival which accompany the capitalistocratic emphasis on giving priority to the aggregate financial value of trade.

Essentially, the quantum economics focus seeks to facilitate a development emphasis on those production flows which operate in concert with the laws of nature towards *minimising* negative impacts on quality-of-survival. It seeks to foster and achieve from production initiatives and benevolent flows of impacts on human survival.

The quantum economics focus also starts from the proposition that the programming initiatives on behalf of economic development achievement will be taken towards also facilitating and executing a societal framework of rights and equity. Therefore, unlike the assertion of the positivist market economics, quantum economics does not regard the execution of a context of social justice as an attainment that is separable from the achievements that economic development is supposed to generate.

However, historically, the "traditional (market) economics" has relied on the versatility of money to quantify the outcomes which humans have secured from their manipulative interfaces with their environment and its parts. Accordingly, in the context of traditional market economic appraisal, an undisturbed forest is in a state of economic "non-productivity". The associated premise is that when such a forest is subjected to total or near total destruction from clear-cutting efforts by possessors of 'human capital', jobs are created and the 'economy' is served (grows essentially).

That financial-centred appraisal emphasis arises in association with the argument that when the felled trees are used to support technologically refined products, those operations further contribute to the highly desired result of economic growth as indicated by increased 'commercial productivity'. Furthermore, within that appreciational context, when a transnational corporation establishes an industrial plant, the envisaged desirable result is that earnings-centred 'jobs' are created.

The extent to which these created jobs support quality-of-living attainments is marginal to the statistical computation of economic performance which largely emphasises the earnings delivering jobs created and the associated 'lowering of unemployment' However, historically delivery of the short-term profit horizons, at which commercial enterprises aim, has usually been accompanied by notable physiologically negative 'high impact' results on delicate ecosystems. Capitalistocrats, for example, typically neglect to recognise the extent to which rainforests generate the predominant amount of the world's supply of oxygen that is vital to life of planet Earth.

Typically, the capitalistocrats as promoters of the "private enterprise" interests of "owners of capital", view such a rainforest as being essentially unproductive when it is not generating earnings for an "owner of capital".

In contradistinction, 'quantum economics' sets out to apply and accommodate the measurement of economic development to a framework which concentrates on the flows of critical survival-centred services that become available to the mass of the individuals that make up a society. In addition, by virtue of its emphasis on quality-of-survival, the quantum focus examines the extent to which the respective forthcoming technical flows arise within an environmental 'low impact' approach. Therefore, quantum economics emphasises a co-ordinated survival-centred 'management of scarcity' towards *technical levels* of deliveries which accommodate/portray the access of individuals to enhanced quality-of-survival.

The primary focus of quantum economics *is not* on the computed level of the totality of exchange operations which arise in the respective legitimated market arrangements that governments use money as a produced institutionalised instrument to facilitate. The market value of trade data shows the association that has arisen between exchange decisions which individuals have made and this versatile supreme type of created property that is called money. That communication is not the principal concern of the quantum economics focus. Rather, its focus is on the success of the society in fostering or servicing the access of its members to mixes of (critical) technical components that service the targets in quality-of-survival that they have.

The quantum economics focus is therefore also on the extent to which an aggregate economic development directorate takes initiatives to mandate that prevailing production and trade operations (inclusive of those that deliver the survival-centred technical services) also preserve a survival oriented relative balance in prevailing eco-systems.

Towards facilitating delivery that arises in concert with optimal environmental expression, the quantum economics appraisal context draws on scientific appraisal input from respective technical areas which include biology, chemistry and physics. The quantum economics appraisal context also draws on computations in social science disciplines that allow the appraisal of efficiency in the allocation of time by conscious individuals. In addition, it accommodates and emphasises the extent to which management operations are appropriately constrained by the tenets of constitutional law.

In the process of making appraisals that draw on the critical input of these background scientific areas, the quantum focus implicitly also examines the extent to which prevailing development management takes seriously its responsibilities for budgeting the carrying capacity of the environment out of which an ecology of survival arises. Therefore, the quantum economics focus does not accommodate the natural environment as being primarily a backdrop with 'raw materials' and 'human capital' that may be used in support of generating 'commercial activity'.

The interpretation of growth which the quantum focus appraises is therefore not restricted to conclusions regarding the size of the enhancement that has occurred in the production of commercial goods and services from 'raw materials'. Instead, 'quantum economics' is concerned with supporting growth as realised human self-development by conscious human economic agents.

Notably, the quantum economics emphasis on 'low impact' environmental approaches is somewhat analogous to an approach towards economic development that evolved among the aboriginal peoples in Canada and also in some other traditional societies. The tactic of those societies of aboriginal peoples was to strive to use available technology in development approaches which minimised disturbance effects on ecosystems and would thereby promote a posterity-oriented human survival in the society.

Indeed, that focus of those "traditional" societies appeared to be aimed at encouraging the use of resource-manipulative initiatives that would promote a symbiosis of the society and its members with their environment. That approach by these aboriginal peoples was more than simply what now passes as a type of 'sustainable development'.

The currently accepted "sustainable development" approach is largely one which seeks to use environmental dominance in strategies which are most consistent with the long term delivery of market profit from saleable "outputs" and "trinkets" which the environment can be 'coaxed' and 'massaged' to deliver.

In contrast, the emphasis on symbiosis with their environment which was found in the approach of the aboriginal peoples in North America was not aimed at financial balance sheet results. Rather, the formal and informal resource management and control systems of these aboriginal societies were aimed within the technical understanding of their reality at the delivery of survival-supportive output for *the* members of the society. Their management systems were aimed at preserving (for themselves and their heirs) the technical capability of the environment to respond complementarily with the delivery of outputs which were supportive of their survival targets.

Quantum economics is correspondingly a multidimensional (joint qualitative and quantitative) analytical framework. It draws on performance computations that address the environmental budgeting responsibilities of the aggregate economic development directorate. It also draws on computations which recognise individuals as budgeting their time and financial resources towards achieving in the living a high quality (consciousness directed) interface with reality.

As a result, the quantum focus essentially challenges the framers of aggregate economic development strategies to recognise that their *raison d'être* is not necessarily to foster buoyant commerce. Rather, it is the discharge of their responsibility to focus on the protection of the capability of the environment to deliver the critical complements to the achievement of a high quality-of-living to the members of the prevailing polity.

The aggregate economic development directorate is required to *use its* custodial responsibilities in respect of the common property resources as well as its coalitional responsibilities in respect of the trade that accompanies monetisation to promote, facilitate and require resource manipulation on behalf of the environmental symbiosis which is human development.

Statistical Computations of 'Economic development'

The 'Quantum Economic' critique is that the orientation of traditional economics to development comprises of an ideological encouragement of a concentration on financially-centred results. This ideological focus of traditional economics is based on a type of utilitarianism which is indifferent to the degradation and destruction of the 'natural environment'. As a result, the traditional economics focus is essentially dysfunctional and inimical to human survival interests. Yet, the 'quantum economics' context also recognises the presence and the convenience of monetised trade and exchange of skills and services.

Consequent to the production efficiency that accompanies division of labour, monetised exchange operations are the norm in a modern society. The flexibility that money offers when items are acquired through trade is undeniable. However, the quantum focus does not use the aggregate market value that is associated with prevailing features/operations as the indication of the importance of respective facets that are associated with trade and exchange. Instead, in spite of the fact that individuals can make technical substitutions among respective items which they use, quantum economics focuses on *the mixes of technical services that become available* through production, trade and exchange.

The quantum economics focus is also additionally mindful that frequently there are market prices which are associated with many of the components on which individuals seek to draw to satisfy their quality-of-living achievements. Yet, the quantum economics focus notes that the output of scarcity management includes the market-equivalent value of trade *as well as* the levels of access to critical components of their survival that persons without high levels of financial income need to secure. Accordingly, the quantum economics focus challenges the orthodox market stewardship of economic development directorates. Specifically, 'quantum economics' questions what achievement *on behalf of executing its responsibilities for fostering a high quality-of-life* has that directorate executed, if individuals in the society who are without high financial incomes do not at the same time have access to the critical survival-centred outputs and services.

Under normal competitive market conditions, there is usually a recursive linkage between the prices of resources that are required in the delivery of forthcoming outputs and the price of those outputs. As a result, resource prices tend to operate as regulators of the output commitments to which they will be directed. Mindful of that circumstance, the quantum economics focus *explicitly* recognises the presence of resources which governments hold in common on behalf of the society (common property resources) that must be *responsibly* managed among potential outputs. When that does not occur, the use of those resources is not necessarily likely to be consistent with the access of members of the society who are without high financial income to opportunities for enhanced quality-of-survival.

How the aggregate economic development directorate deals with the pricing features which enable it to budget the non-environmental parts of the common property resources among the critical components on behalf of quality-of-life delivery is elaborated in the book entitled *Work, the Economy and Human Development*. However, mindful of those dual sets of outputs from trade (as market value and service mix), the quantum economics focus offers a supportive approach on behalf of an 'aggregate economic management arrangement' which accommodates the access of those who are without high financial income to the critical components of at least minimum standards of quality-of-life attainments.

As a starter, the quantum economics focus construes a unified conception of individuals as being indivisible 'economic' agents as well as political citizens. It recognises that in their private attempts to use trade as a strategy to acquire the wherewithal for their living, individuals make use of the convenience of money. However, the quantum focus that is being presented here argues an emphasis on the holistic aggregate economic development responsibilities of government. The measurement focus explicitly argues that in addition to its responsibilities in the arena of monetised trade, government has an obligation to protect the survival-centred integrity of the eco-system which becomes accessible to the humans who make up that trading environment.

Therefore, a government will need to collate its responsibilities for monetary management for protecting the survival-centred integrity of the environment of aggregate exchange. Accordingly, if a government neglects to include facilitating the access of individuals to the complements of stipulated minimum standards of survival centred achievements, the extent to which it is operating consistent with its *raison d'être* is questionable.

Quantum economics concentrates on the effectiveness of the survival-centred budgeting of environmental capacity that the macroeconomic management directorate executes. It is argued that the macroeconomic and other co-ordination which makes a viable exchange environment possible also have the responsibility to be supportive of the delivery of technical components which are consistent with access of individuals to a high quality-of-survival. To that end, the quantum economics approach presents to respective aggregate economic development directorates an alternative appraisal context to the utilitarian earnings-centred 'human capital' focus that governments now apply to economic management co-ordination.

Quantum economics expects development managers to focus on the extent to which mixes of at least minimum technical levels of components that make for quality-of-life attainment are accessible to the members of the society. These deliveries include ensuring (for example) universal access of individuals to health care and other critical public services such as justice irrespective of the personal financial resources of these individuals. Corresponding access to components which satisfy the need for food, shelter and clothing and critical living-centred environmental conditions are also features that are to be included when appraisals are being made as to whether a high quality-of-survival is being fostered.

The result is that the quantum economics focus includes as management outputs effective civil rights as access to critical services in respective matters of justice) as well as 'equity' as material access to critically targeted levels of respective outputs.

An additional feature in quantum economics is the recognition that the prevailing market economics context by virtue of its overwhelming emphasis on market pricing and available private wealth as the access-rationing device overlooks the time-pricing in respect of opportunities for living that individuals include in their budgeting. Yet, how that time-pricing is being satisfied forms the pivot to the quality-of-life assessments that individuals make as they pursue their targets in human development.

Additionally, quantum economics recognises that as individuals make their survival-centred assessments, their experience as members of societies also leads them to make distributive judgements regarding what they have achieved. As a result, quantum economics also brings these distributive features into the performance appraisal context which an aggregate economic development directorate must use as it seeks to facilitate human development. However, the accommodation of that (distributive centred) performance appraisal emphasis is addressed in *Work, the Economy and Human Development*.

Within its emphasis on performance indicated by the access of individuals to critical services, the quantum context emphasises human economic agents as sentient beings that have a survival-centred 'free will' which they exercise when they make their time and other resource allocated choices. Aggregate economic development directorates are therefore invited to be mindful that although individuals make utilitarian choices when they budget their finances, they also use underlying extra-market (living-centred) pricing relationships when they make exchange choices.

Holistic aggregate economic development directorates are therefore invited to be especially aware that in the light of the variety of sources from which quality of life attainment flows, development initiatives which service the targets of capitalistocrats do not have priority. It will also be necessary to foster the delivery of results and (time-use) opportunities which promote the symbiosis which conscious individuals seek to achieve from their time and resource management operations in their environment.

In the execution of their responsibility to budget the coping capacity of the environment, these aggregate economic development directorates must therefore focus on:

(a) Constraining (via appropriate monitoring and policing) the extent of assaults on the environment
(b) Causing remedies to such assaults on the eco-system.
(c) Monitoring the extent to which the prevailing usage of common property resources facilitates the delivery of outputs that are necessary for access of individuals to a high quality-of-living.

These economic development directorates are therefore invited to guide their development initiatives by drawing on statistical data which report on:

(a) The levels of *deficits* in the access of responsible individuals with low earnings in the society to critical technical output flows that are pivots to forthcoming quality-of-living but have so far been overlooked
(b) The extent of the departure from optimality which accompanies the eco-system in which prevailing tolerated (critical and other) outputs arise

———•———

Quantum Economics and a Quality-of-living Index (QLI) or 'Q index

A proposed Quality-of-living Index (QLI) (or 'Q index') to complement 'Quantum economics' looks at the statistical data that portray prevailing technical quantities of critical services. The delivery of these technical services must complement quality-of-life of responsible citizen-partici-pants of 'economic society' inclusively. The performance that an aggre-gate economic development directorate has fostered is then construed in terms of the pattern of relative deficits in technical quantities for individ-uals and 'households' in optimal survival-centred environmental states out of which a high quality-of-living becomes accessible.

The respective forthcoming mixes and levels of outcomes (as technical quantities) will be consistent with a high quality-of-living only if their creation, delivery and usages are also so complementary. Therefore, per-formance appraisal must monitor the extent of that complementarity of tolerated production techniques and usage patterns.

A computed 'Q Index' may be used to portray variations in the results from aggregate economic development management. However, the sourc-es of the variations in production and delivery, out of which enhanced quality of living will be forthcoming, will arise out of two distinct (but not necessarily statistically independent) *sets* of pivotal features. These sources are respectively identified as:

(a) *Locational/environmental features* that arise in the geo-graphic space at hand
(b) *Human factors* that arise from activities which humans execute consequent to their sentience, socialisation, history and technology that they develop and they may adopt.

Performance will be indicated by (or will pivot on) the technical lev-els of the target components to the quality of living expression that the society targets. In addition, although changes in the delivered levels of technical outcome may arise as a result of commercial initiatives, it is not the market value of the prevailing technical features which indicates their quantities or their impact on the 'Q index'.

An aggregate economic development management will also need to have as its fundamental target the promotion of resource management and usage out of which delivery of the sought technical flows to quality-of-living attainment will be forthcoming.

Required statistical information must therefore be able to guide the development directorate to make management and/or oversight decisions which will be necessary to foster access to those technical flows.

An additional feature is that although variations in the technical levels of these pivotal human as well as locational outcomes may *appear* as market results, they are significantly in response to the tolerances in the budgeting of environmental carrying capacity that the economic development directorate practices. Accordingly, quantum economics recognises an aggregate economic development directorate as having a number of definitive responsibilities.

The aggregate economic development directorate will need to monitor and police how the prevailing common property resources of the society are being utilised. It will also need to specify assaults on the eco-system and environment (that accompany or are a result of production and resource management decisions) which will NOT be legitimated.

The Quantum Economics focus argues that the accessible (as compared to the delivered) quantities as technical data levels for respective mixes of critical targeted outcomes are essentially "economic quanta" at the particular time and place.

These technical data that report on deliveries are disparate in their substance and configuration. However, the quantum economics focus recognises that there are living-centred time-use-management principles which are involved and around which forthcoming aggregates may be computed. It also recognises that in the substitutions which individuals make among alternative commitments of their resources and efforts, they are guided by matters in respect of the effectiveness of their time-use.

Aggregate economic development directorates may also draw on those living-centred time-use efficiency relationships that individuals make to guide their programme selections toward maximising the benefits to the diverse public from policies which are aimed at fostering deliveries of the technical outputs that portray economic quanta.

Notably, the maximum effectiveness of programme commitments towards the delivery of *critical* targeted mixes of technical services is not indicated by the aggregate market value of these delivered services. What these delivery levels are will not necessarily have been in response to expected profit opportunities that their deliveries will yield. An economy that is managed on behalf of quantum attainments needs not be managed to complement the market-profit targets of capitalistocrats. That reference group does not pay attention to survival associated with quality-of-living targets of the diverse public inclusive of the poor in addressing disparity in the society.

The respective parts for any forthcoming computed 'Q index' which is associated with environmental budgeting practices of an aggregate economic development directorate encompass the following:

(a) The location or geographic area of measurement (L) and the particular point (or duration) in time (t) for which a legitimated economic development directorate is executing targets in environmental budgeting.

The component, L_t, identifies the region and time where the critical quality-of-life components are expressing themselves. For example, 100 km^2 in an area in northern Alberta, Canada, as of September 1, 1998 or 5km^2 in Hong Kong, China over a 9 year period from 1992 to 2001.

(b) The change agents (scientific or policy centred) in that region which are impacting on *how* the *respective* technical features that contribute to quality-of-living express themselves.

(c) The principal *sets* of Human (H) and of Environmental-provided (E) support features or services which produce or are respectively contributory to technical flows out of which quality-of-life arises. These sets are identified here as comprising of variables/components E_t, and H_t.

The statistical frame that is used for the prevailing performance analysis will need to identify the mixes of critical technical flows on behalf of quality-of-life (as economic quanta for a location) that belong to the respective sets. At the same time, the society will need to identify and focus on the levels of access of individuals to these technical attributes and relationships which it will seek to preserve and facilitate on behalf of the opportunities of its statistically typical member to secure access to a high quality-of-life.

The aggregate economic development directorate will need to aim at promoting environments/ecosystems and technical flows of quantum components in E_t and H_t which will be as close as possible to optimal survival-centred technical levels.

Scientific analysis as well as societal commitment will be involved in specification of what are the optimal levels for these respective human and environmental services. Within that background, the quantum economic development focus therefore argues and is mindful of the following:

$$Q(max) = [(L_t, \#E_t) : (L_t, \#H_t)]$$

Q refers to the attainable 'Quality of Living' and '(max)' identifies the presence of an upper attainable limit.

L refers to the location or geographic reference area for which computations about the effectiveness of resource allocated performance are being made and t identifies the referenced time period for which the appraisal is being computed.

E refers to the set of the respective technical components in the natural and material environment (and/or eco-system), from which respective technical features (variables) arise that make for the availability of a high quality-of-living.

#, 'delta' identifies the principle that it is a change in quantity
of the particular neighbouring variable in the set that
is being measured.

H refers to *the set* of respective (identified) technical components in the material and social ecology to human survival as the built environment which will be brought
into the outcomes that will be prioritised.

The argument is that quality-of-life for any stipulated location and
time period will vary in direct relationship to two sets of *conscious-
ness-referenced* interface data.

One data set comprises of items that occur or have been caused to occur in critical features from the natural eco-system and environment (environmental factors). The other set comprises of changes in data points or
sought/manifest results that accompany what people as technical agents
do (human factors).

For each reference quantum factor in *E* or *H*, the community will
need to identify or delineate, as the achievement target, an optimal reference configuration or environmental budget target. Additionally, the
achievement/expression for each reference quantum factor will have its
own scientific technical units in which its existence and changes in it will
be measured.

To execute or approach a maximum status to "*Q*", the society will
need to set out to emphasise and promote the achievement/delivery of
quality-of-living to which it is committed for any member of the society.
In particular, the society is *required* to *stipulate* and make a list of the
respective critical quantum factors in *Et* and *Ht* for which it has targets
and will use its common property resource management and other constitutional governance responsibilities.

For example, take a natural environmental factor such as tree density.
The departure from an idealised norm for this quantum factor can be
computed only after the community (with the guide of prevailing best
scientific information) first sets a stipulation of what will be the reference
tree population and how changes in its level and its environmental supportive function will be computed.

For each quantum factor, scientific background information can be drawn on to identify the sources that are respectively responsible for the positive and the negative forthcoming variations in them. Therefore, for each technical (quantum) factor, scientific guidance will be needed to stipulate a number of features in respect of:

(a) The normal undisturbed level of environmental presentation of the particular technical feature
(b) The technical manifestation of the optimal survival-centred reference state for the particular (human or environmental) quantum feature
(c) To compute the extent of the prevailing deviation of each technical feature of focus from these optimal quantum impact states.

Development management must be seen as being directed towards taking management initiatives to foster the delivery of respective critical quantum features from the environment and from human activities at levels that are as close as possible to an optimal expression.

Performance will therefore be indicated by the relative technical closeness of the accessible outputs from prevailing resource management operations to the target optimal levels for the respective mixes of quantum factors. The swapping of pollution between industrialised countries and the developing societies that are willing to accept environmental "poisons" for a fee will not be accommodated as a legitimate development technique.

The quantum focus does not seek to homogenise, as market economics does via the *conceptual* principle of "equilibrium market prices", an aggregate statement of output from the variety of technical outcomes that portray attainment. Although the quantum economics focus recognises the technical variety among the capacities of individuals, it at the same time emphasises that fostering the opportunities of individuals to have high quality time-use interface is the development target.

Essentially, Quantum Economics is a measurement context which stimulates a society to examine the opportunities for living that it is fostering/generating. In particular, via its emphasis on the stipulation of component technical targets at the time-use interface, quantum economics prompts the society to focus on *where* deviations from preferred survival norms exist and are therefore in need of correction.

The imputation is that the objective of programming and policy initiatives must be to bring the pivotal environmental as well as human factors into optimal technical balance with the quantum goals. The society, as an indication of the social and cultural milieu towards which it is headed, may therefore decide to make priority groups of respective quantum factors.

In the exercise of its stewardship in matters that are related to human survival, the society may then stipulate impacts on the environment and may also stipulate delivery levels of human factors where it will use its stewardship of the common property resources of the society to help become available.

Development costs will be calculated as the departures of respective critical quantum components from the optimal levels for the survival-centred state (or time-use interface) that respective management initiatives have generated. Notably, the levels of many environmental costs that arise in association with 'quanta' in the 'E' set are usually due to human activities.

Outcomes for which the status of the 'E' quanta may be computed include critical features such as the 'pristineness' of water quality for human consumption and wildlife habitation, 'access to ground water', 'air quality', 'precipitation', 'population of indigenous animal species', 'population of indigenous trees, plant and other fauna over an area' and aggravation of the 'Ultra Violet' light spectrum.

Programming which aims to correct the departures from the optimal states for these and other features will draw on a variety of resources, effort and time commitments by the society and its members. Furthermore, these resources that will be drawn on to make corrections are likely to be relatively scarce such that they are likely to have market prices. As a result, the levels of the resource commitments which will be necessary to bring respective quantum departures back towards the optimal state are likely to have parallel market costs.

When societies decide to take initiatives to re-balance respective quantum components, the resource commitments that the management directorate will make will initially be guided by the social priorities that the society places on the attainment of respective quality-of-life (quantum) features. However, there are also economic efficiency conditions (which are elaborated elsewhere) which a society may apply to its selections of resource commitments among alternative departures from their quantum targets.

However, as a first stage operation, the focus is on the respective mixes of features on which an aggregate economic development needs to focus (if it intends to manage the common property resources as well as execute its co-ordinating responsibilities) so as to promote quality-of-life targets in a monetised environment.

There is technical variety to the respective quantum components and the quantities of resources as well as time which respective quantum components will require to correct departures from their optimal delivery levels. That pervading variety makes it difficult to compute an aggregate achievement which is based on the technical interfaces as attained quanta out of which quality-of-living becomes accessible. Yet, in a first stage appraisal, achievement may be framed as the *relative* success of the society in causing mixes of quantum targets to be forthcoming.

At its optimal targeted technical level, each technical feature that is included as a quantum component may be given a quantum index of 1.000. Relative departures from that optimal state of presentation are then graded downwards. Therefore, a ten percent access of optimal attainable level is an index quantity of 0.100 or 100 'quanta'.

Although it is tempting to consider outcome as indicated by a simplistic aggregation of index levels, high performance may not be indicated by including and then aggregating index levels across many quantum features in the 'Q' index because quantum economics addresses the interface with survival as the pattern of contribution to quality-of-life attainment. It does not seek to resolve questions regarding whether a society has more or less material output from resource commitment.

Each society will need to stipulate the technical complements for which it will have access targets and for which indices of relative deliveries may be computed. However, a tentative list of such proposed quantum components that are to be delivered at optimal technical levels which are consistent with a high quality-of-life may include features as indicated in the following sample of a Quantum Economic statistical analytical and measurement framework.

Please note that the listed variables can be adjusted accordingly by communities and societies via a consultative process concerning quality-of-life attainments. The standardisation of certain specified technical delivery features associated within the 'quantum economics' QLI measurement framework by member countries of the United Nations would provide a basis of potentially constructive cross-societal comparisons. Notwithstanding this, QLI is posited as a flexible measurement framework which is responsive to the quality-of-life attainments of respective communities and societies. QLI is posited as an alternative to the market-based GDP-oriented measurement indices.

QUANTUM ECONOMICS
Holistic Aggregate Management

[SPACE-TIME Relationship] (Lt)

i.Natural and Material Environment Factors(E)

A. Conservation of the Natural Ecology

Tree Density of an Area	1.000
Indigenous Animal Species Conservation	1.000
Indigenous Species Conservation	1.000

B. Freedom from Diseconomies

Relative absence of Surface Water Pollution [Water Purity]	1.000
Relative absence of Air Pollution [Air Purity]	1.000
Ozone Layer Conservation	1.000
Quality of Survival supporting Ultra Violet Index	1.000
Quality of Survival supporting Precipitation	1.000
Pollution-free ground Water	1.000
Toxicity-free Land	1.000
Top-soil Conservation	1.000

Industrial Pollutants and Environmental Degradation

(Freedom from industrially released
Carcinogenic Substances/Pollutants

Carcinogenic Substance 1	1.000
Carcinogenic Substance 2	1.000
Carcinogenic Substance 3	1.000
Carcinogenic Substance 4	1.000

Relative Freedom of Population from Chronic Health Problems

Health Problem 1	1.000
Health Problem 2	1.000
Health Problem 3	1.000
Health Problem 4	1.000
Health Problem 5	1.000

ii. Human/Built Environment Factors (H)

A. Access to Food, Clothing, Shelter and Healthcare

(Food)
Access to (specifiable) to High Quality Foodby Indicatable Type: (each)

	1.000
Access to High Quality Starchesby Indicatable Type: (each)	1.000
Access to Other Specifiable Food: (each)	1.000
Access to Carcinogenic-Free Foods	1.000
Access to Genetically-Engineered-Free Foods	1.000
Access to foods made with only organic ingredients	1.000

(Clothing)

Access to Basic Clothing	1.000

(Shelter)

Access to Basic Shelter	1.000

(Health Care)
Access to Universal Public Healthcare   1.000

B. Economic Disparity

Freedom from Economic Disparity   1.000

[i.e. 0.910 would indicate much less economic disparity than 0.240. For example, Denmark with among the least economic disparity in the geo-political West would be closer to 0.910 and the U.S. would be closer to 0.240]

C. Public Health

Public Sanitation Standards   1.000

(Freedom from Carcinogenic
Substances in Foods)
Carcinogenic Substance 1   1.000
Carcinogenic Substance 2   1.000
Carcinogenic Substance 3   1.000
Carcinogenic Substance 4   1.000

D. Personal Safety/Crime

Nonviolent Crime Free   1.000
Violent Crime Free (Non-homicidal)   1.000
Homicide   1.000
Prison Population   1.000

E. Consciousness-Driven Self-Direction

Freedom of Consciousness   1.000
(i.e. *Canadian Charter of Rights and Freedoms* guarantees Freedom of Consciousness)

Involuntary Unemployment   1.000
Involuntary Underemployment   1.000
(Calculated based upon formal education and choice relative to employ-
    ment occupation)   1.000
Constitutional Protection of Privacy   1.000
(Anti-Discrimination)
Minorities: Freedom from Institutionalized Racism   1.000
Freedom from Sexism   1.000
Employment Equity Representation in Workforce   1.000
Freedom from General Institutionalized Discrimination   1.000

F. Opportunities for Facilitative Organisational participation opportunities and Synergy

(Governance)
Degree of citizen-participation in government via no-coerced turn-out
    during elections   1.000
Degree of citizen-participation in daily operation of government via con-
    stitutional instruments   1.000
Degree of participation by labour in the organizational managerial direc-
    tion of private-enterprises   1.000
Constitutional Government(i.e. Does government have legal limits on its
    powers?)   1.000

(Community Interaction)
Discretionary Opportunities and Resources for membership in Voluntary
    Associations

Labour Organisations   1.000
Political and Social Clubs   1.000
Family and Religious Organisations   1.000
Capital Intensive Team Sports   1.000
Capital Intensive Individual Sports   1.000
Individual Sports   1.000
Music and Dance as Communication   1.000

Access to Territorial Space and Permissible Informational Travel	1.000
(Organisational Control of Information) Access to Information)	1.000
(Uncensored) Newspapers and Cinema	1.000
Public Libraries and Continuing Education	1.000
(Access to Formal Education and Skills Development)	
Access to Schooling; Primary (years)	1.000
Access to Schooling; Secondary	1.000
High Level, (University) Education	1.000
(Public Direction/Control of Common Property Resources)	
Relative Public Control of Water Resources	1.000
Facilitative Public Control of High Water Quality	1.000
Relative Public Control of Hydro/Electricity	1.000
Facilitative Public Control of a High Air Quality	1.000
Facilitative Public Participation in Mass-Media/Broadcasting	1.000
Facilitative Public Control in Agricultural Resources	1.000
Facilitative Public Control in Land Conservation Management	1.000

The foregoing presentation of quantum components, as indicative in the provisional list of complements to quality-of-living, draws attention to the fabric of the *tapestry* of living, which a holistic aggregate resource management directorate supports rather than the prevailing financial-equivalent wealth "score". Quantum Economics emphasises the living-centred attainment of individuals as the outcome of a holistic aggregate economic development context. Quantum Economics also emphasises the ecology of survival in a holistic aggregate economic development context that supports human survival and quality-of-living attainments.

There are efficiency tactics that the holistic aggregate economic development directorate will also need to execute as it balances resources among approaches to respective quantum states. These efficiency tactics will need to correspond with and will also need to be informed by the strategies which individuals use in a cosmopolitan political economy as they manage their time-use commitments so as to secure human development from their interface with prevailing reality. However, elaboration of matters in this regard is presented in the book entitled *Work, the Economy and Human Development.*

CHAPTER 15

Quantum Economics Retrospective: Towards Renaissance

⸎

Q UANTUM ECONOMICS via the posited Quality-of-Life Index (QLI) presents a rejuvenated analytical context towards a rejuvenated New Economy. Quantum Economics provides a critical basis for addressing the dysfunctional effects of the market-based economics paradigm on the guidance of public-policy making in the international political economy.

———•———

Public Policy, "Globalisation" and the developmental quandary of the so-called 'Third World'

Does the market-based economics provide the best framework to critically guide developmental considerations in the so-called 'Third World'? To help consider this question, consider the apparent trends. Has the introduction of market-based economy via privatisation and International Monetary Fund (IMF)-related austerity policies alleviated economic disparity in so-called developing countries? *Apparently not* – The institution-alisation of the 'market' economy in these societies has by and large wors-ened economic disparity and poverty. Has the institutionalisation of the market supported critically needed environmental conservation? Once again, apparently not. The institutionalisation of the market in these areas has in fact accelerated environmental degradation in the so-called 'Third World'. These trends continue to endanger the quality of human survival, animal habitats and numerous plant species that human and animals depend upon for survival. Indeed, societies which used to have very sophisticated resource management practices are currently facing humanitarian disasters. These cited sophisticated resource management practices refer to the indigenous systems of knowledge which evolved from millennia of cultural wisdom about human ecology in relation-ship to economic-related development. Humanitarian crises have been induced by the apparent "intrusion" of activities associated with market capitalism Humanitarian crises have also been induced by correspond-ent dysfunctional 'market indices of growth' that have side-tracked the economic directorates of societies. Numerous studies, including well-re-searched television documentaries, have attested the apparent socio-eco-nomic dysfunctional effects of the "intrusion" of market capitalism in the so-called 'Third World'.

———•———

The implications of enlarged political economic blocs on governance and work

The proponents of 'market capitalism' via "globalisation" champi-on the ascendance of enlarged political economic blocs. Perhaps the well-developed of these blocs include the European Union. However, ex-amples of such bloc arrangements also notably had included the North American Free Trade Agreement (NAFTA) toward the current *United*

States-Mexico-Canada Agreement (USMCA). The proponents of 'market capitalism' have championed the ascendance of such blocs towards an integrated "economic globalisation" regime based on diverse claims. Among these claims is that the ascendance of such blocs of "liberalised trade" bring forth "prosperity to all" and the "strengthening of democracy" internationally. These blocs indeed make it easier for transnational private enterprises to do business and make money in general. However, the advantages of such enlarged blocs to the diverse publics of the societies who are subjected to these enlarged blocs are far less substantiated.

It has been well-documented that while these blocs benefit the ownership interests of private transnational enterprises, they also dysfunctionally affect the ability of democratically elected "sovereign" governments to serve their constituencies. These enlarged political economic blocs are based on an apparent informal "Corporate Charter". This apparent operational "Corporate Charter" marginalises the public interest concerning the quality-of-life to the extent to which that 'public interest' conflicts with the vested interests of corporate ownerships. In other words, numerous documented evidences indicate that the enlarged political economic blocs either support democracy, where these blocs have been formally established, or the 'spread of democracy'. In addition, the ability of corporate ownership (in an ascendant capitalistocracy) to secure additional financial benefits from such enlarged political economic blocs have been at the expense of the quality of survival of subjected diverse publics. *This has occurred as the vested interests of the transnational enterprises have concentrated economic power to such an extent that they have compromised the representational integrity of responsible constitutional government.*

The erosion of labour law, inclusive of union collective bargaining rights by governments in Europe, Canada, and the U.S., has been symptomatic of pressure exerted by the ascending concentrated economic power of transnational enterprises against constitutional government. The prolific growth of *sweat shops* which exploit individuals throughout the so-called 'Third World' has been symptomatic of the erosion of the ability of officially 'sovereign' governments in these societies to protect its citizens from the subversive effects of transnational enterprise lobbyists. The proliferation of "sweat shops" throughout the Third World suggests that "democracy" in general and the well-being of employed individuals are not a substantive consideration of transnational enterprises. The existence of the "sweat shops" is not confined to the so-called "Third World". "Sweat shops" also exist in the geo-political West. The employed individuals of these "sweat shops" are frequently immigrants who can be coerced into such working conditions under threat of deportation because of a legally precarious immigration status. As the pressures mount on corporations to achieve insatiable profit expectations, workplaces become the frontlines of corporate efforts to achieve maximised profits by undermining workplace conditions. The "sweat shop" represents a *market* idealised workplace for the corporations which abandon their facilities in the geo-political West, laying-off many hundreds of thousands of people in the process. The depressed wage context and anomia associated with "sweat shops" are becoming more prevalent in the cultures of the workplaces in the West as dysfunctional mercenary profit related pressures continue to mount on corporations.

————•————

Smaller political economic regimes are more supportive of quality-of-life attainments

Why are smaller political economic regimes more supportive of quality-of-life attainments? A smaller political economic regime provides the basis for potentially greater accountability to individual constituents than comparatively enlarged political economic blocs. Thus, a political economic regime of 4, 000 will provide a more optimised context for accountability than a regime of 400, 000. A regime of 400, 000 will provide a more optimised context for accountability than a regime of 4, 000, 000. With this in mind, a regime of 4, 000, 000 will provide a more optimised context for accountability than a regime of 40, 000, 000. This is because small political economic regimes are more inherently responsive than larger regimes. Notwithstanding this, larger regimes can be made correspondingly responsive with a more pro-active approach to facilitating a governance context of responsiveness. The current creation of enlarged political economic blocs appears to principally respond to the 'market' interests of Big Business rather than quality of living. A posited rejuvenated conception of a New Economy would be facilitated by the creation of smaller governance structures of accountability rather than large blocs via "globalisation". Such smaller local governance units aided by correspondent analytical evaluations would be able to more responsively monitor environmental sustainability and quality-of-life attainments in support of self-actualized human development.

―――――・―――――

Towards a Quantum Economic analytical context in support of a rejuvenated 'New Economy'

A posited 'Quantum Economic' analytical context is cognisant that attributed 'market efficiency' does not ensure the distribution of goods and services that are needed to support the high quality of survival for individuals without prejudice. Indeed, the attributed "efficiency of the market" does not provide a desirable efficiency for a dynamic pluralistic society. Attributed "market efficiency" also does not necessarily support the distribution of access-opportunities, on which individuals rely for quality-of-life attainments in a modern pluralistic society. Attributed "market efficiency" also does not support redressing sexism, institutionalised racism and other forms of institutionalised discrimination. Such institutionalised discrimination continues to have dysfunctional effects on quality-of-life attainments in relationship to human development. Institutionalised discrimination has persisted and has, in fact, been reinforced by 'market capitalism' within the pluralistic societies of the West and internationally. A culture of Social Darwinistic tribalism in market capitalism (explored in a proceeding) has indeed reinforced the persistence of institutionalisation discrimination of access-opportunities in the international political economy.

———◆———

The apparent logic of 'the market'
The mythology of "value-free" economics

Protagonists of 'the market paradigm' claim that its approach to economics is simply empirical without any "value judgements" that would undermine 'objective assessments' of data. With this in mind, protagonists of 'the market paradigm' attack public policy considerations to alleviate social costs via social programmes and environmental conservation as "interfering" with the market. Milton Friedman and other adherents of the Chicago School's market paradigm champion the notion that "the market" best operates towards a desired "market efficiency" with the least "interference". These adherents also champion the idea that government involvement in the economy should be limited in highly circumscribed areas. These areas include 'maintaining law and order', a monetary policy that complements support to financial markets that critically include the stock markets and national defence via the maintenance of a military.

While protagonists of the market proclaim a value-free approach to economics, it is apparent that values are inextricably apart of the 'market paradigm'. It is these 'market' values which have relegated work as a function of a 'wage earning' market operation. This 'market approach' deprives individuals of responsible constitutional government that can actively establish, affirm and enforce a system of economic rights.

What is the apparent logic of the market? The market is an essentially envisioned commercial milieu of buyers and sellers who are pursuing their self-interest goals via trade. The market operates within a legitimated legal framework. The market is driven by the perpetuation of a culture of activity associated with economic agents in pursuit of "profit" and "wealth".

Within this context, the apparent logic of the market is that owners of private enterprises should strive for the achievement of 'market efficiency'. This critically relies on managerial efforts to depress wages in order to help maximise insatiable profit expectations by shareholders. 'Wages' and overall working conditions should be depressed in association with 'work' as a 'market operation' rather than an exercise of conscious individuals pursuing a high quality of survival in living. Pursuant to the apparent logic of the market, 'wages' and working conditions should be depressed when legally feasible and commercial expedient to business enterprises in relation to '*the market*'.

Champions of the 'market paradigm' claim that when left alone free of 'government intervention', the market fosters healthy competition. Such healthy competition is supposed to support the optimised availability of the goods and services to-wage earners. However, the apparent logic of the market legitimates and encourages predatory and related unlawful business practices via a sought elimination of market competitors by Big Business. Market competitors are viewed to undermine the ability to maximise profit on behalf of a constituency of shareholders. Corporate take-overs result from efforts by a constituency of shareholders to reduce market competition that depresses insatiable profit expectations. These corporate take-overs often result in mass-layoffs, further efforts to depress wages and overall working conditions where possible and the further ability of corporations to 'control the market'. Efforts to 'control the market' are evident in the apparent organised rising of gas prices by oil companies and the rising costs of renting apartments in urban areas that have resulted in the growing pervasiveness of homelessness and worsening 'wage slavery'.

The drive of insatiable profit by shareholders also creates a dis-incentive to the production of long-lasting high quality products. This apparent trend is evident in the declining durability of products since the 1950's and 1960's despite advances in technology that could support even more improved durability. This has been referred to as "planned obsolescence" by Ralph Nader who is a famous consumer advocate. Within the market paradigmatic logic system of planned obsolescence, why continue to make a product that can last for 15, 20, 30 or 40 years when a product that can be made that only lasts 2, 3, 4 or 5 years? In doing so, the corporations can encourage the more frequent buying of products to replace the products that have built-in sub-standard quality. This apparent planned obsolescence also in turn accelerates the use of resources for wasteful production and the further degradation of the environment from non-recycled and dumped wasted materials.

The 'market' left on its own without legislatively accountable intervention by responsible constitutional government does not inherently operate in a manner that complements quality-of-life attainments. The profit ethos of 'market capitalism' supports the calculated indoctrination of materialism via societal socialisation in 'popular culture'. Such indoctrination further encourages wasteful buying patterns. 'Wasteful buying' further drives "wage earners" into worsening conditions of 'wage slavery' via indebtedness. 'Wasteful buying' further supports 'wasteful production' in order to support maximised profit-earnings. Protagonists of the market paradigm essentially advocate divesting 'the market' from intervention by *responsible government*. Such intervention on behalf of human rights in a manner that alleviates social costs has been substituted for a market regime of indoctrination and ensuing control by capitalistocrats in pursuit of 'profit' at whatever costs.

———•———

Replacing the 'market'-based conception of economics with an 'agora' of complex-interdependence and living

Instead of a focus on human survival that is linked to quality-of-life attainments, 'market'-oriented economics bases its elaborated formulations and theories on an erroneous, mythological and essentially propagandised premise. The 'market'-based economics implicit premise is that the so-called "profit-motive" is the primary drive for human civilization and uses that base to legitimate essentially commercial-driven 'market operations' rather than quality of survival. That focus has taken human civilization on a course that is oblivious of critical human survival considerations linked to quality-of-life attainments. If, for example, someone is sick and is on life-support in the hospital, which option would such an individual more likely choose: someone giving such an individual some money with no medical treatment or someone giving such an individual medical treatment that promises his/her immediate recovery from being on life-support and being ill in general? *The Chicago School 'market' economics based paradigm prescribes such a choice-matrix in which such profit-considerations override quality of survival considerations.*

Indeed, the Chicago School market-based paradigmatic context drives the American private-oriented healthcare system. It has prescribed a context in which commercial considerations override human survival considerations that are linked to access-opportunities to flows of services that yield quality-of-life attainments. Americans without the money to pay for-profit-associated "market-based" pricing on their health are denied healthcare including medication. Other Americans who have the money up front to pay for their emergency healthcare needs are forced into bankruptcy or near bankruptcy with other debilitating impacts on their quality of survival. Other Americans simply forgo critically needed healthcare. Individuals who forgo such needed healthcare endanger their health and the survival of others in what is a 'complex interdependent' socio-economic milieu *where choices of conscious individuals have impacts on each other in a joint-survival context.*

The book entitled *Constitutionalizing Universal Public Health in Canada: Integrating quality-of-life considerations into the Charter of Rights and Freedoms* explores the world renowned Canadian universal public healthcare system as providing a model of healthcare that is consistent with quantum economics. The dominant Chicago School market paradigm that drives "economic globalisation" leads human civilization on ensuing destructive paths of economic development de-sensitised to quality of survival as the economic driving force.

Towards a posited rejuvenated 'New Economy', quantum economics argues that in the light of their awareness, conscious individuals engage with each other so as to operate as inheritors of a commitment to survive.

The dynamic of a commercial-focused "market" is based on an insatiable drive for profit by agents squandering the human development potential. Human economic agents are turned against each other in tri-ballistic adversarial and mercenary constellations in the so-called "free market" regime. These constellations are associated with market-induced social factionalism, pseudo-feudalistic strife and attrition in this regime. The essentially predatory context of 'the market' squanders survival-related precious resources into dysfunctional adversarial competitive interests with short-term profit horizons.

The 'quantum economics' context recognises that humans are social beings. Accordingly, as social beings, the nature of conscious individuals un-coerced by the adversarial context of market capitalism is to work in association with each other in their human development.

The axiomatic "profit-motive" context of market-based economics dysfunctionally squanders precious, often non-renewable resources that are a permanent loss to humanity into the essentially venal pursuit of instant gratification and self-aggrandisement. Alternatively, quantum economics posits the re-orientation of the organisational development of society away from a survival-squandering "alleged "profit motive" into a "sustainable equilibrium" focus. A 'sustained equilibrium' focus is based on human development context sensitised to the ecology of survival.

Within an organisational context, the drive for 'market' profit creates a propensity for the organisational management structure to commercially exploit employed human economic agents oblivious to their health and general well-being. The correspondent pricing that manifests from the market reacts to the servicing of a critical mass of human economic agents with relative elevated levels of purchasing power circumscribed by a 'market' regime of 'supply' and 'demand'. The pricing that ensues from the drive for profit is particularly evident in developing societies with increasing economic disparity as a result of "economic globalisation" is frequently more than socio-economically disenfranchised individuals can afford. The quality-of-survival needs that individuals are disenfranchised by a reliance on "market forces" without access to social programmes that alleviate the social costs of the market. The reliance on so called "free market" forces has become the basis of growing levels of poverty and social malaise both in the geo-political West and the so-called "Third World".

———◆———

Towards a posited rejuvenated 'New Economy'

An economy which supports the quality of survival needs of human economic agents inclusively will have a greater capacity for robust synergistic development from the contributions of conscious individuals than an economy in which such participation is marginalised.

'Quantum economics' posits a human development context in which organisational development pursues sustainability freed from the dysfunctional resource-squandering 'market' pressures. In such a milieu, organisational development would be focused on facilitating a synergistic environment of human development and a resource management context that in turn is cognisant of the 'complex interdependence' of the ecology of survival. The alleviation of the pressures of a 'materialistic society' driven by dysfunctional adversarial human inter-personal and organisational relationships and wasteful mercenary resource management practices would help a milieu that facilitates human development.

———◆———

Raymond Samuels

Technology in a market-based economics in relationship to a posited 'quantum economics'

'Quantum economics' also recognises the importance of technology in development as the market-based economics paradigm. However, the 'quantum economics' focus of 'complex interdependence' associated with the 'ecology of survival' and the development of technical capabilities has distinctive outcomes. The deployment of technology within Chicago School market-based economics is enveloped within its short-term profit horizons. Thus, the deployment of technology within a raison d'être of profit is implicitly aimed at enhancing the squandering of re-source-based survival opportunities. As technology is further developed within Chicago School market-based economics, so is the squandering of resource-based survival opportunities accelerated. Within a 'quantum economics' developmental paradigm, technology is developed to support the *conservation* of survival opportunities. Such an economics is based on an organisational development context of ecologically sensitised and human development focused 'sustainable equlibria' rather than profit.

————•————

Addressing the apparent dysfunctional societal development effects of market-based economics

The so-called "profit ethic" is the apparent social psychological intellectual manifestation of 'dis-associative' societal organisational development. Individuals and individuals within institutions pursuant to a development paradigm associated with the "profit ethic" are engaged in adversarial Social Darwinistic competition with its debilitating survival consequences. A 'quantum economics' context of 'complex interdependence' is a developmental context supportive to 'associative' human economic development. Such an 'associative' and 'mutualistic' based economic development supports individual and related collective survival considerations. Such a milieu that is cognisant of 'complex interdependence' is 'associative' and 'constructive' rather than ' dis-associative' and 'destructive'. Market-based economics leads to a correspondent 'market drive' for commercial utilitarian conquests that may "require" war at the expense of human survival considerations "to help expand markets". The dis-associative context of the market also reinforces racialist tribalism. Apparent racialist tribalism manifests in the continuing substantive indifference of market-based European societies to critically alleviating institutionalised poverty in African and other non-European societies worsened by "market" capitalism. Its context from the same mentality also encourages crime that manifests from the 'dis-associative' context of market economics with a correspondent drive for "market opportunity".

Indeed, increased crime has frequently developed following the expansion of 'market capitalism' based on its 'dis-associative' context. Alternative to the market-based legitimated context of corporatized 'economic globalisation', a 'quantum economics context supports the human development associated with conscious individuals as social beings into a socio-economically facilitative cosmopolitan association. An inclusive-focused developmental regime of a robust and dynamic cosmopolitan society is cognisant of the synergistic productive potentials of a human development context. Such a human developmental context that facilitates interdependent citizen-participants to constructively support their individual and combined quality-of-life attainments in comparison to the mercenary market-based developmental paradigm is comparatively facilitative to synergistic productive potentials.

————•————

Raymond Samuels

Economic Disparity and a Quality-of-living Index (QLI) or 'Q index

Economic disparity refers to an environment in which there is a substantive gap between "the rich" and "the poor" of a society. Market-focused economics associated with the contributions of the Chicago School has totally marginalised the redressing of "economic disparity" as a critical analytical consideration of economic development. This omitted substantive analytical consideration has been further manifested on a globalising scale via efforts to institutionalise "economic globalisation".

Economic disparity is critically linked conceptually to the quality-of-life considerations. Economic disparity in the market economy is the outcome of an iniquitous public policy framework. This public policy framework is in turn supported via the continued use of a dysfunctional market-oriented analytic context. Such a framework legitimates exploitative developmental practices carried out by constituents of the most financially wealthy who rely on an ever growing pool of cheap "human capital" to support greater levels of profit. Economic disparity rises in a roughly proportional manner to the commercial utilitarian usage of 'human agents' and 'natural resources' by a capitalistocracy in a manner that *institutionalises poverty via the disenfranchisement of access-opportunities.*

Economic disparity is associated with a pattern of institutionalised economic decision-making that is indifferent an inclusive developmental context associated with a quality-of-living framework. The economic disparity that is legitimated by the market economy condones predatory exploitation of "human capital" and "material capital". The predatory exploitation of "human capital" and the correspondent commercial utilitarian exploitation of material capital associated with natural resources that are critical to sustaining communities lead to dysfunctionalities that undermine quality-of-life attainments.

The insatiable drive for profit that is associated with predatory and commercial utilitarian exploitation legitimated in the paradigmatic framework of the market economy encourages the wasteful allocation of resources into commercial schemes of self-aggrandisement. When these resources have been totally depleted in the name of maximised profit of commercially savvy entrepreneurs, the result is a permanent loss of what may very well be a life-depending resource that is critical to human survival. The society, if not the globe in general, within an ecosystems context incurs a long-term socio-economic loss as a result of such environmental degradation. Environmental degradation is indeed marginalised within the privatised short-term profit-horizon calculation context of the "market economy".

Economic disparity supports a regime of poverty for the disenfranchised poor. That outcome supports a milieu of social malaise and alienation that in turn supports a milieu that often includes homelessness, drug addiction/substance abuse and ensuing crime. Such a regime can also support the evolution of extremist ideology that may promise some form of salvation from repressive destitution associated with prevailing disparity in the form of terrorism. The Quantum Economics context presents an analytical context that supports the addressing of the manifestation of such terrorism via progressive social policy that complements high quality of survival. The market response to such a milieu of rampant crime and terrorism is the "police state". The police state is a fascistic political economic approach to ostensibly maintain "law and order" in a manner which enhances authoritarian social control. In the process, the police state is aimed at subverting *responsible government* on behalf of the security interests of 'capitalistocracy'.

A rejuvenated developmental paradigm associated with the quality-of-life requires an analytical framework that addresses economic disparity. Quantum Economics posits such a rejuvenated analytical framework.

A proposed Quality-of-living Index (QLI) (or 'Q index') to complement 'quantum economics' looks at the prevailing technical quantities of critical services associated with the 'ecology of survival' that will complement the quality-of-life access of a diverse public. Such a rejuvenated index of economic development must critically include the currently most economically disadvantaged of society to truly support a needed inclusive quality-of-living attainment framework. A QLI that incorporates the analysis of the institutionalised features of an economy that has created socio-economic marginalising (via predatory exploitation of "human capital" and correspondent exploitation of material capital) can address the shortcomings of a market-focused economic growth measurement context. The posited QLI that is presented as an alternative to GDP related indices of economic development is explored in the preceding Chapter.

QLI related performance will be indicated by or will pivot on the technical levels of the target components to the quality of living expression that the society targets critically concerned with the most economically disadvantaged of society and by departures from them. In doing so, the inclusive participation of citizens in a political economy which contributes to the dynamism and robustness of a pluralistic society can be maximised while alleviating dyfunctionalities associated with economic disparity. The market-focused paradigm that legitimates predatory exploitation substantively measures economic performance on the balance sheets of the most successful entrepreneurs and trivialises the atrocious social and environmental costs of short-term profit horizons.

While the market economy provides the basis of society of wasteful economic strife between adversarial interests competing for an insatiable drive for short-term horizon focused monetary profit, "quantum economics" presents a rejuvenated paradigmatic context for fostering a more synergistic and robust economy. Such an economy supported by a quality-of-life index framework that helps guide public policy maximises the participation of citizens in a political economy. These citizen-participants with affirmed human rights as economic agents are presented with in a rejuvenated QLI analytical attainment context complementive of alleviating institutionalised poverty and correspondingly assisting public policy in the societal pursuit of a high quality of survival. Quantum economics recognises a complex independent ecology of living that is in contradistinction to market-based economics which fails to deal to illuminate an analytical context and formulation of survival-related economic public policy considerations.

A rejuvenated aggregate economic development management context will also need to have as its fundamental target the *promotion* of resource management and usage related to the 'ecology of survival' out of which delivery of the sought technical flows (measured by required statistical information) to quality-of-living attainment will be forthcoming. The posited academic-professional area of 'Quantum Economics' would seek to analyse the tolerances in the budgeting of environmental carrying capacity that the economic development directorate practices.

By virtue of the responsibilities which the institutions of governance have regarding the quality of the environment of survival, quantum economics does not have, as its primary focus, the rate of growth that has been occurring related to financially augmented trade. Rather, it recognises a survival-focus of conscious individuals pursuing economic development. This axiomatically includes developmental effects on health linked to the protection of the "currency of survival" of ecosystems associated with human ecology. Therefore, quantum economics critically addresses the strategies which governments need to execute within the governance context of society in the facilitation of high quality of survival by conscious individuals.

A 'quantum economics' perspective focuses on the idea that an economy is an infinitely complex and interdependent ecological system. The success so-to-speak of an institutionalized quantum economics context of development is the ability of human economic agents as conscious individuals to balance quality-of-living attainments associated with a complex interdependent 'human-made' and 'natural environment'. These quality-of-living attainments are fundamentally based upon supporting human health and survival within a broad ecology of survival context of the 'human-made' and the 'natural environment'.

BIBLIOGRAPHY

Becker, Gary (1975); "A Theory of Allocation of Time", The *Economic Journal* Vol. LXXV, pp. 493-517.

.... ed) (1972); *Human Capital Policy Issues and Research Opportunities* Fiftieth Anniversary Colloquium VI, (New York: National Bureau of Economic Research).

.... (1964); *Human Capital*, (New York: Columbia University Press for the National Bureau of Economic Research).

Berger, Peter L., (1964), "Some General Observations on the Problem of Work" in *The Human Shape of Work* Peter L. Berger, (ed.), (New York: The Macmillan Company, pp. 211-241).

Bognar, Jozsef (1969); *Economic Policy and Planning in Developing Countries*, (Budapest: Akademiai Kiado).

Borner, Silvio, (1992) with Aymo Brunetti, and Beatrice Weder; *Institutional Obstacles to Latin American Growth*, Inernational Center for Economic Growth, Occasional Paper no.24, 47 pp.

Braverman, Harry (1974), *Labor and Monopoly Capital: The Degradation of Work in the Twentieth Century*, (New York: Monthly Review Press).

Breton, Albert (1974), *The Economic Theory of Representative Government*, Harry G. Johnson (ed.), (Chicago: Aldine Publishing Company).

Canadian Conference of Catholic Bishops (1983); "Ethical Reflections on the State of the Economy", (Ottawa: Canada: *Catholic New Times*).

Carby-Samuels, Horace R. (1983) "The Human Development Basis of 'Ethical Reflections'", (Toronto, Canada: circulated but unpublished manuscript).

.... (2002) *Work, The Economy and Human Development*, Ottawa, Canada, Agora Publishing Consortium, (ISBN 0-9681906-1- 8

Dalton, George, (1968), *Primitive, Archaic, and Modern Economies*, Essays of Karl Polanyi, (Boston: Beacon Press).

Feyerabend, Paul, (1963), "How to be a Good Empericist", in Philosophy of Science *The Delaware Seminar, Volume 2*, Bernard Baumrin (ed.); (New York: Jon Wiley & Sons, pp. 3-39).

.... (1970), "Against Method", *Minnesota Studies in the Philosophy of Science Vol, IV*, Michael Rander, and Stephen Winokur (eds.); (Minneapolis: University of Minnesota Press, pp. 17-130).

.... (1970), "Problems of Empiricism, Part II"; *The Nature and Function of Scientific Theories*, Robert Colodny (ed.); (Pittsburgh: University of Pittsburgh Press, pp. 275-353).

Fisher, Irving, (1930) (1961), *The Theory of Interest* (New York: Augustus M Kelley).

Frieden, Karl, (1980), *Workplace Democracy and Productivity*, (Washington, DC: National Center for Economic Alternatives).

Friedman, Milton, (1957), *A Theory of the Consumption Function*, (Princeton: Princeton Univrsity Press).

.... (1953) *Essays in Positive Economics*, (Chicago: University of Chicago Press).

.... (1960), *A Program for Monetary Stability*; (New York: Fordham University Press).

Freire, Paulo (1970), *Pedagogy of the Oppressed*, Myra Bergman Ramos (tr.), (New York: The Seabury Press).

Galbraith, John Kenneth (1973), *Economics and the Public Purpose*, (Boston: Houghton Mifflin Company).

.... (1967) *The Economics of the New Industrial State*, (Boston: Houghton Mifflin Co.).

Galtung, Johan, (1972), "A Structural Theory of Imperialism", *The African Economic Review*, Vol 1, No. 4, pp. 93-138.

Habermas, Jurgen (1971) *Knowledge and Human Interests*, Jeremy J. Shapiro (tr.) (Boston: Beacon Press).

Hirshman, Albert O. and Michael Rothschild (1973) "The Changing Tolerance for Inequality in Development", *Quarterly Journal of Economics*, Vol. LXXXVII, pp. 544-566.

Jonas, Hans (1969) "Economic Knowledge and the Critique of Goals", in *Economic Means and Social Ends*, Robert Heilbroner (ed.) (Englewood Cliffs, New Jersey: Prentice -Hall Inc.) pp. 67-87.

Kuhn, Thomas (1962), *The Structure of Scientific Revolutions*, (Chicago: The University of Chicago Press).

Kuznets, Simon (1963) "Parts and Wholes in Economics" in *Parts and Wholes*, Daniel Learner (ed.), (New York: The Free Press of Glencoe).

Leontief, Wassily, (1971), "Theoretical Assumptions and Nonobserved Facts"; *American Economic Review Vol. LXI #1*, March 1971, pp. 1-7.

Linder, Staffan (1969), *The Harried Leisure Class*, (New York: Columbia University Press).

Machlup, Fritz (1962), *The Production and Distribution of Knowledge in the United States*, (Princeton: Princeton University Press).

.... (1980), *Knowledge, Its Creation, Distribution and Economic Significance*, Vol. I, (Princeton: Princeton University Press).

.... (1984) *The Economics of Information and Human Capital* T. W. Schultz (ed.), (Princeton, Princeton University Press).

Macpherson, C. B., (1962) *The Political Theory of Possessive Individualism: Hobbes to Locke*, (Oxford: Oxford University Press).

Magnuson, Warren G. (1968) and Jean Carper *The Dark Side of the Marketplace, The Plight of the American Consumer*; (Englewood Cliffs, New Jersey: Prentice-Hall Inc.).

Marshall, Alfred (1890), (1964) *Principles of Economics*, Eighth Edition, (London: MacMillan).

Merleau-Pontey, Maurice, (1962) Colon Smith (tr.), *Phenomenology of Perception*, (New York: Humanities Press).

Myrdal, Gunnar (1965), *The political Element in the Development of Economic Theory*, Paul Streeten (tr.) (Cambridge, Mass.: Harvard University Press).

.... (1958) Paul Streeten (ed.), *Value in Social Theory*, a Selection of essays on Methodology; (London: Routledge Keegan & Paul).

North Douglas C., (1992); *Transactions Costs, Institutions, and Economic Performance*; San Francisco, International Center for Economic Growth, Occasional Paper No. 30, 32 pp.

O'Toole, James, (1974) *Work and Quality of Life*, Resource Papers for Work in America; (Cambridge, Mass.: M.I.T.Press).

Polanyi, Karl (1968) "Our Obsolete Market Mentality", in *Primitive, Archaic, And Modern Economies: Essays of Karl Polanyi*, George Dalton (ed.), (Boston, Mass.: Beacon Press), pp. 59-77.

.... (1964) *The Great Transformation*; (Boston: Beacon Press).

Polanyi, Michael (1966) *The Tacit Dimension* (Garden City N.Y.: Doubleday Book Company).

Ricardo, David (1817), (1911), *The Principles of Political Economy and Taxation*, with an introduction by Michael Fogarty, (Everyman's Library, London: J.M. Dent and Sons Ltd., New York: E. P. Dutton & Co. Inc.).

Rifkin, Jeremy (1980) *Entropy*, (New York, N.Y.: Viking Press).

Schultz, T. W. (1972), *Human Resources*, Gary Becker (ed.) Fiftieth Anniversary Colloquium VI, (New York: National Bureau of Economic Research).

.... (1961) "Human Capital", *American Economic Review*, Vol. 51, March , pp. 1-17.

.... (1964) *Transforming Traditional Agriculture*; (New Haven, Yale University Press).

Smith, Adam (1776) (1937) *An Inquiry Into the Nature and the Causes of the Wealth of Nations*, (New york: Modern Library Edition).

.... (1759) (1966) *The Theory of Moral Sentiments* (New York: Kelley Reprints; Augustus M. Kelley Publishers).

Stewart, James B. (January 1995) "Time use, Psychic Duality and the search for Authentic Development by Peoples of African Descent", (Manuscript: currently unpublished).

Toulmin, Stephen (1972) *Human Understanding*, Vol. I, (Princeton, New Jersey: Princeton University Press).

Tucker, Robert (1961), *Philosophy and Myth in Karl Marx*, (Cambridge: Cambridge University Press)

Turkel, Studds (1973), *Talking to Myself* A Memoir of My Times; (New York: Panthenon Books).

Wicks, Rollo (1958) *Man, and Modern Society*, (New York, McGraw Hill Book Company)

Wilber, Charles, and James Weaver (1975), "The Role of Income Distribution in the Process of Development", *Economic Analysis and Workers' Management*, Vol IX, No. 3-4, pp. 202-221.

Agora Cosmopolitan

The Quantuum Effect

Raymond Samuels

The Quantuum Effect

Raymond Samuels

www.ingramcontent.com/pod-product-compliance
Lightning Source LLC
Chambersburg PA
CBHW051711020426
42333CB00014B/941

* 9 7 8 1 9 2 7 5 3 8 5 0 0 *